BEFORE THE LIGHTS WENT OUT

The 1912 Triangular Tournament

PATRICK FERRIDAY

FOREWORD BY DAVID FRITH

First published in Great Britain by
VON KRUMM PUBLISHING
21 Brooker St
Hove BN3 3YX
VonKrumm@britpost.com

A CIP record of this book is available from the British Library.

Cover and all interior graphic design by Stewart Karl Davies

Printed and Bound in Great Britain
by MPG Biddles Ltd. King's Lynn

ISBN 978-0-9567321-0-1

Acknowledgements

Books

David Higham Associates – Empire, Denis Rudd
Penguin Books – Empire, Niall Ferguson
Orion Publishing Group – The Triangular Tournament, EHD Sewell
MCC – Minutes
ICC – Minutes
John Dos Passos – The 'newsreel' idea preceding each chapter in part II (all extracts there are from the *Times*)
Permission has been sought, where required by copyright, for all other quotations and the presumption is, in the case of failure to reply, that permission is granted. If this is not the case any publisher concerned should contact the author.

Images

Roger Mann Collection: 173, 202, 203, 211, 215, 278
David Frith Collection/Roy Minnett Album: 212, 224, 242, 270
Topfoto: 170, 171, 190, 191
Getty Images: 10, 178, 261
The Daily Graphic: 206, 234, 256, 267
The Triangular Tournament – EHD Sewell: 189, 227, 229, 243, 250, 252, 253, 258
Sussex CCC: 240, 279
Kent CCC: 43
Melbourne CC: 82, 84
Longden Family Records: 168
Where not otherwise specified, from the author

Help

Libraries: Jubilee (Brighton), British (St Pancras), British Newspaper (Colindale), Scottish National (Edinburgh) and MCC (Lord's).

A number of individuals have been very generous and offered help often before it was requested and then provided it in a manner and quantity that was a pleasure to behold – Rodney Ulyate, Roger Mann, John McKenzie, Ruth Earnshaw, Martin Ferriday, Richard Parry, Stewart Davies, Stephen Chalke and Bill Longden.

Special thanks are due to three people – David Frith for generous use of his time and expertise over 18 months and a foreword to top it off, James Mettyear for endless evenings in The Sussex Cricketer by the Tate Gates at Hove plus afternoons lurking in the slips and Rebecca Ferriday for just about everything else.

Contents

Foreword

Cricket's Triangular Tournament in England in 1912 will always stand out as an event of great significance and hypnotic interest. The fulfilment of a shared dream of staging a three-way challenge between the world's only Test nations early in the 20th Century, even though the weather was sometimes unsupportive and even though Australia's team was depleted, was a significant staging post.

It was to be over half-a-century before a multi-nation 'World Cup' worthy of the description came to fruition – and even then it materialised in limited-overs rather than Test format. The delay stemmed from a multiplicity of reasons: two world wars, a shortage of administrative vision, and the emergence of more and more Test nations around the globe. There came a time when it would simply have been illogical to propose any repeat Test tournament or carnival. With all these Test teams it would be much too unwieldy.

The 1912 event therefore remains unique. It also assumes a beguiling sepia charm as its centenary approaches. The event was quite well chronicled, but has since lain somewhat limply towards the rear of cricket's consciousness, partly because of the aforementioned drawbacks. Yet there was a lot of entertaining cricket played, and some of the cricketers in action remain household names.

Patrick Ferriday has produced here one of the most lucid and penetrative studies of the period that I have ever read, and he portrays the 'Golden Age' in a slightly less golden light. Withal, the Triangular Tournament is placed expertly into context, and a highly enlightened context at that. There is no room here for rose-tinted glasses.

Before the Lights Went Out tells of the link between cricket and Australia's federation in 1901, with reflections on the bond that existed between Mother England and her 'offspring' Australia, a picture which might perplex those who are too young to remember those links. And the South Africans too, with their complex racial mix, are brought to life, their master figure, Abe Bailey, being the chief architect of the enterprise.

The match descriptions have just the right amount of detail, and the pace is good. This is no easy task. Writers and researchers sometimes fall into a trap: 'I've worked hard to unearth all this, so it must go in!' The Ferriday way is to be economical and elegant while yet offering a broad picture. An important additive is the setting of cricket into its wider environment of political and social events. This is no two-evenings' research job; and importantly there is a masterly summing-up.

In 1938, Eddie Paynter was out leg-before for 99 in a Test at Lord's, and many years later, still somewhat rueful, he confided that he had actually nicked the ball from O'Reilly onto his pad. This, in terms of the complete and fine detail, seemed to be a uniquely gruesome fate. But I've now learned from this book that Charlie Macartney was also the victim of almost an identical form of miscarriage, also for 99, also at Lord's, also in an Anglo-Australian Test. And who was the scarcely-known

Ernie Hume, who was close to the Australian touring team, and died that summer? The answer's here. The reader will be struck by how leisurely and uncomplicated was cricket a hundred years ago. There can be no going back to it. As the majority of us well know, in terms of behaviour by cricket's participants and onlookers, the game always reflects the world around it fairly accurately, even though the walls that enclose cricket grounds ought really to be sufficient to shut out the turbulent outside world. There will be few readers of this book who will not at least once in a while wish they were there, at Lord's or The Oval or 'up north', watching the cricketers of three lands thrash out their 'world championship'.

While the Triangular Tournament of 1912 might not have been as great a success as a cricket event as its organisers had wished, it was a significant landmark in history which now lends itself to a broad and absorbing and colourful analysis by Mr Ferriday.

David Frith

Guildford, June 2010

Australia had become a very different place to live. The experiences in Melbourne had been bad enough to transform the way business, and even life, was done. Gone was the flamboyant exuberance; respectability and thrift were the new watchwords. It was not just in Victoria, the whole continent was coming to terms with a new order where success and prosperity could no longer be assumed. Prior to the late 1880s gloom, not only was Australia one of the wealthiest regions on earth but she was also one of the fairest. The profits created from the traditional agricultural endeavours were considerably more evenly distributed than in any of the European industrial nations and the country could proudly point to lower rates of infant mortality and higher rates of adult literacy than anywhere else in the world. It was no socialist utopia and many suffered hardships, not least the indigenous population, but there was a sense of a country pulling in the same direction where the interests of employee and employer were largely shared. This balance was relatively easy to maintain in the times of plenty, but as the recession began to bite there was an air of inevitability in the way that haves and the have-nots were thrown against one another.

Withholding of labour by the sheep shearers of Queensland set the ball rolling, but it was the legendary Maritime Strike of 1890 that represented the first high-water mark of industrial action. Mine, power and transport workers joined the dockers in a challenge to the colonial governments unprecedented in the short span of Australian history. The response was hard; police and troops broke the strikes and within a few years organised working class action had been crushed. But the violence and anger could not be forgotten as employers absorbed the lessons learned and began to combine to protect their interests. The working class responded in a similar fashion; suspicion and antipathy towards both employers and the authorities that were seen to have taken their side abounded and a state of 'us and them' came into being that, by and large, had not existed 20 years earlier. A boisterous economy had hidden the cracks that permeated society and when the mask was removed the depth of the fissures became visible; this exposure did nothing to cure the problem.

A party political upheaval was the most tangible upshot of this side-taking, beginning with the formation of the Labor Electoral League in New South Wales which as early as 1891 held the balance of power in the assembly. Within a decade a national Labor Party had made dizzying progress, radically altering the political landscape. The older parties combined as an anti-Labor group thus establishing politics as intensely class-based with a divide increasingly crossing all levels of society. Incredibly enough this fledgling party had graduated to power within a decade of its first appearance; a rate of progress bemusing for European Labour Parties still embroiled in a long-winded infancy.

Slightly less tangible, but no less important for that, was the culture of 'mateship' – the belief that only friends and workmates were trustworthy – and with this came a commensurate distrust of any representative of capitalism. The great industrial struggles of the 1890s all seemed to include legends of strength in adversity, loyalty to the point of fanaticism and an almost religious belief in supporting a mate and sharing with a mate. The fact that many contemporary writers and artists represented this development cemented it into the heart of what was a relatively youthful culture. The Australian man liked this essentially masculine image – hard but fair, eschewing affectation, free-spirited and anti-authoritarian. If there had to be a bad guy it was, inevitably, the bureaucrat, the banker or the boss profiting from the honest sweat and toil of the working man or, worst of all, the strike-breaker or scab. Elements of this 'mateship' are evident in the frontiersmen of North America or the working class solidarity of industrial Europe but only Australia gave it a name and kept it for over a hundred years.

The speed of change in Australian society during the last two decades of the nineteenth century was blinding and the results almost revolutionary without a revolution. Not only was society confronted with recession and its consequences but also, running almost parallel, was a drive towards federalism

New South Wales was totally dominant in terms of size at the beginning of the nineteenth century but gradually bits had been snapped off to form further 'colonies'; South Australia in 1836, Victoria in 1851 and Queensland in 1859. Each of these had local assemblies but remained, of course, answerable to the Queen and her government. In Britain the argument over free-trade and protectionism had crossed party lines but in Australia it was contained within colonial boundaries. Victoria favoured tariff barriers while New South Wales traditionally stood on the opposite side. Nothing better encapsulated the differences and consequent inefficiency of such a system than the 'Australian' rail network. New South Wales adopted the Irish gauge while Victoria and South Australia favoured the English version. Queensland and West Australia thought neither suitable and chose other alternatives. It was a situation that favoured no-one and was sometimes crippling; and yet it was not to be changed without first damping the fires of inter-colonial rivalry and convincing all parties that their interests would be better served in a federal state. The British Government needed no convincing, on the contrary there was persistent encouragement for a unified and efficient Australia which represented a potentially mighty trading partner and military ally. Sir Henry Parkes, prime minister of New South Wales, was the first major figure to take the bull by the horns and call for a united Australia and, despite dissent from many quarters, his call struck a chord and the progress towards his avowed goal was rapid. With the example of Canadian Federation only 20 years earlier, the first meeting of the Federal Council of Australia took place in 1886 and a mere 15 years later victory had been achieved with the declaration of the commonwealth on 1 January 1901. A number of factors had facilitated the pace of this complex change, the most basic of which was its essential good sense. A highly literate population was constantly informed of the current political debates and undoubtedly felt intimately involved in a transformation that would affect the whole population. While there was fear in each of the colonies of somehow losing out (a natural fear bedevilling all such moves towards unity), most influential politicians came to the conclusion that federalism was, sooner or later, inevitable and that it was preferable to influence its course from the inside rather than moaning from the outside.

External events also combined to influence the process. Encouragement from Britain, the model of the newly unified Germany and even the fear engendered by the Japanese crushing of China in 1895 served to highlight the vulnerability of a nation without national defence that was being made increasingly aware that British

States had altered the balance of world power and while the man on the Clapham omnibus may have been largely unaware of the changes taking place, the powers behind the British throne were well aware that challenges were coming and would have to be met head on.

The traditional British political parties had been torn apart firstly by the question of Irish Home Rule and then, a decade later, by arguments over protectionism and free-trade and very soon they would be confronted by the rise of a new party representing the working man. Still mostly unenfranchised, the working class faced a hard struggle for survival even though many of the worst abuses of the industrial revolution and the population shift towards the new industrial heartlands, as described by Dickens and Engels in the 1840s, had been eradicated. Reforms in education and health, protection of the destitute and infants, progress in sanitation and transport and improvements in conditions and hours at the workplace had made everyday life more tolerable but, by and large, the working classes were badly housed, badly nourished and had little hope of escaping the slums. If the late Victorians and Edwardians could not solve the problems of poverty they were at least good at recording them. From the writings of Charles Booth to Masterman's *The Condition of England*, published in 1909, images of poverty and desperation in both the cities and the countryside abounded. The portrait of Edwardian Britain as one of shooting parties and country-house cricket is in violent contrast to what was the actual experience of all but a tiny elite.

The Liberal Government that had been returned with such an enormous majority in 1906 was now under huge internal pressure. There was the problem of Ireland, the principle of Home Rule and the question of Ulster. The introduction of the Home Rule Bill in 1911 gave opposition leader Bonar Law a whip with which to flay his opponents across the floor and as Unionist resistance grew in Ulster it seemed that civil war might follow. Then there were the Suffragettes with a campaign of destructive militancy and organised protest that taxed the police and prison authorities to the limit. When hunger strikes and force-feeding were added to the agenda it seemed that, like the crisis in Ireland, a bloody denouement was a probability rather than just a possibility. Lastly, Asquith and Lloyd George were faced with the spectre of mass labour unrest from 1910 onwards. The introduction of 'a shining procession of social reform' such as the Workmen's Compensation Bill and the Old Age Pension Act had not been able to disguise the fact that the working class were, in real terms, worse off in 1910 than they had been a decade earlier. The flood of South African gold had accelerated inflation ahead of wage increases and with large capital investment abroad rather than at home the situation in the industrial heartlands was bleak. The passing of the Trades Dispute Bill which freed unions from liability for damage claims in case of a strike meant that organised labour was now back in the arena and the unions began to flex their muscles. Ramsey MacDonald noted 'One felt as though some magical allurement had seized upon the people'. These vast movements combined with great scientific and social advances told of a society in flux, desperate for change but sometimes unsure of how to achieve it, dragging the remnants of Victorianism into a new century while simultaneously trying to cast off the heavy burden of tradition and fear of the unknown.

The 1911 London Transport Workers strike brought the conflict into sharp relief.

The 1909 budget was only forced through by the threat of creating new peers as the government attempted to pay for the naval improvements and sweeping social reform with death tax, increased income tax and a new super tax on high earners. It wasn't that British production or exports weren't increasing, and often in an impressive manner, it was the rate of increase of her main rivals that was the point of concern. British growth between 1893 and 1913 of 131 percent in steel production or 100 percent in manufactured goods may sound quite impressive but when measured against 522 percent for steel in Germany or 500 percent for manufacturing in the United States then the problem becomes apparent. FW Taylor's work into the rationalisation of the workplace in America showed just what could be achieved by well organised mass production and the Model T Ford was the first great example of his theories in action.

Some economists thought that British industrialists had become lazy and set in their ways while others pointed to a high level of investment in other countries that left British trade and industry looking tired and old. Fortunately the annual trade deficit was easily covered by invisible earnings as London remained the centre of financial markets and sterling continued to represent solidity and good sense; put simply, sterling was as good as gold. The fact that Britain provided nearly one-third of the world's manufactured goods in 1870 tells a story of phenomenal achievement and industry. Equally the fact that this figure had shrunk to just 13 percent by 1913 is indicative of a huge relative decline, Britain could no longer outbuild the world.

It was hardly surprising then that, from 1880 onwards, successive British Governments should cast their eyes abroad with renewed suspicion and consider their place in the new world order that was forming around them. Lord Salisbury's famed policy of 'splendid isolation' was less a policy than a position forced on him by a lack of suitable alternatives. Agreements and ententes with the United States and France were signed in the early years of the new century but, crucially, the aims and ambitions of Britain and Germany never seemed to coincide happily. The last great reform of the Balfour government was the establishment, in 1904, of the Committee of Imperial Defence which later, under Asquith, became the blueprint for a response to a European war. As the Edwardian decade passed it became increasingly apparent that Germany had progressed from an annoying industrial rival to a frightening military force and potential opponent in a European war. In the words of Niall Ferguson, 'settling old disputes on the periphery was a way of freeing British resources to meet the growing continental challenge from Germany'. For exactly the same reason the Empire needed to be drawn together. Given these transformations and the military inadequacies exposed by the Boer War (not the least of which was the rejection of 30 percent of all volunteers on medical grounds) huge efforts were made to improve Britain's ability to defend herself. It was indeed, according to GM Trevelyan, 'a somewhat sobered John Bull who picked himself up off the pavement the morning after the Mafeking debauch'. Ironically it was to Germany that many looked for the model of how a nation could maximise its potential through national efficiency in industry, education and social welfare. A country could only be as good as its component parts and therefore fitness and literacy became causes of national concern. No longer could the playing fields of

Eton or Harrow sustain the Empire and guarantee safety from aggressive foreign powers. War, if and when it came, was going to be more total than anything that had gone before. Those that gave the matter thought, blanched at the possibilities of modern weaponry but none predicted its scale and brutality.

But if Britain was struggling to compete on her own she did at least have some mighty support at her shoulder, didn't she? While it was taken for granted that Britain should continue to discharge her duties to her colonies, many began to wonder just what this Empire was achieving. Was it the vocation of the Englishman to improve the lot of others in the far-flung reaches of Africa or Asia? To boldly go and build churches and railways, to dig mines and dam rivers? To promote civilization and Christianity and teach the gospel of prosperity? And could one expect co-operation and loyalty in return? Insurrection and violence from India to Egypt and from the Sudan to Transvaal and Jamaica showed the answer to at least one of these questions was a resounding 'No'. Yet surely the Empire was still crucially important to the mills of Manchester and the exchanges of London? The question was, did Britain need to commit either politically or economically to ensure that the wheels of industry and commerce continued to flow?

Colonial secretaries Chamberlain and Churchill were suitably enthusiastic about the potential of colonies in terms of trade and even possible military conflict but, to some degree, these colonies needed to be self-reliant and independent of a protection that Britain could no longer afford to offer. The 1900 Colonial Stocks Act gave significant impetus to investment with the aim of building powerful self-governing republics whose loyalty would, in the future, lie with Britain. Mutual benefit was seen as the way of binding the Empire together as a popular institution and there was precious little opposition to the granting of dominion status to the four 'European' colonies of Australia, New Zealand, Canada and South Africa. Over the previous 30 years efforts at tightening the ties had been spasmodic in the extreme. Colonial conferences in 1887 and 1897 had been arranged to coincide with two jubilees and it was only in 1902 that an agreement to five-yearly meetings was reached. Even then progress was scant; the Committee of Imperial Defence was a significant move but the efforts of Alfred Lyttleton to form an Imperial Council died through lack of interest, before being partially resurrected in the offices of the Dominion Department of the Colonial Office.

By 1911, the 1912 conference having been brought forward by the death of the King, there was increasing solidarity between the four self-governing dominions but also an overall decentralisation. The ties may have been rather loose and sometimes scarcely visible but there was still a will to stick together based on sentiment, loyalty, culture, history and money. Trade throughout the Empire had remained buoyant during the Edwardian period and when the loyalty of the dominions came to be tested from 1914 onwards they were not found wanting.

The ability to keep the Empire tightly unified through such turbulent times was one of the greatest achievements of diplomats, statesmen and civil servants who used all means at their disposal ranging from brute force to conciliation via intimidation and diplomacy. This desire to exploit all avenues inevitably brought sport into the political arena and cricket was, as the national game, perceived to be the most potent weapon. Sport was no longer just a plaything of the idle rich or an opiate for the masses, it was an integral part of society and as such was fair game in the process of building and binding an empire.

By 1908 sport had been introduced into many elementary schools and trainee teachers were now instructed in the rudiments of teaching PE while in the same year Robert Baden-Powell's *Scouting for Boys* made its first appearance. Outside the schools however sport had bloomed, taking advantage of the newly won half-holidays enjoyed by the working class, although the majority were still passive spectators rather than active participants. Cricket was now forced to compete with football and rugby as a mass spectator sport and the Empire was able to deliver All-Black and Springbok rugby touring teams as well as allowing the well-heeled to enjoy the delights of the Indian import of polo.

At the heart of the decision-making process in English cricket during this period lay Marylebone Cricket Club whose 16-strong Ordinary Committee's method of electing its own new members led to its being composed of a self-perpetuating clique. The aristocracy was the dominant force with a smattering of well-connected barristers and industrialists. It hardly needs saying that Eton, Harrow and the Oxbridge colleges were the educational establishments feeding into this most exclusive of clubs. The sale of life-memberships in the 1890s did create a more egalitarian atmosphere and, furthermore, around 50 percent of the committee were usually men with experience of first-class cricket. This may just have been one of the reasons that England was spared the hiatus that afflicted the Australian game when the players came into conflict with their Board of Control. The appearance of the imperially inclined Lord Harris in the mid-1890s led to a significant shift in emphasis and he was quick to draw in like-minded men such as Lord Hawke, Pelham Warner and Henry Leveson Gower. Harris, born in Trinidad, patron and player of Kent, investor in South Africa and governor of Bombay was clear in his mind as to the role of the Empire and the role that cricket had to play within it.

> 'England….had undertaken to educate oriental people on western lines, to imbue them with western modes of thought, and to encourage them to admire and to strive at the western systems of government.'

There was perhaps more than a grain of truth in the contemporary joke pillorying the three main colonial powers: the first act of the French is to build a restaurant, the Germans construct a road and the English a racecourse followed closely by a cricket ground.

Within a short time MCC had taken control of foreign tours and one of Harris' most trusty lieutenants was entrusted with the captaincy of the first MCC trips to both Australia, in 1903, and South Africa in 1905. If any man could outstrip his mentor in both enthusiasm and commitment then it was Pelham Warner.

> 'Cricket has become more than a game. It is an institution, a passion, one might say a religion. It has got into the blood of the nation and wherever British men and women are gathered together there will stumps be pitched.'

One hundred and more years on, declarations of this type can read as a sub-Shakespearean call to arms or an eerie religious tract but there can be no doubting the conviction behind the words. Cricket had its followers in all branches of the Empire. In religion, CT Studd, having represented England in Australia while still an undergraduate, devoted his life to missionary work in China, India and Africa. Cricket was also credited as a great moral force among the natives in Tonga and the Gilbert Islands. In politics, Alfred Lyttelton was appointed colonial secretary in 1903 having prematurely curtailed his cricket career to concentrate on his legal work though not before taking 4-19 bowling underarm in an Australian total of 551. He would have been brought on earlier but for being the wicket-keeper.

The supremacy of the British white man hardly needed reinforcement in schools although text books describing West Indian natives as 'lazy, vicious and incapable of any serious improvement' drove the message home. The fact that the Empire was so colossal was proof enough and, despite the odd reverse, the continuing expansion was empirical evidence that the British were born to govern. It also seemed quite in the order of things that the colonies should happily accede to such intrusion; Pelham Warner noted the Cingalese enthusiasm for 'the qualities of the ruling race' during a brief stay in 1903 and Joseph Chamberlain was categorical that 'the British race is the greatest of governing races that the world has ever seen'.

There were numerous challenges to this order from within and without but the 'Johnny-come-latelies' in the colonial arena were always playing catch-up while the revolting natives could always be knocked down should the need arise. Gradually though things changed as the Victorian age morphed into the Edwardian. The Boer War was a rude awakening and the German threat was real. Britain needed to adapt to the new challenges and that meant a new approach and even a leaner and more efficient Empire.

Australia and South Africa

Cricket in Australia was quick to take hold and spread during the nineteenth century in the same way that civilised urban society had been, and when the first group of English cricketers made the long journey south the reception on arrival was ecstatic and, largely, deferential. These were men from the 'mother country', an innately superior country, arrived to entertain and inform their distant cousins, but with each trip the Englishmen found the opposition stronger and public awe of the visitors dwindled.

The first sight of the cricketing colossus WG Grace, in 1873, did nothing to arrest the decline; while all were in agreement that he was the finest cricketer ever seen, some of his practices both on and off the field attracted scathing criticism from the Australian press. The *Wallaroo Times* felt his behaviour concerning games in South Australia had been unforgivable.

> 'Mr Grace has done no good to the 'manly game of cricket' in these colonies, for instead of his brilliant and skilful play being remembered, his name will become a synonym for mean, cunning and systematic fraud.'

Strong words indeed and hardly the kind of thing that any English newspaper would ever have countenanced and certainly indicative of the new-found confidence of the hosts.

The real turning point came in March 1877 with victory for Australia in the first Test match. The theme of 'blooming Australia' was omnipresent, summed up in the *Australasian*:

> 'The event marks the great improvement which has taken place in Australian cricket; and shows, also, that in bone as muscle, activity, athletic vigour, and success in field sports, the Englishmen born in Australia do not fall short of the Englishmen born in Surrey or Yorkshire.'

The *Age* took it even further, calling the result:

> '....a crushing reply to those unpatriotic theorists who would have us believe that the Australian race is deteriorating from the imperial type, or that lengthened residence under the Australian sun must kill the Briton in the blood.'

Interestingly here, one newspaper refers to 'Englishmen born in Australia' and another the 'Australian race'. This was the era of emancipation as, gradually, the inhabitants of Victoria and New South Wales began to see themselves as Australian and not British – the fact that there was a national cricket team, even though the nation had not yet come into existence, was simultaneously symptomatic and catalytic.

There is no doubting the pride in the performance of the Australian cricketers but equally there is little doubt that these men were only now beginning to see themselves as actually Australian (it is questionable whether such a thing existed in polite society) – they had been, and to a degree still were, Englishmen temporarily displaced and prospering in the colonies even though the majority had never seen Britain. What a curious dichotomy, patriotism for a country in name alone. So curious that it had to change, and change it did. Only months after this celebrated Test the Australian players were plying their trade in England with dramatic results. The famous victory in a day over MCC at Lord's was celebrated in the English press as:

> '....all of our own flesh and blood and we welcome their prowess cheerfully as proof that the old stock is not degenerating in those far-off lands.'

In that very 'far-off land' the hope was expressed that the team would prove:

> '....the colonials are worthy descendants of the good old stock from which they have come.'

The imagery is stiflingly arboreal, the cutting from the solid English oak (and a slightly diseased cutting at that) flourishes in the merciless heat far from the mother tree; a compliment to both parent and child alike and a subject for mutual rejoicing. Sport had also brought the first individual national heroes into the public eye. The sculler Edward Trickett was welcomed by 25,000 people on his return from a world championship victory in London. Cricket would have to wait for Victor Trumper, earlier champions such as Spofforth and Murdoch were much praised but never quite attained the required level of innocence and they also had inter-colonial rivalry to contend with which tended to militate against the creation of national heroes in team games.

The initial euphoria could not continue as, during the 1880s, touring parties sailed back and forth and familiarity began to breed, if not contempt, then certainly a feeling of parity. Australian cricket had become nearly the equal of English, the grounds at Melbourne and Sydney were more than a match for anything to be found in London or Manchester but money and class structure were becoming increasingly divisive issues. For Australians the combination of amateur and professional in visiting English sides was a reminder of a less egalitarian society – the champagne supping Pommie was born. For the English gentry the Australians could often seem boorish and lacking in due deference but they in turn could point to the democracy of their teams and the hypocrisy of alleged amateur gentlemen earning more than their professional team-mates.

Yet in 1883 Richard Twopeny wrote with justification in *Town Life in Australia* that:

> '….all ages and classes are interested in it [cricket] and not to be interested in it amounts almost to a social crime.'

The national game was throwing a mirror onto the relationship between the mother and her child and the child had plenty to say, as evidenced by the *Bulletin*:

> 'The Australians, whether amateur or professional, will never consent to be spat upon by dirty little cads whose soap-boiling or nigger-murdering grandfathers left enough money to get the cads' fathers 'ennobled' and to enable the cad himself to live without working.'

Ironically the class structure that was being so vilified in some sections of the Australian press was far from absent in the Australian game. It was no coincidence that when two English sides toured simultaneously in 1886-87 it was the elite Melbourne Cricket Club that invited the 'amateur' side of the two. This was to be followed by the increasing influence of the administrators whose determination to wrest control from the players was to result in the battle that was to ultimately wreck the national team in time for the 1912 Triangular Tournament.

The 1890s saw a further shift in attitudes as the whiff of federalism ironically led to a new found cordiality between the two nations. Crucial to this was the fact that the British Government was at least as keen as the new colonies on the idea of a federal Australia. When Lord Sheffield presented the Sheffield Shield, to be competed for by the three main colonies, he explained to John Cresswell, secretary in South Australia, that the feeling in London was that the colonies should be forging closer links with one another with an eye to a federation that would reduce administrative and trade complexities at a stroke. At the same time the cricket associations in Victoria and

Meat and fruit rotted on quaysides, food shortages bit and the union triumphed, receiving recognition, wage increases and reduction in hours. Within weeks Liverpool docks were paralysed and then the rail network was hit. By the end of the year union membership had risen by 600,000 and 10 million working days had been lost to strike action. The prospects for 1912 were no brighter. A national mineworkers stoppage in support of a minimum wage brought the country to its knees in the early part of the year before a tearful Asquith begged Parliament to pass a Minimum Wage Act. A national transport strike was only averted in the summer because most union coffers had not recovered from the dispute of the previous year. The figures made even grimmer reading than 1911. Over one million involved in industrial action and 38 million days lost. And yet, in essence, only a temporary shoring up had been achieved. The working class was as mad as hell and they weren't going to take it. The great mediator of the time Sir George Askwith commented:

> 'There may be movements in this country coming to a head of which recent events have been a small foreshadowing.'

Home Rule, women's suffrage and labour relations; all three issues lay unresolved and would remain so for many years as the challenge of German military ambition dwarfed all others.

Even the posturing of the Spithead naval review back in 1897 had been partly an exercise in blustering through the challenges that had developed to the British domination of the sea. Although the navy remained a mighty force and huge investments had been made since the mid-1880s as awareness of the rival strength of Germany, the United States and Japan increased, the two-power standard, by which the British navy should equal the combined strength of her two nearest rivals, was unsustainable. Even the considerable sums coming from Australia, New Zealand and South Africa for naval upkeep, in what amounted to a vast protection racket, were not enough. The money was quite simply not there, or at least not in the quantity which was being made available in some other countries. Kaiser Wilhelm II's naval obsession combined with the drive of Admiral von Tirpitz ensured the construction of no less than 14 battleships between 1893 and 1903 and from 1906 the British response was Admiral Fisher's Dreadnought programme. The enormous fire power of this new class of ship would render obsolete anything Germany could offer – this was about effectiveness and efficiency rather than the pomp and posture that had dominated the previous 20 years.

In many ways these new sea monsters were symbols of their age. Power, speed, and militarism were all contained in these ironclads and they were welcomed by a country becoming fearful and even paranoid of the German threat. The Hague International Peace Conference of June 1907 could hardly have provided a starker illustration of the mood of the age. Half an hour was spent discussing peace and four months on the rules of war! The only wonder is that European conflict did not come sooner than 1914. Each new invention was seen through its military potential: motor cars, aeroplanes, cameras and even great art movements such as the Futurists ('war – the world's only hygiene') reflected a drive towards violence or the potential for violence.

section', a 'culture section' which revolved around technical education and a grand sporting contest encompassing 'running, rowing and cricket'.

> 'such a contest between carefully selected representatives of the English-speaking race would command more general attention and be more popular than any other contest....and it should popularise the idea of Empire, which is at present only latent in an organised form in the English mind; but especially it would encourage the sentiment of union.'

India and the East were to play a conspicuous part in a street pageant! Some claimed optimistically that this lit the spark for Pierre de Coubertin and 15 years later Astley Cooper was still banging the same drum.

The British Government, unlike that of the United States, was loath to become involved in the new Olympic venture despite the arguments of pro-Olympians that a leading role could further British prestige. The haphazard organisation of the 1896 Games in Athens and the 1900 gathering in Paris did little to encourage the Foreign Office to provide either funding or encouragement. But when Rome was unable to stage the event in 1908, the British Government saw an opportunity of at least furthering the ties of the 1904 Anglo-French entente by adding the athletics contest onto the Exhibition of Science, Arts and Culture that the two countries were jointly sponsoring. Britain, by virtue of having the largest team, was rewarded with the highest gold medal tally and the White City and the stumbling exhaustion of Dorando Pietri's marathon finale entered sporting folklore.

Astley Cooper returned to bemoan the 1908 Olympics as 'a side show to the Franco British exhibition' and worried that 'our colonial brethren are saying that it is evident the Briton at home prefers the Continental to them'. He then enlisted the support of CB Fry who proceeded to rubbish the Games in Athens, Paris and St Louis before proclaiming:

> 'I believe there would be greater success achieved and better ends served by aiming, not at a world wide, but at a Pan-Britannic Olympia. The reasonable function of the Olympia idea is to foster nationalism; as a means to cosmopolitan understanding it is of doubtful value.'

Here was certain evidence of the lack of understanding as to which way the world and its sporting links were turning. This was 1908 and not 1888 and the Olympic Games was not about to disappear, it was imperialism that was not just on the back foot but ducking and weaving as well.

The British Empire had developed into a complex and constantly changing entity consisting of a variety of contradictory elements and, in the words of KP Sandiford, 'This attachment to Anglo-Saxon values was the ultimate triumph of Victorian imperialism'. Jack Williams concludes that 'acceptance of white English cricket mores by those who were not white was seen as proof of white English moral excellence.' For Benny Green

'It seems to have been a typically English compromise between a religious manifestation and an instrument of policy, occupying a misty hinterland in which ethics and biceps merged into a third entity, an exquisite refinement of the other imperial concept, the White Man's Burden.'

There was the need to keep the natives at arms-length while espousing the virtues of fair play and democratic government. There was also necessity of keeping the Empire united while allowing some of its constituent parts an autonomy that would increase their potential as trading and military allies. Insecurity and aggression are familiar bedfellows for the Englishman abroad and the Empire builders were no exception. Like their ex-patriot cousins of the twenty-first century they revelled in creating familiar surroundings in far-flung outposts.

As the brief span of Edwardian years swung by, the need for imperial unity became ever greater. The industrial threat of the USA and Russia was replaced by the even greater significance of a German challenge to British naval supremacy. With German military and industrial expansion rapidly outstripping that of Britain it was clear that splendid isolation was no longer an option. The hugely successful *The Expansion of England* by JR Seeley caught the mood and in turn influenced no lesser figure than Joseph Chamberlain in the belief that the Empire was Britain's only way of competing with the new industrial giants. The day might soon come when Britain would need allies and those she could most rely on were those that had been in receipt of British 'largesse' for the previous hundred years or more. When, in the aftermath of the Boer War, Rudyard Kipling lambasted the upper classes for their inability to defend the Empire, he cited, amongst other things, their obsession with the 'flannelled fools at the wicket'. He was wide of the mark (although in his defence he was attacking the stay-at-homes), those flannelled fools had played their part in drawing an Empire together little knowing that the fruit of their labours would have its resolve so appallingly tested in Belgium, France and Gallipolli.

3

The Counties Awake

With the Empire expanding inexhaustibly during the second half of the nineteenth century, the greatest of its games now began to take root and flower in terms of organisation, skill and professionalism. If one were to try and find a pivotal year in the development of English cricket, it would be hard to ignore the credentials of 1864. Before this there were amateurs playing for fun and touring professionals eking out a living in a largely unregulated sport. Afterwards there was regular county cricket, contracts, purpose-built grounds and international cricket.

The change didn't, of course, happen overnight but three things mark out this year as a watershed in the game that led to a rapid acceleration away from the 'middle ages' towards what we now recognise. Firstly, overarm bowling was finally legalised following Edgar Willsher's provocation and challenge to obviously obsolete rules. This excused umpires from judging whether or not the bowler's roundarm delivery had snuck above shoulder height and with this the potential art of bowling was instantly transformed. Secondly, 1864 saw the first appearance of *Wisden*; the influence on the expansion of the game that this yearly compendium of scores, performances, statistics and opinions brought can scarcely be overestimated in its cementing of the game in the public psyche. And then came Grace. In 1864 the Champion himself, William Gilbert Grace, made his first mark in 'big cricket' by registering scores of 170 and 56 for the South Wales club against the Gentlemen of Sussex while just shy of his sixteenth birthday. Over the next 10 years he transformed the art of batting and where batting went bowling had to follow. His influence is incalculable but to take just four of the elements that CLR James identified suffices. He killed bullying fast bowlers; he showed that large crowds could be attracted; he made the Gentlemen vs. Players fixture competitive again and he showed that one batsman could play forward and back, off and on, attacking and defensive. It was only as his bulk outgrew his strength that the others caught up and by that time he was well into his forties and cricket had left the backwaters of the repertory theatre and had taken its place in the West End.

The County Championship, the kernel of the domestic game, was still a quarter of a century away at this stage but the increasing frequency and competitiveness of inter-county fixtures throughout the 1870s and 1880s made a formal competition an inevitability. Indeed, 1864 marked the first year when enough games were played (24 between eight 'first-class' counties) for the sporting press to talk of a champion county. The results were, however, somewhat bemusing. Cambridgeshire won their three matches but were outpointed by Surrey's six victories in eight matches and Kent finished bottom, losing seven from seven while Hampshire lost only four of four. The fixture lists were far from random but remained mildly eccentric, geography certainly playing an important part as did relationships between various patrons, committees and other men of influence. Then there was the question of money; professionals needed paying and amateurs needed expenses. Nottinghamshire, for example, were far keener to risk defeat in front of a large crowd against Yorkshire than give Hampshire a thrashing for virtually no monetary gain. Furthermore, fixtures were often discontinued and then picked up again as arguments raged over umpiring, division of receipts or even the disputed 'ownership' of a player's registration. The latter was addressed by the leading counties in conjunction with MCC when qualification rules were formalised in 1873.

These were some of the trials and tribulations of the embryonic county game but despite them the growth remained steady if not exactly spectacular. The true blossoming would have to wait another 30 years and then it flowered for two decades until the First World War stopped cricket, and everything else, in its tracks. In this golden age the work of the early pioneers such as Grace, Shaw and Ulyett was taken up by some of the greatest and most redoubtable names in the history of the game; Rhodes and Hirst, Fry and Ranji, Hayward and Hobbs, Blythe and Woolley.

From the pivotal year of 1864 onwards the first half-century of the county game can be said to have been dominated by four teams and each, in their own way, illustrates how the game developed and became what it was by the time of the 1912 Triangular Tournament.

Alfred Shaw and Nottinghamshire

The Nottinghamshire domination of the early years of inter-county cricket was not total but they were, by some distance, the most consistent and successful team for over two decades. Their record of 113 victories and only 38 defeats tells of consistent strength over 23 years and is also a testament to a lack of fixtures; they averaged less than 10 games a season. Yorkshire and Surrey were the most keenly awaited opposition while Gloucestershire, Middlesex and Lancashire were worthy rivals. This period of domination could have begun earlier had William Clarke not poached the county's best players for his wandering All England XI but his efforts nonetheless left their mark in Nottinghamshire; the Trent Bridge ground was established and playing cricket as a way of earning a livelihood became a possibility.

Richard Daft was the first major figure of the period – a batsman reared on unpredictable and scary pitches with a reputation for straight-bat orthodoxy that enabled him to smother shooters and lifters with equal panache, a prerequisite in terms of both scoring runs and protecting life and limb. The preparation of pitches

A strong professional base to the team was crucial to any extended period of success. Even a cricketer as far ahead of his contemporaries as WG Grace could not single-handedly carry a largely amateur team for any length of time on his broad shoulders. The golden age of Edwardian cricket is often defined through the extravagant amateur talent of men such as MacLaren, Fry or Mason and any combination of statistics and contemporary accounts leaves no doubt as to their outstanding abilities, but the point remains that most could not sustain a cricketing summer year after year; consistency required a professional backbone.

The Kent team is the finest example; only when they became settled through contracted professionals did they start winning titles. Their first success in 1906 was described as 'a result due to the brilliant character of their play and their splendid sportsmanship' – the 'brilliant character' refers largely to the batting of the amateur Hutchings but behind him was a strong paid and trained contingent. The same can be said of the Yorkshire side; for every thrilling innings by Jackson, Taylor or Mitchell there were dozens of match-winning bowling performances by Rhodes, Hirst and Haigh. And so further back to Lohmann and Shaw – it might be possible for amateurs to sustain a glorious month, or even a season, but the glory was always temporary without a Shrewsbury or a Blythe year-in and year-out.

A further addition to the professional armoury was the fact that bowling rested largely in their hands. There were some exceptions such as quick bowlers Brearley and Kortright, the originator of the googly, Bosanquet and the Champion himself but even this illustrious quartet would be humbled by Fielder and Richardson or Attewell and Wilfred of Kirkheaton. With this dominance came the reliance on professionals to win matches because then, as now, that is what bowlers do. Sussex were able to boast two of the greatest amateur lights of the golden age in Fry and Ranjitsinhji and this pair double topped the national batting averages on no less than five occasions yet not one title resulted. Yorkshire romped to the Championship in 1901 without a batsman near the head of the averages and Surrey's greatest period was clearly built around the skills of Lohmann, Lockwood, Brockwell and Richardson. This balance of power has never really changed, as the Surrey team of the 1950s attests; seven successive Championships with only one top-class batsman, in Peter May, but a bowling attack of Bedser, Laker, Loader and Lock.

The issue of captaincy is certainly one where the paths of these four great sides parted. Kent's two, Marsham and Dillon, were neither spectacularly endowed as players or tacticians but seem to have allowed their fine side to function freely. Lord Hawke was a moderate cricketer and, according to his friend CB Fry, 'the story of his being a great captain was a myth' but with the team at his disposal it would have been difficult to fail. It would, however, be churlish to ignore his work behind the scenes and the enormous energy which mark him out as the father of Yorkshire cricket. Shuter was a reliable and adequate bat and commanded the respect of his Surrey team while Daft and Shaw could actually lead by example.

In wicket-keeping, however, there was a huge similarity. All four teams enjoyed the benefits of men of great ability and longevity able to forge partnerships with the key county bowlers. The vast figure of Mordechai Sherwin of Nottinghamshire, Harry Wood of Surrey, David Hunter of Yorkshire and Fred Huish of Kent (the first two named played for England just seven times between them while the latter pair were never capped). All were remarkably resistant to injuries which, given the pitches and equipment, is a marvel and none were particularly inspiring batsmen. Hunter was a regular number 11 for Yorkshire while Sherwin averaged a meagre seven in a 20-year career.

What does stand out time and again in the story of these four county sides is the importance of money and the ability to invest it wisely in attracting and retaining the best available players. With a huge increase in the popularity of what had become the national game, these men could provide enormous profit through success on the field and thus continue the process of recruitment and retention. For better or for worse cricket was no longer just a sport, it was business as well.

4

Advance Australia Fair

❧❧❧

Although finances remained tight for the smaller counties in England, the domestic game had, by and large, prospered during the fifty years before the outbreak of war in 1914. Undeniable was that the Championship, and the competition, rivalry and support it engendered, had become part of the British summer both in saloon bars and London clubs. Each new season was eagerly anticipated and if there was no touring team then the prospects for the counties were predicted and discussed with renewed vigour. The development of the game in Australia ran simultaneously and rapidly but took many different pathways. The connection with the game in England was equally complex but it was precisely this connection that drove the game forwards in terms of finance and prestige.

By the time of the 1912 Triangular Tournament, Test cricket had reached a high level of maturity having stumbled and waltzed through a variety of setbacks and leaps forward. The idea of an eleven-a-side game of cricket between England and Australia would have been unthinkable only forty years before 1912 despite the fact that two touring parties had already travelled south and been well rewarded for doing so. Yet within a short space of time attitudes had changed – XXIIs were replaced by XVs and then XIs and touring teams started to experience the bitterness of defeat. Organisers became aware that it was no longer feasible to fill berths with well-intentioned but hapless amateurs while relying on a few top-class players to secure the desired results.

The first report of cricketing activity in Australia came in 1804 as members of the officers and crew of the HMS *Calcutta* did battle in Sydney. With the encouragement of governor Macquarie and the enthusiasm of visiting army regiments, the game began to take hold in and around Sydney during the 1820s. With the games came the clubs, the prestige and the social standing. The prize fixture was that between the two main groups, military against civilians, and these matches were often attended by crowds of thousands and competition, driven by a cash prize on the field and betting in the rings, was intense.

Melbourne wasted no time in embracing the game with the Cricket Club's formation in 1838 coming only three years after the establishment of this new settlement. The 1850s saw a boom in the young nation's major urban centres: in Sydney the

Albert Club was soon followed by the Warwick while further afield Newcastle and Albury became homes to new ventures, in Melbourne the Union and Brighton clubs started to threaten the pre-eminence of the Melbourne Cricket Club which had the misfortune to have its ground bisected by Australia's first railway line. But in a metropolis awash with money from the first gold rush there was plenty to go around to purchase and develop the land of the MCG. With this in place, suitable opponents were required and only one would really fit the bill – New South Wales. Victoria had been playing Tasmania since 1851 but the commencement of the great 'inter-colonials' in 1856 was to give the game an enormous fillip, feeding on the lust for sport and the burgeoning rivalry between the two power-houses of Australian life and prosperity. Crowds of up to 15,000 descended on the MCG and with it the potential for mass entertainment and mass marketing came into being. Only one other development could top this – international cricket.

Stumbling Steps

The first cricket team to cross an ocean had been the 1859 vintage led by George Parr to North America. Not long afterwards Australian hoteliers and restaurateurs Felix Spiers and Christopher Pond began to hatch cunning plans to appropriate the popularity of cricket and thereby promote their chain of establishments. Their first choice of celebrity guest was Charles Dickens but even their generous terms were insufficient to entice him into making the long journey. A somewhat cheaper alternative was a cricket team.

WB Mallam was dispatched to England by Spiers and Pond with instructions to bring back 12 players for the summer of 1861-62. He alighted on England's finest, engaged in a North versus South fixture at Birmingham, and laid before them the terms of £150 plus travelling expenses. The Nottinghamshire players, led by George Parr, perhaps chastened by his torrid experiences in America, rejected the offer but the southern contingent were more impressed and signed up to the venture under the leadership of HH Stephenson. The lack of Parr, Daft and Caeser certainly took away some of the lustre but the others confidently expected to beat all-comers as they boarded the *Great Britain* in Liverpool on 20 October 1861.

The entire tour was a roaring success from the moment the players disembarked until their departure three months later. Huge crowds gathered at the dockside in Melbourne to welcome the conquering heroes on their arrival and they had to be spirited away to practise in secret. Spiers and Pond could rub their hands with delight as no less than 15,000 paying customers attended the first day of the first game against XVIII of Victoria. By the end of this match the entire expenses of the whole tour had been recovered and despite the staggering amount of 'champagne receptions' a profit of £14,000 accrued to the entrepreneurial pair which they used to set themselves up with a chain of successful London refreshment rooms. The players received more than double the original terms and were so flush they were able to turn down a further £100 to prolong their stay by a further month. The English season was calling all but one; Charles Lawrence decided to accept terms of £300 per annum to coach at the Albert Club in Sydney.

The die was cast – if nothing else, the sheer weight of money ensured that further tours wouldn't be long delayed and better terms could be offered to attract the cream of English cricket. And there were more enticements. One of the English team, Roger Iddison, best summed up the players' experiences saying: "Well I don't think much on their play but they're a wonderful lot of drinking men". Certainly the standard of Australian cricket was meagre but the best English professionals were accustomed to touring and thrashing inferior opposition in their own country and it was more fun and better rewarded to continue the practice in Australia. The hospitality and the amenities at the major centres were quite superb even if conditions at places such as Geelong and Ballarat were rather more rudimentary. The difficulties of travel were minimised by keeping to a largely coastal itinerary to avoid arduous overland travel as much as possible. These professional cricketers were tough, rising to the unfamiliar challenges of heat and mosquitoes with aplomb. The effect on many of those who watched these men was hugely important in terms of the development of the game. Here was the standard to aspire to, these were the skills to learn and Australia was not lacking in raw, if untutored, talent. The appointment of Charles Lawrence in Sydney was a pivotal moment. By the time his career finished, some 36 years later, he had taught and worked with virtually every leading player and the first generation of Test stars, Murdoch, Bannerman and Spofforth, had been and gone and placed Australian cricket on a par with the English game.

The first English tourists receive a heroes' welcome on arrival at the Café de Paris in Melbourne – 24 December 1861.

In monetary terms, Spiers and Pond had made their killing and now other eyes were greedily cast at the popularity of the game and the business to be made out of it. But was it just about the sport or did the visit have a deeper significance? Why had a crowd of 10,000 gathered at Port Melbourne to greet the tourists? Why had the majority of the city's population turned out to line the streets around the Café de Paris, where the official reception was held, in a scene compared to the Athenians arriving in Corinth? Somewhere in the answer lies the nature of the relationship between the Australian colonies and Great Britain in the latter half of the nineteenth century. These cricketers were men from the 'mother country' and as such were heroes, mates and brethren rolled into one. Most members of this crowd still regarded Britain as home even though many of them had never seen her green and pleasant land and presumed they never would. This was an opportunity to touch Englishness, to feel a certain affinity to 'home' and to celebrate the old world while showing just how far the new world had progressed. There was pride in the Australian colonies, and their achievements, mixed with a certain measure of deference and recognition of the inherent superiority (in cricket at least) of the visitors who would provide sporting entertainment in a country prosperous enough to enjoy such extravagance. Nationalism did not cloud the enthusiasm of the multitudes gathered, for they saw themselves as, in essence, British; residents of Victoria but certainly not Australian. Cricket would have an important part to play in establishing a national identity but only later, when Victoria and New South Wales and then South Australia combined forces, would the idea of an Australian team beating an English team become realistic. Then there would be time enough for patriotism.

Given the success of the initial Australian adventure it was short odds that another would soon follow and only two years later George Parr, having no doubt rued his decision to decline the first tour, was invited by the Melbourne Cricket Club to gather together a second group of players. Melbourne was rapidly becoming the driving force behind the widening of the game as developments such as underground drainage allowed professional Sam Cosstick to produce the first lush green outfield in the country. Such a venue deserved top-class cricket and Parr had no difficulty assembling a talented professional team augmented by one amateur, EM Grace. There was little discernable improvement in the standard of the home players and once again the tourists were able to ride roughshod over local XXIIs while enjoying their hospitality. However, appearances were deceptive and it was in fact the greater playing strength of this second touring party that enabled the dominance to continue at the same level. The fast bowling of Jackson and Tarrant made a huge, and often frightening, impression on opponents and spectators alike while the eminent figure of Grace was celebrated by a waxwork in Sydney. Once again the colonies were enamoured of visitors from the old country, showing their appreciation at train stations and docksides before paying good money to see them perform. And perform they did, completing no less than 19 matches in a 14-week stay that included a first trip to New Zealand.

This was the game as it should be played and there in the crowd, thrilled by the pace and aggression of George 'tear' em' Tarrant was a youthful Fred Spofforth, destined to return the complement in spades by tormenting English batsmen throughout the first decade of the Ashes. But perhaps the greatest gift to Australian cricket was William Caffyn's acceptance of an offer to coach at the Melbourne Cricket Club. Charles Lawrence had stayed in Sydney two years earlier and now Melbourne it spent the next 40 years on his mantelpiece.

In 1884 the redoubtable Billy Murdoch was back in England again, aided and abetted by the seemingly inexhaustible Fred Spofforth. This time there was no touting for fixtures, the successes of the previous four years having ensured nationwide popularity which even MCC recognised by granting three Test matches. The *Standard* captured the mood of grim determination when calling for players and officials

> 'to sink all county, university and club considerations and combine to form practice teams to check, if possible, the advance of the Australian invader.'

It was now deemed inappropriate to mention the 'M' word but money it was that would overshadow the summer. The squad had convened as a private enterprise without the backing of Australian associations and as such the finances were tight to begin with and very carefully regulated thereafter. Fortunately the team performed well despite being weaker than its predecessor, eventually losing the series 1-0, the only result being in the first ever Lord's Test. It was this match that caused the furore when it became public knowledge that the gate receipts of £1,334 had all been paid to the tourists. Some newspapers began to drop the 'Mr.' prefix that had always been applied to Australian visitors although it's doubtful that any players found this particularly disturbing. The nature of the undertaking was clear and the Australians remained somewhat bemused as they became caught up in the English class system of professional and amateurs. Australian players were in a sense amateurs in that they all had other jobs and were granted leave of absence to tour. Exceptions such as Alick Bannerman existed, but there was no question of the separate dressing room and different hotel charade that was customary for the English team. These players had risked time and money on the tour and thought it perfectly natural to receive due reward for their labours even if these rewards sometimes amounted to five times the annual salary of their 'real' jobs. Not that it was easy to ascertain what had actually been earned. Critics of the 1882 tourists claimed £700 and defenders £250. The Australians either failed or, more likely, refused to understand the nuances having seen at first-hand how much money the best English amateurs could 'earn' and how little, by comparison, the professional was paid. Certainly there was a more egalitarian instinct in Australian society and this was reflected by the press that, this time, supported its men and questioned why the term professional should carry any stigma. English professionals could apparently only cast envious glances at their counterparts. Some twenty years later nothing much had changed when the erudite Albert Knight exercised his pen:

> 'Not until we have a real and vital principle underlying our own amateurism – in lieu of grotesque semblances fostered by amiable laxity and shuffling expediency – can we fairly rebuke Australian practices.'

Just six months later money was to cause further head-shaking and hand-wringing but this time it was in Australia and was heavily laced with an Antipodean flavouring. The first Test at Adelaide should have been a great occasion as the sterling work of Jesse Hide and secretary John Creswell came to fruition in a ground boasting a magnificent new stand but it proved to be a financial disaster for the South Australian Cricket Association as a seemingly under-prepared home side were well beaten. The second Test was blighted even before it started when the Victorian Cricket Association offered only £20 per man; these terms were promptly refused by all the leading players bar Spofforth and a weak team was comfortably brushed aside. As if this weren't enough, English manager Alfred Shaw disputed the division of the gate money pointing out that the Australians had been more than generously treated in England and now was the time to reciprocate. The local press was inclined to support this position and once again Billy Murdoch became the pantomime villain for his part in 'the gate money racket'. Waters were temporarily smoothed and the best of Australia levelled the series, helped by England's star bowler William Barnes' refusal to bowl in the third game, but Australia fell apart again before the final game and were beaten by an innings and with it the series was lost by 3-2. There was no doubt that the potential quality of the teams was abundant but the series was a grim one with the alleged cynicism of the players being reflected in the press. The public were not impressed and crowds fell and the future look decidedly less bright than it had done two years earlier, particularly in Sydney where club cricket was suffering such a decline that the future of many was thrown into doubt. In Melbourne the cricket community was still reeling from the fire that had entirely destroyed the MCG pavilion in 1884.

The two teams had remained evenly balanced until 1886, now it shifted dramatically one way as the first generation of great Australian players, Spofforth and Murdoch in particular, left the stage. Despite the continued excellence of George Giffen and the discovery of the twin tyros Turner and Ferris, the Australians could manage only one victory in the next five years. This was an imbalance that would lead to cash-flow problems that in turn would jeopardise the future of international cricket, reliant as it was on clicking turnstiles.

In 1885 the South Australian secretary, John Cresswell, opened negotiations with the NSWCA and VCA with a view to combining forces to promote the next tour of England. The idea stalled, as many others were to, and the upshot was that many leading players did not make the 1886 trip. This tour was led by Henry Scott and his weakened and ill-disciplined squad proved no match for a star studded team of Grace, Shrewsbury, Lohmann, Peel and Briggs.

The next English team to Australia was likewise too good, winning both Tests and this, allied to the poor weather and deepening recession, led to falling attendances. Worse was to follow when two English sides toured simultaneously in 1887-88 in a display of appalling organisation and foolishness. Financial disaster was the inevitable result as the already tarnished golden goose was overcooked. With the colonies constantly suffering the loss of leading players to international fixtures, the VCA set out to regulate and promote inter-colonial fixtures even if that meant curtailing the amount of tours taking place. This was not a new concern; as early as 1881 the NSWCA annual report described the inter-colonial matches as 'a matter of first importance and one to which all others should be made subservient'. The meeting on 21 December 1887 where the three major colonies discussed these initiatives, together with recommendations to alter the lbw law and introduce the six-ball over,

'Owing to the disturbed state of the country, we had ten days kicking our heels and were then telegraphed for to go to Johannesburg to play there to turn people's mind from the raid.'

A week later they found themselves surrounded by Boer militia playing cricket in the buzzing capital of Transvaal having met and played cards with some of Jameson's incarcerated men. They also met the taciturn President Kruger and tried to persuade him of the beneficial effects of a day at the cricket. Only one failure, in Natal where the British lieutenant Poore scored a century, preceded the first Test in Port Elizabeth. Lord Hawke had been so impressed with Poore that he invited him to play for England but a combination of Poore's commanding officer and the local newspapers ensured he would remain committed to South Africa. The logic of this may be hard to fathom but is indicative of a fascinatingly complex relationship between mother country, military and colony. Here the imperial gesture was to support the beleaguered colony (or at least the white non-Afrikaner part of it) against England. So Poore played for South Africa but he could do little to help his country of temporary adoption as George Lohmann took 15-45 in a rout. The other two Tests followed the same course and Lohmann finished with 35 wickets at 5.8. If ever a series was a one-man show then this was it. Even more remarkable was the fact that Lohmann had been diagnosed with tuberculosis three years earlier and had become a regular visitor to the dry warm air of Matjiesfontein as guest of self-made millionaire James Logan. The influence of Lohmann continued to be felt throughout South Africa during the few remaining years of his life as he and the likes of Billy Bates and George Gunn spent time at the Wanderers' Club. William Brockwell and Len Braund were invited to coach in Pretoria and, with the help of such outstanding players, within a decade South Africa were approaching a semblance of parity with England and Australia. Despite the one-sided nature of the 1896 Tests, Sammy Woods was impressed enough to remark that: 'These young fellows will be as good as the Australians before many years are out'. Woods was himself Australian! Many South African's were, however, distinctly unimpressed with Lord Hawke and his men; the attempt to poach Poore, the failure to appear at a smoking concert held in their honour at Pietermaritzburg, the sale of equipment and biographies at inflated prices, complaints about conditions and umpires and also the distinctly dubious bowling action of Fry all gave the press plenty with which to fill their columns.

The Jameson raid and subsequent resignation of Cecil Rhodes as prime minister of the Cape Colony had done nothing to quell the various grievances of either the Uitlanders or the Afrikaners in Transvaal. As South Africa lurched towards bloody conflict the blissfully unaware Lord Hawke arrived back in 1898, commenting naively that 'less disturbed political conditions' were prevalent. Meanwhile, back in London, Lord Milner and Joseph Chamberlain were discussing the advisability and inevitability of all-out war. The tourists, again bankrolled by Logan despite his experiences with Walter Read, were the equal of the previous groups, the cracks this time were amateurs Frank Mitchell and Pelham Warner and professionals Schofield Haigh, JT Tyldesley and the ex-Australian Albert Trott. Once again the matting wickets caused problems for the batsmen, so much so that Hawke would not allow Western Province to field visiting professionals Fred Tate and Syd Barnes; probably a sensible, if not particularly sporting, move. Hawke reported that 'unpleasantness' and 'ructions' led to the cancellation of two Tests in Johannesburg; the real reason was a period of bitter in-fighting between the various cricket associations in South Africa. The countries finally met at the Wanderers' in February and, for the first time, England were pushed hard thanks to a magnificent century by Jimmy Sinclair and, despite Warner carrying his bat through the second innings, the hosts were set a mere 132 to win. They failed, as Trott cut them to ribbons, but it was a brave and narrow failure and a large crowd had witnessed what was possible and that, in Sinclair, they had a player of the finest class. The Uitlanders remained sternly pro-South African in their allegiance, a fact no doubt influenced by the lack of Afrikaners in the national team.

After trips to Bulawayo, Mafeking and Kimberley and having survived a terrible train crash, the tourists arrived in Cape Town for the second Test where things once again started badly for England. The hero of the first Test, Jimmy Sinclair, once again scored a century and this time also displayed his bowling skills, helping to dismiss the visitors for 92. As the fortunes favoured the home side so the crowd grew to witness Johnny Tyldesley lead an English recovery. However, at lunch on the third day the South Africans were seemingly well placed on 11-0 chasing a total of 246 to win with a thrilling final two sessions in prospect. Half an hour later they had lost, bowled out for just 35 by Haigh and Trott. It was a bitterly disappointing finale but the South Africans could at least take comfort from having twice shown that they could compete for most of the game effectively at an international level, albeit against a weak English side. If only they could sustain their progress into the fourth innings. Any attempt to make this final leap was by necessity postponed as the much predicted and provoked Boer War finally broke out. Two of Hawke's party, the Yorkshire amateurs Franks Mitchell and Milligan, elected to stay behind in South Africa and both became embroiled in the conflict. Mitchell served with the Yorkshire Dragoons, returned to Yorkshire cricket and then accepted the position of secretary to Abe Bailey in 1903 before going on to captain South Africa on two English tours, the second of which was the 1912 Triangular Tournament. Milligan was shot and killed while serving with Colonel Plummer's force in the relief of Mafeking.

The New Century

Towards the end of 1900 it seemed as if the influx of British and Empire troops was finally crushing the Boer resistance and a tour of England, again sponsored by Logan, was organised. The party left the plague-ridden city of Cape Town in April 1901 and immediately and inevitably sailed into controversy. The Boer War had not finished but had rather entered its most ugly phase of guerrilla actions on one side countered by scorched earth and concentration camps on the other. The tourists had been weakened by hostilities with Tommy Routledge still fighting, Peter de Villiers incarcerated as a prisoner of war in Ceylon and Jimmy Sinclair only just managing to make the boat after escaping his Boer captors. The players were accused of trivial pursuits when they should have been attending to matters of Empire, a view expressed most eloquently by a great lover of cricket, Sir Arthur Conan Doyle. The South African Cricket Association had, for its part, wisely distanced itself from the entire project, pointing out that it was essentially Logan's private venture which it indeed was; he even selected his own son. The team did, on arrival, take the time to answer their critics by pointing out that most had already seen action including JJ Kotze who was an Afrikaner but had fought on the British side.

Despite the dissenting voices the tour went ahead and after a shaky start the form of the tourists improved in what was an almost exclusively first-class programme. What was lacking was consistency and strength in depth. Sinclair, Hathorn, Shalders and LJ Tancred (younger brother of AB) attracted plaudits while Kotze was reckoned to be faster than anyone bar Charles Kortright which goes some way to explaining the wonder surrounding the name of wicket-keeper Ernest Halliwell who stood-up to him. Unfortunately six players don't make a team and the South Africans suffered from the lack of Sewell and Llewellyn who had been poached by Gloucestershire and Hampshire and could not be co-opted for the summer. South Africa had now reached the level of a good county side but were still inferior to Yorkshire or Surrey let alone a representative team. Given the political and military situation a Test match on this tour would have been deemed less than appropriate even if the tourists playing strength had merited it. In July, while the tourists were struggling at Old Trafford, one of the most bizarre games ever was taking place at the Nondescripts' Ground in Colombo between the Colombo Colts and the Boer prisoners – truly an imperial event.

The tour lost money, not that Logan would have been overly concerned, and soon after its completion it lost its manager. George Lohmann, having settled in Matjiesfontein, had realised the dry South African air was prolonging but not sparing his life and he took the decision to pay a last visit to friends and family on this tour knowing full well that the weather and stress would be likely to accelerate the progress of his illness. He died a month after his return to South Africa aged 36; in the words of CB Fry 'a truly great figure in the great cricket of his time'. His contribution to the art of bowling, the status of the professional cricketer, Surrey CCC and the development of the game in South Africa was immeasurable.

The great supporters of South African cricket were inclined to bemoan climatic disadvantages, matting wickets and a lack of interest in the game outside urban centres but nonetheless South African cricket was creeping closer to parity with the big two. Enormous strides had been made in a mere 13 years and behind the best of it was the work of the professional English coaches. Just as Australia had benefited hugely from the work of Lawrence, Caffyn and Hide so the efforts of Lohmann, Brockwell, Braund and the founding father Frank Hearne had had a huge impact from Port Elizabeth to Johannesburg. South Africa still contained a large number of Randlords for whom the hiring of British players, and thus the improvement of cricket in their area, was something of a status affair and the professional was more than happy to swap the winter sleet of Accrington or Newark for the warmth and remuneration of Pretoria or Durban. A similar movement was also now underway in India as rival princes sought kudos through cricket. Even the journey to Cape Town was no longer prohibitive as faster steamships reduced the journey from three weeks to two making it easily possible to spend five months in South Africa while cricket in England was taking its winter break. The geography, organisation and even culture in Australia militated against a similar arrangement; the Melbourne or New South Wales clubs were less likely to import English coaches when men such as Bannerman or Giffen were becoming available to work in this capacity.

It was now high time for the South Africans to test their metal against the other Test-playing nation, something that had been mooted for many years. Soon after Major Warton's first English touring side had left South African shores, letters were being dictated with the idea of attracting further touring sides, not only from the mother country but also from Australia who, by this time, were more than a match for England in terms of cricket if not prestige. It was, however, nearly 13 years before the many laid plans came to fruition as all attempts foundered on the twin rocks of money and seasons.

Tours by English teams had always enjoyed the generosity of individuals but there was less readiness to bankroll an Australian visit until Abe Bailey stepped into the breach. The Australians for their part were technically amateurs, taking time off from their 'day jobs' to tour, and they had traditionally required and received a generous allowance for their efforts especially as they were always a crowd puller in England, virtually guaranteeing handsome gate receipts. The same certainty did not exist in South Africa and the seasons dictated that tours there would mean that leading players would be absent from the prestigious inter-colonial games involving Victoria, New South Wales and South Australia which were, in turn, great money-spinners. It was only in 1902 that a window of opportunity was found by tacking a short stop-over on their return from an English tour, thus allowing players to return to 'state' cricket, a term that had come into being with the Federation of 1901.

The English summer of 1902 had been wet and miserable but the doings of Trumper and Jessop had cheered the hearts of all cricket lovers and when the Australians boarded the *Dungeven Castle* bound for Cape Town they were given a rousing send-off. Just 17 days later they docked with a juddering crash, literally, in a country that only four months earlier had seen the Treaty of Vereeniging finally end the Boer War. The boat journey was followed by three days in trains and there they found themselves; at an altitude of 1800m in searing heat on a grassless red soil field surrounding a matting wicket. The contrast to Manchester or Sheffield could hardly have been more extreme and it is little wonder that the Australians struggled to acclimatise. For two days the visitors were baffled by the matting wicket and the left-arm spin of Charlie Llewellyn. The Australians were forced to follow on, a luxury that South Africa would not enjoy for another 50 years. Order was soon restored as Australian batsmen recalled their youths spent on artificial surfaces and Clem Hill led them to the safety of a draw. Despite the obvious advantages the South Africans had enjoyed, they had every reason to celebrate their first Test match against a truly representative international side and an exceptionally good one at that. Giant Australian bowler Hugh Trumble had had enough of watching the ball bounce over the stumps and he was happy to take his pregnant new wife home to Australia but the rest of the team were in Pretoria on the following day where Victor Trumper smashed a double-century against Transvaal for whom Jimmy Sinclair replied in kind.

Without a rest day the Australians were back in Johannesburg for the second Test match and once again the South Africans more than held their own in the early stages with the spin of Llewellyn, the pace of Kotze and the hitting of Sinclair enabling the hosts to establish a first-innings lead. Once again the effort couldn't be sustained, Warwick Armstrong scored a century and Jack Saunders and Bill Howell cleaned up the South African second innings for just 85. In the final Test, at Cape Town, the best efforts of Llewellyn with the ball and Sinclair with the bat helped little as Australia coasted home by 10 wickets. And after just one month they were gone.

The South Africans had glimpsed the brilliance of Trumper and the brutal efficiency of Hill and Armstrong. The Australians for their part were favourably impressed with the standard of play they encountered even if the matting wickets came in for criticism. Victor Trumper expressed the view, later echoed by Warner and Hobbs amongst others, that until turf wickets became the norm then South Africa would struggle to keep pace with the other major cricketing nations. South African opening batsman Louis Tancred, writing a decade later, emphasised the 'snap' that the visiting team showed; always alert, always ready to seize an opportunity or exploit a weakness and playing hard and giving no chances. This was disciplined cricket that had only been hinted at by the previous English visitors. The Australian reward was £250 a man, a reflection of the crowds drawn not only by the brilliant tourists but also by the thrilling hitting of Jimmy Sinclair. A return visit proposed by Melbourne CC in 1905 foundered on the dislike of the professional tendencies and a general antipathy towards Australians at a time when many were arriving in South Africa to seek their fortune.

In 1904 Abe Bailey again placed his considerable financial strength behind the third South African tour of England and freed up his secretary, Frank Mitchell, to lead it. Six of the 1901 tourists were again present and once again the budget allowed for three weeks of practice on turf before the first match. This tour proved to be another considerable step forward as the tourists were beaten just three times in 26 games. The team was totally dominated by the Transvaal contingent and Reggie Schwarz was the revelation, with 96 wickets at 14 each, ably supported by new men Gordon White and Sibley Snooke. The secret was the googly which Schwarz unveiled early in the tour in the nets at Cambridge, having learnt it from sometime team-mate and inventor Bernard Bosanquet, and which became his stock delivery for the rest of his career. Although still struggling against the strength of the best counties the tourists proved themselves more than capable when, for example, they easily beat an England XI including such luminaries as Ranji, Jessop and JT Hearne. Unfortunately the public and press were still unconvinced and the crowds never approached those attracted by the Australians, a fact not helped by the lack of a Test match and counties such as Lancashire and Nottinghamshire resting key players. MCC were nonetheless impressed and within 18 months they were, in their new role as tour organiser, dispatching a very capable mixture of amateurs and professionals, having first negotiated an underwriting of any financial loss by the South African authorities. With a five-Test series in prospect, it seemed that South Africa had now become a significant part of the cricket establishment, it was now time to do more than sportingly compete – in order to climb the next rung it was necessary to win regularly.

16 July his memory of the meeting was somewhat different.

> 'On inquiry I found that several members of the committee had been simply directed to support the MCC and voted accordingly but are by no means in agreement with the deduction which the MCC have drawn from their votes....We have, I think, been at cross purposes throughout; the MCC promoting this scheme under the idea that it was the strong wish of the counties, while the counties acquiesced under the idea they were obliging the MCC.
>
> I find it difficult to reconcile the position taken up by the MCC with the statement to the Australian Board of Control, that an objection on the part of the latter to a triangular contest should not be reason for refusing a visit from them in 1909.'

Remarkable. Virtually unintelligible, devious or stupid, Denison had apparently slept through the previous meeting as MCC's position was made clear. How could he think he was being loyal to MCC and how could he, and others, have misunderstood the meaning of the 23 June cable which had been read out at the 3 July meeting? At least it was becoming clear that the counties were ready to act to rectify their error. The *Times* expressed the desire to show the beleaguered Australian Board proper support, particularly as 'practically an invitation' had already been issued. Within days Essex, Derbyshire and Lancashire were clamouring for a further meeting of the AC-CC. For some reason Yorkshire advocated an Australian visit in 1910 but they had an agenda and finances peculiar to themselves.

Confusion reigned even in the press as the *Manchester Guardian* lamented the inevitable passing of this 'beautiful scheme' and somehow concluded that 'the MCC was for forcing them into the triangle' which had never been the case. In the days leading up to the meeting the delegates were bombarded with propaganda. A cable from Melbourne encouraged them to stay firm and promised they had the backing of Australian players. The *Observer* meanwhile continued its campaign of picturesque vitriol:

> 'These counties in their perfunctory dabbling with a great question endangered a great cricket friendship by coquetry with a whim of a millionaire.'

The AC-CC meeting was hurriedly convened for 29 July with Lord Harris in the chair and a stenographer from the Metropolitan Reporting Agency present. This time everyone would be accountable for what they said. The long and sprawling events were faithfully recorded – Denison claimed that the motion he had supported meant that if the Australians didn't visit in 1909 then South Africa should not be invited as an alternative which was fair enough as far as it went. Jessop attempted to establish whether or not MCC had formally invited Australia before the counties intervened. Lord Harris tried to confirm that CB Fry had been in the room when the vote was taken and nobody seemed to know who the dog was and who should wag its tail. MCC were the ruling body but in the matter of international fixtures they were powerless to act without the counties who provided the players, the grounds, the fixtures and thus the money. Finally a resolution was proposed by Horner of

Lancashire and seconded by Jessop, ratified by the MCC committee later in the day and cabled to Australia the following day:

> 'That the Advisory Cricket Committee of the Counties request the MCC to invite the Board of Control in Australia to send a representative team to England in 1909.'

The *volte face* was complete and on 6 August the reply came back:

> 'Invitation accepted, subject to approval of draft programme and terms. Board request you in conjunction with Mr. Poidevin to draw a draft programme, making provision for a rest prior and after Test matches.'

The proposed Imperial contest had been replaced by a standard Ashes series and the *status quo* restored – or so it seemed to all except a certain Mr Bailey. Within two weeks he was charging off, like the proverbial bull in a china shop, on a new tack. The Johannesburg correspondent of the *Sportsman* was reporting that a new scheme was being formulated and it would soon be made public. A week later Bailey released the details which were far-fetched in the extreme and couched in terms guaranteed to antagonise. His idea was that after the 1909 Ashes series in England both teams should sail to South Africa and play a Triangular Tournament there.

> 'We will take all the risks and provide all the guarantees. We want to do away with any and every excuse for not making a beginning with the great contest….The Cornstalks have not shown the true sporting spirit in the negotiations [and] if you ask the real cause, I think it is that the Australians are afraid of us, and afraid we may displace them in public favour in the Old Country….The South African climate is at the bottom of it all…. Perhaps you and I will not live to see it, but the people of this part of the globe will grow to be the strongest race in the world.'

Presumably Bailey thought that such an aggressive throwing down of the gauntlet would goad Australia into accepting the challenge or maybe he just believed he could buy everybody off. He was wrong on both counts; they scarcely gave it the time of day and by the end of the year the South African Cricket Association was busy trying to distance itself from the entire episode and was 'quite content to wait a year or two.'

1909 - 1911

Cordial relations between London and Sydney had been restored and the stage was set for an Imperial Cricket Conference during the summer of 1909 to establish a pattern of international fixtures which would hopefully include a Triangular Tournament at some future date. Although the formation of the ICC may have been of some consolation to Bailey it can only have been scant. As a sportsman and South African patriot his real interest was in the cricket and the ICC was a nice by-product; the major concern was that the South African team had already peaked and that any delay in staging a Triangular Tournament might catch them in decline.

When the dust had finally settled, Sydney Pardon was able to reflect in *Wisden* on what had occurred and he did not mince his words.

> 'The counties, of course, laid themselves open to criticism by going back on themselves but public opinion was clearly with them. Everyone felt that the change of front, however sudden, was better than the persistence in a wrong course. The credit of putting things right belonged mainly to Mr Jackson. But for his timely action the relations between English and Australian cricketers might, after thirty years of friendly rivalry, have become very strained….For the most part, the case was fairly argued from every point of view, but certain over-zealous people in Johannesburg, including it would seem Mr Abe Bailey himself, went so far as to suggest that the Australians declined the Triangular Tournament because they were afraid to meet the South Africans. This attitude would have been offensive if had not been so transparently absurd. The Australians have their faults, but lack of courage is assuredly not one of them.'

As Monty Noble's men arrived in England in April 1909 to begin their defence of the Ashes, JC Davis of the *Referee* took up the same theme.

> 'Was it sportsmanlike of South Africa (or Mr Bailey) to evolve a Triangular Scheme cut and dry its details with (unofficial) England, and yet not consult the views of, or even communicate with Australia? It is hardly 'playing the game' and, considering the relative positions of the two Colonies in the world of cricket, it was perhaps a little absurd.'

Despite the residual bitterness, the 1909 tour was full of cricketing interest and behind the scenes bridges were being built and plans were being made to regulate the future of Test cricket. On 15 June the representatives of the three countries thrashed out an agreement at the inaugural ICC meeting:

> 'That the principle of Triangular Contests is approved (providing the following arrangements have been made)….for England to visit South Africa in 1909-10 and South Africa to visit Australia in 1910-11 an effort should be made to have the first Triangular Cricket Contest in England in 1912 subject to South Africa waiving its claim to come alone that year; and to further this object England pledges itself to visit Australia in 1911-12.'

A further meeting of the ICC was set for 20 July at which the schedule of Test matches was extended to 1917 and a 'scheme for the triangular cricket contest' was formalised. The three teams should each play one another three times, the gross gate money of each game (admission 1s) to be split between the two participants, both visitors to play each first-class county and not more than three days allotted to each match.

With Australia, contrary to expectation, having retained the Ashes in 1909 it now remained for MCC to plan tours to South Africa and Australia before hosting these two in England in 1912. In the meantime South Africa would finally be seen on Australian turf. Or so it was hoped. In May 1910, with the tour only months away, the South African Cricket Association unaccountably demanded a 'fixed guarantee' for their visit to Australia. This was rejected and only intervention by Abe Bailey saved the tour and with it the Triangular Tournament which had always been conditional on a South African team visiting Australia before 1912.

Of prime concern to the authorities in England were the selectorial traumas of 1909 and a determination not to repeat these mistakes. With this in mind, the Test Board of Control met in November 1910 to 'formulate a scheme for arranging trial matches in 1911 in order to help the Selection Sub-Committee to make their selections for the Triangular Contest in 1912'. Three fixtures were arranged in addition to making provision for the two Gentlemen vs. Players matches to be hijacked for trial purposes. The absurdity of the plan was manifest in that the games would take place 12 months before the matches being trialled for, with the little matter of a full tour of Australia in the intervening winter to consider. The 1910 *Wisden* had called for new men, fearing that the generation of MacLaren and Hirst was in terminal decline, but in 1911 the editor then thundered at the shortcomings of the trial system that the Board had implemented:

> 'It is in every way a matter for congratulation that the question of securing the best possible England team for the Triangular Tournament in 1912 has been taken in hand but I do not see that much good can come out of the trial matches….What advantage can there be in making Tyldesley, Hobbs, Blythe and KL Hutchings, for example, play in trial games a twelve-month before the real business begins?....Far more important, however, than anything that can be done in 1911 is the recognition of the fact that the method of selection of England elevens for Test Matches must be altered. In other words the authorities are at last condescending to organise. We may be sure that in connection with the Triangular Tournament we shall have no repetition of the wild follies for which such a price had to be paid in 1909.'

As the 1911 English season began, further plans were afoot. Lord Hawke proposed limiting county fixtures to two long days during 1912 to facilitate the presence of two touring teams. His idea was blocked and the impracticality would be revealed in 1919 when post-war austerity forced the system on the counties for one season. Then came the business of setting dates and venues for the nine international fixtures. With such a bumper crop to be harvested, the Board of Control was inundated with requests to host a Test. The Grange Ground at Edinburgh, Cardiff, Brighton and, more reasonably, Edgbaston threw their hats into the ring while Lord Harris spoke optimistically of crowds of 50,000 at Dover. In the *Sporting Life* EHD Sewell sniffily suggested that the Woodbrook ground in Ireland or even the Parc des Princes would be as suitable as Cardiff or Edinburgh. The Board duly stuck with its favourite five and the list was approved by the ICC on 30 June 1911.

May 27th (Whit Monday) - Australia v South Africa at Manchester
June 10th - England v South Africa at Lord's
June 24th - England v Australia at Lord's
July 8th - England v South Africa at Leeds
July 15th - Australia v South Africa at Lord's
July 29th - England v Australia at Manchester
August 5th (Bank Holiday) - Australia v South Africa at Nottingham
August 12th - England v South Africa at The Oval
August 22nd - England v Australia at The Oval

With the big matches now arranged, the finer details of entrance fees and trial matches in London were confirmed. On 18 August the Board of Control now came to consider the possibility of extending the period of play:

> 'It was decided that the Test Matches shall be for three days only but that if after the second match between any two countries neither side has secured an advantage the third match shall be played to a finish.
> The Secretary [Lacey] pointed out that no provision had been made to meet the contingency of two countries tying for first place.'

Neither the Board nor the ICC saw fit to heed Lacey's warning although the latter did bring forward the ninth and last Test to 19 August 'to enable the game to be continued if necessary beyond three days without a Sunday intervening'. No points system was proposed and the presumption was clear that somehow everyone would know who had won and if they didn't then there wouldn't, and shouldn't, be a winner. This was not to be a championship or league, this was an imperial event to be played in a spirit of healthy competition with the play, not the result, being paramount.

The entire process had been pretty unpleasant and in the centre of it all stood Bailey, now Sir Abe Bailey, knighted in the 1911 New Year's list for his contribution to the cause of South African Union. In many ways this was a microcosm of Bailey's career; his vision and ambition were laudable, his finances well-managed and wisely invested but he displayed a total lack of tact, diplomacy or even common sense. This, allied to too many vested interests and some absurd confusion in London, brought international cricket to its first brink of the century.

Fortunately the day had been saved and the fixtures were now all arranged but first there was the little matter of an MCC tour of Australia. As the autumn of 1911 crept in, the deeds of Pelham Warner's team in Australia began to dominate the cricketing minds in England. Hovering in the background was the prospect of a glorious jamboree bag of cricket in the form of the Triangular Tournament of 1912.

8

Pricing It Up - 31/12/1911

❦

I f bookmakers had been preparing odds (and maybe some were) for the upcoming Triangular Tournament on New Year's Eve 1911, they would have had plenty of evidence in the shape of recent form, players' performances and selectorial conundrums to ponder. The form was:

1905 England vs. Australia 2-0
1905-06 South Africa vs. England 4-1
1907 England vs. South Africa 1-0
1907 -08 Australia vs. England 4-1
1909 England vs. Australia 1-2
1909-10 South Africa vs. England 3-2
1910-11 Australia vs. South Africa 4-1
1911-1912 Australia vs. England 1-0 (4 to play)

Australia: won 11 drew 5 lost 5
England: won 8 drew 7 lost 14
South Africa: won 8 drew 2 lost 8

England v Australia

The English and Australian teams had been largely evenly balanced over the previous decade with series often heavily influenced by the vagaries of the climate on uncovered pitches but for now the Ashes were in Australian hands.

Behind the scenes the new Australia was now seeking to unify cricket under the Board of Control which would henceforth oversee all foreign tours and thus bring to an end the practice of the team sharing the profits amongst themselves and leaving nothing for either the development or administration of the game at home. The Board was also facing up to the reality that, though the worst of the recession had passed, a new enemy had arrived as other sports began to eat into cricketing revenue.

Joe Darling might have had a strict religious upbringing but as far as money was concerned it had taught him discipline and not disdain. The embryonic Board had, despite its best efforts, little say over the 1905 touring party where Darling's luck ran out: five times he faced the man born on the same day as himself, England captain Stanley Jackson, and five times he called wrong. Jackson then proceeded to top both the bowling and batting averages in a 2-0 win. When Jackson arrived at the Scarborough festival in September he found Darling stripped to the waist ready to wrestle for choice of innings. Jackson nominated George Hirst as his 'captain for the day' and Darling decided to revert to the coin – Jackson again called correctly! Not for the first time suggestions were made that Tests in England should now be played over four days, pitches being much easier to score on unless attacked by rain. The Test at The Oval was a case in point as it became clear early on that a draw was inevitable on a lovingly prepared flat wicket although it did give CB Fry the satisfaction of puncturing the Australian theory that he could only play on the on-side; a large number of his 144 was driven and cut through a flimsy off-side defence.

With the Australian Board of Control still suffering birth pangs, MCC declined their offer to entertain a touring side in 1906. Apparently things had improved by the following year and AO Jones led a side including young Jack Hobbs and Sydney Barnes but lacking the likes of Hayward, Tyldesley, Jackson, Fry and Hirst. The teams were quite evenly balanced even if the record books show a 4-1 home victory as England lurched from triumph to disaster seamlessly. The sterling efforts of late substitute George Gunn couldn't stop Australia winning the first Test by two wickets. The next game was even closer as England put on 73 for the final two wickets and Gerry Hazlitt missed his Joe Solomon moment with a wild throw when a tidy return would have ensured the first tie in Test cricket. This was to prove the high point for England and thereafter it was the power of Hill, Armstrong and Roger Hartigan and the brilliance of Jack Saunders on flat pitches that flattened an increasingly dispirited touring party. Cricket had come a long way in half a century, only one game on this tour was not eleven-a-side and even Western Australia joined the list of states included on the fixture list. Considerably less encouraging was the nature of many games; the run-rate of only 43 per hour gave, in the words of Harry Altham, 'the first unmistakable evidence of the logical implication of matches without time-limit'. Colonel Philip Trevor, manager of the MCC team, commented 'now is the time to redeem the Test match from the familiarity which breeds contempt' before passing an even darker judgement:

> 'Risk, dash, personal sacrifice, and a slight element of personal danger have combined to make cricket the national game. The traits which are now too often distinguishable in it are rather un-British. Stolidity in practice with a business result in prospect smacks of the German.'

Worse still for the 'old country' was to lose at home in 1909 to Monty Noble's underrated team. After being embroiled in disputes concerning money and selection, as the Board of Control began to exert its statutory powers, the tourists were trounced in the first Test. Two bowlers who hadn't been on the previous tour, Hirst and Blythe, shared all 20 wickets. Why on earth the Australians had been underestimated is hard to fathom with the proven talent of Trumper, Armstrong and Noble being joined by the youth of Charlie Macartney and Vernon Ransford and they duly came into their own while the English selectors tinkered their way to defeat. They constantly managed to find the wrong attack for the prevailing conditions in a display of sustained ineptitude that had *Wisden* commenting that that their work 'touched the confines of lunacy'. Archie MacLaren once again proved himself to be a thoroughly ordinary captain both as tactician and motivator and also thoroughly unlucky. Where Jackson won all five tosses in 1905, Archie managed to lose all five in 1909 and the series was lost by two to one. It seemed that the old guard of English cricket was nearing the end. MacLaren managed only 85 runs in five Tests and fellow veterans Tyldesley and Hayward were scarcely more effective even if, in their defence, one could point to the wet wickets and the relative failure of even Jack Hobbs. Of the bowlers, Blythe, Hirst and Barnes prospered but all three were well into their thirties by this time.

The Australians had good reason to feel satisfied. Under unfamiliar conditions they had not only deservedly won, they could also point to the 'coming men' who had, seemingly, already arrived. The old guard of Trumper, Gregory, Armstrong and Noble were not at their very best but new boys Vernon Ransford and Warren Bardsley picked up the slack. The bowling was left mainly in the hands of Cotter, manager Frank Laver, Armstrong and young Charlie Macartney. Each managed at least one brilliant performance and it was the latter's 11-85 which won the third Test. England found themselves in such apparent disarray that one wit proclaimed 'if we don't buck up we'll have to content ourselves with supplying the umpires when Australia and South Africa are here in 1912'.

After the drama and disaster of the selection process in 1909, picking an MCC squad to tour Australia two years later was inevitably a tortuous process, particularly in the area of captaincy. Everybody in the press wanted Fry. His batting was seemingly as brilliant as ever and his reputation and popularity were apparently unrivalled. Commitment remained a weakness, however, particularly as he was closely involved with the training ship *Mercury* and, not being a wealthy man, he had to consider the financial aspects of a winter away. In July 1911 he was offered the captaincy and finally, a month later, declined it despite a public appeal intended to raise money for the *Mercury* thus freeing Fry for the tour. Reggie Spooner and a resurgent Gilbert Jessop were also forced to put business before pleasure and England had lost her best spinner as well with the international retirement of Colin Blythe, although Rhodes and Woolley could turn their arms at a pinch!

With Fry out, the mantle passed to Warner who had led England to victory down under eight years earlier and was batting as well as ever. His vice-captain, JWHT Douglas, was a sound choice as bowling all-rounder while Barnes, Rhodes, Hobbs, Strudwick and Frank Foster were all obvious selections. George Gunn's previous good form in Australia counted him in and Frank Woolley was now almost an established Test player. The second wicket-keeper had to be 'Tiger' Smith of champions Warwickshire. These 10 players were clear enough but the remaining six places were closely contested with a series of trial matches to help.

In the first of these games the greatest impact was made by Gilbert Jessop with a typically rapid century. JW Hearne, Relf, Seymour and Warner all made runs with the best bowlers being Woolley and Hirst. The second game was more informative. Fry batted brilliantly, a century by Hardinge of Kent advanced his claims, good all-round work by Iremonger was duly noted and Foster continued his outstanding form with nine match-winning wickets. But it was the form of Fry that drew the eulogies from Hamish Stuart in *Cricket* and with his decision on touring still pending he wrote:

> 'Fry is as great a batsman as ever and in point of masterful assertion of superiority over bowling is second to none....the match showed what a great captain Fry is.... it is to be hoped that he will go to Australia and will lead England....'

It was not to be.

The two Gentlemen vs. Players games that followed were also closely observed by selectors. Sydney Barnes finally agreed to an examination and of course passed with flying colours, 9-132. Big centuries were hit by Hobbs (a certainty), Spooner (a refusal) and Sep Kinneir (a hopeful). On the downside, failures by Tyldesley, Hardinge, Hirst and Hayward probably finished their chances of touring. Iremonger was soon added to the growing squad, having bowled well for the Players, followed by Kinneir on the back of his century. In mid-August Phil Mead was invited after some heavy run scoring for Hampshire closely followed by Bill Hitch the Surrey fast-bowler. The final two places were given to Joe Vine and JW Hearne and by mid-September the squad was complete. One or two men could, on form alone, feel aggrieved. George Hirst was still the leading all-rounder and Harry Dean had had an outstanding season for Lancashire. In fact, of the top 20 in the English bowling averages for 1911 only one man was picked to tour Australia that winter and that man was Jack Hobbs! Middlesex's ex-Australian Frank Tarrant might well have been a good choice on form but the political ramifications meant that, despite his keenness, it was never really a possibility.

Both teams had solid reasons to feel optimistic as MCC set sail in their quest to regain the Ashes in the autumn of 1911. Australia still had most of their old faithfuls and even the loss of Monty Noble was balanced by the return of Clem Hill who had been unavailable in 1909 and now took over the captaincy. Two men unknown to the English, Hordern and Kelleway, had fitted comfortably into the team that had played South Africa and it seemed a perfect mixture of experience and youth with which to confront the old enemy.

The tourists made a fine start but suffered a grievous setback when captain, Pelham Warner, was taken seriously ill and the leadership reverted to Johnny Douglas. The first Test was won handsomely by the home side with the anticipated mixture of experience and youth proving irresistible. Hill, Armstrong, Trumper and Minnett prospered with the bat and Herbert Hordern took 12 wickets in his first Ashes game. Douglas was never again foolish enough to deny Sydney Barnes the new ball. The second Test started on 30 December and the first hour was one of the most memorable ever witnessed. The conditions were overcast with patchy rain showers but there was nothing in the pitch to tell Clem Hill not to bat on winning the toss despite the protestations of Tibby Cotter. With the new ball in his hand and fortified by a half-bottle of red wine the brilliant SF Barnes proceeded to dismantle the Australian top order and in a trice Bardsley, Kelleway, Armstrong and Hill were dispatched. Nobody observed proceedings closer than the other bowler, Frank Foster, who wrote to his parents

> 'Just think on a perfect wicket, and, mind you, a wicket fifty times as good as the best of our wickets at Edgbaston, he got five of the cream of the Australian batsmen out for six runs. It was magnificent.'

All out for 184 and by the close of play MCC had made good inroads for the loss of one wicket. With the next day a rest day the prospects for New Year's Day 1912 were interesting to say the least.

England v South Africa

South Africa could be said to have arrived at the Test table by defeating the MCC tourists 4-1 in 1905-06 but English apologists had any number of excuses to draw on. A team lacking Fry, Jackson, Tyldesley, Rhodes and Hirst could hardly be considered fully representative even if this was, by some margin, the best set of players to visit the Cape. Warner's men had scarcely contemplated defeat as they were buffeted about the stormy Atlantic but they were to find South African cricket considerably more muscular and mature than it had been 18 months earlier.

The tourists started in fine fettle, winning their first five games in quick succession before the game against Transvaal provided a stark revelation that was to have a lasting impact. The English were faced with Reggie Schwarz's googlies on a matting wicket and they also came face-to-face with the first South African 'great', Aubrey Faulkner. When it came to the first Test it was these two that were called on to open the bowling by new captain and wicket-keeper Percy Sherwell in a game that was evenly balanced until the closing stages. South Africa were set 284 to win, a not impossible target, and this time the batsmen held their nerve in the last innings. First Gordon White and Dave Nourse (another English ex-soldier) guided them close to victory but, with wickets falling regularly, 45 were still needed when last man Sherwell joined Nourse at the crease. With the Wanderers' ground packed, the deficit was slowly eroded until finally the release came as Sherwell gratefully banged a full-toss to the boundary. Within seconds the rolled red gravel outfield was covered with celebrating spectators and Nourse and Sherwell were chaired to the pavilion.

If the English tourists had been guilty of underestimating the opposition, no such excuses could be offered in the next two Tests as England were increasingly comfortably beaten by a talented side that batted down to 11 and boasted four of the best wrist spinners in the world. The final two Tests were played on the matting over grass pitches at Cape Town which favoured the visitors who had struggled with the pace of the matting laid on baked ant-hill soil of Johannesburg. Colin Blythe immediately came into his own as England won the fourth game before losing the last by an innings as the fatigue of extensive travelling, culminating in four Tests in a month, began to tell. For the 10,000 spectators in Cape Town this 4-1 series victory (using just 11 players) was the final proof that South African cricket could now be ranked with the best in the world and in Aubrey Faulkner they had an all-rounder to rival Stanley Jackson or Monty Noble. Pelham Warner's account of this trip gives a fascinating insight into the Edwardian amateur's genuine pleasure in watching the birth of a cricketing nation. After being defeated in the first Test, he wrote:

> '….defeat in such a struggle was glorious, for the first test match will be talked of in South Africa as long as cricket is played there.'

Despite this South African victory in their own country, the Springboks were given little chance of success in 1907 on English turf pitches. They were offered a full tour complete with three Test matches although the financially nervous MCC insisted that the costs should still fall on the shoulders of the South African Cricket Association. Cricket had now voted to follow its rugby counterparts of the previous winter by adopting the Springbok emblem and the green and gold colours thus furthering the sense of a national identity in the years leading up to the final consolidation and creation of a united South Africa. Financial considerations then jeopardised the entire undertaking as it became clear that the majority of the team required a guaranteed allowance which, after some soul-searching, was provided by Abe Bailey to the tune of £80 per player. This led, not for the first or last time, to some justifiable questioning of the amateur status of the team from some quarters. Another point of controversy was the possible inclusion of Jim Mackay, lately immigrated from Australia, who was eventually excluded because he 'would destroy the South African character of the team'.

Once again the precaution of an early arrival allowed the visitors to adjust to the climate and pace of wickets and form was quick to arrive. Lesser counties such as Leicestershire and Warwickshire were brushed aside before the stronger teams Middlesex and reigning champions Kent were also defeated, and when the South Africans arrived at Lord's for the first Test their reputation had preceded them. No less than 50,000 people paid for entry over the three days, a figure unimaginable only three years earlier. Led by CB Fry, the England team could boast the very best of Edwardian cricket in Blythe and Hirst, Jessop and Tyldesley, and RE Foster and Hayward. Against this wealth of talent, the bowling of Vogler, a valiant captain's innings by Sherwell and the rain enabled South Africa to emerge undefeated. Sherwell's contribution was remarkable and unique; batting at 11 in the first innings, he decided to keep his pads on when the follow-on was enforced and proceeded to hit 115 in 90 minutes. At Leeds the pitch rolled out soft and receptive to the mesmeric skills of Colin Blythe who collected 15 wickets in a 53-run victory. Most experts considered that the pitch had been the difference between the teams as the pace of Kotze was nullified and the bounce of the quartet of googly bowlers severely restricted. Unfortunately the conditions at The Oval for the final Test were similar to those at Leeds. Fry with the bat and Blythe with the ball proved irresistible. Nonetheless South Africa made a valiant attempt to knock off a fourth-innings target of 255 in 160 minutes, abandoning it only when potential match-winners Faulkner and Sinclair were dismissed, a draw being a fair result. The public were quick to appreciate the attractive and aggressive style of the tourists and *Wisden* proclaimed them men 'who treated cricket as a game, not a business' in a thinly-veiled attack on Australian 'priorities'.

This was praise indeed and many now felt that the South African's had their feet firmly under the big table. What might have happened on hard wickets which would have suited the pace of Kotze and the googly quartet? Seemingly there was now precious little to choose between the two nations.

The MCC tourists in South Africa, 1909-10 – Back: GJ Thompson, W Rhodes, FE Woolley, JB Hobbs, H Strudwick; middle: GH Simpson-Hayward, Capt. EG Wynyard, HDG Leveson Gower (captain), D Denton, CP Buckingham, MC Bird; front: NC Tufnell, FL Fane, C Blythe.

Given the level of performance shown by the South Africans in 1907, it was a huge disappointment that such a patchy party was sent south by MCC two years later under the captaincy of Henry Leveson Gower. True, any team containing players such as Rhodes, Blythe, Hobbs and Woolley could scarcely be described as weak but at least five members of the touring group would, under normal circumstances, never have come near to the national side. Quite simply patriotism was not enough. Amateurs such as Fry and Jackson were perennial no-shows when it came to touring while for the professionals playing for England was not always the most financially gainful way of spending the winter. Declining an invitation to tour was, however, no bar to instant resurrection as shown by Stanley Jackson who, having rejected a tour of Australia in 1903-04, was promptly appointed captain for the 1905 Ashes series over the head of Pelham Warner who might justifiably have asked if MCC understood the concept of loyalty. He didn't, of course.

Despite the absences, the two teams disputed a fine series which was just shaded by the hosts whose Ernie Vogler could now justifiably lay claim to being the finest bowler in the world (no doubt Syd Barnes would have disagreed). Vogler had overtaken Schwarz by virtue of his variety; essentially a leg-break bowler with googlies and top spinners, he was far less predictable than the accurate Schwarz who bowled only googlies. Aubrey Faulkner had now moved ahead of Monty Noble as the world's leading all-rounder and shining light of the side. In spite of the brilliance of Jack Hobbs, it was a series of disappointments for MCC. Colin Blythe was only included on his favoured Cape Town matting where he proceeded to bowl England to victory in the fifth Test, his last for England. Denton, Rhodes and Woolley were all found wanting and only the underarm lob bowling of George Simpson-Hayward consistently troubled the home batsmen. The *Referee* extracted a gloomy picture of the future:

> 'It is to the new talents that we must look to uphold our reputation when the Australians and South Africans swoop down upon us....Our cricket authorities, however, are the last people in the world to look ahead....We are sadly in want of amateur batsmen.'

That word 'amateur' again. Albert Knight of Leicestershire put forth his interpretation of current form in his own inimitable fashion:

> 'None the less, skilled critics, anticipating the Triangular contests of 1912....have placed South Africa first, Australia second, and our own decadent isle third. So insoluble is the mystery of players' "form" that prophecy of this kind is utterly futile. One recalls it only to demonstrate the faith in South African cricket so strongly held.'

Even though the South Africans had triumphed and attracted widespread praise, they had concerns. Jimmy Sinclair was no longer the whirlwind of old while two of the googly quartet, White and Schwarz had regressed and even the ever-reliable Dave Nourse appeared to be past his best. Most worrying of all was the lack of new young talent. Much had been expected of men such as Zulch and Stricker but they did little to enhance their reputations. Quite simply Vogler and Faulkner had driven the hosts to victory, they took 65 wickets between them and Faulkner was also the highest run scorer in the series, outgunning even Jack Hobbs. The victory was duly celebrated but to those that cared to look deeper, with an eye to future meetings, the picture was not so healthy. Leveson Gower and Sydney Pardon were both convinced that South Africa would have little chance of seriously challenging Australia on their own wickets the following year. Essentially an ageing team had been carried by the brilliance of two men in beating a disappointing team that still had youth on its side and would only improve over the next few years. The next time the two sides would meet would be in England in 1912.

South Africa v Australia

Despite the many positives expressed on both sides following the 1902 series between South Africa and Australia, it was to be eight years before the two teams would meet again. South African stock had risen enormously following a near miss in England and the victory over England in 1909-10. Now, with the return of captain and wicket-keeper Percy Sherwell and the experienced all-rounder Charlie Llewellyn, the 15-man squad was confidently expected to give an excellent account of the newly created Union of South Africa in their first tour of Australia in a series designed to grease the organisational wheels behind the Triangular Tournament. The reality was somewhat different as the South African decline that had been detectable in the home series against England now became much more obvious.

Even before the tour began money was an issue with South African players, perhaps remembering how well Australia had fared in 1902, objecting to the financial arrangements and the lack of an Australian guarantee against loss. In Australia the South Africans were accused of 'riding the high horse' until Abe Bailey's financial muscle smoothed the waters. He stepped in with an open wallet and generous heart fully exonerating the Australian Board for their refusal to insure the tour. He was well aware that his cherished Triangular Tournament depended on this visit.

The South African tourists in Australia, 1910-11 – Back: Umpire, AW Nourse, COC Pearse, T Campbell, LA Stricker, CB Llewellyn, umpire; middle: SJ Snooke, GA Faulkner, RP Fitzgerald (manager), PW Sherwell (captain), RO Schwarz, JH Sinclair, AEE Vogler; front: JW Zulch, JMM Commaille, SJ Pegler. Absent: CMH Hathorn.

The cricket finally started in November 1910 and the visitors began well with a thumping victory over South Australia as Stricker and Nourse with the bat and Reggie Schwarz with the ball showed an immediate appreciation of the hard and fast turf of the Adelaide Oval. Narrow defeats at the hands of Victoria and New

South Wales and a draw with an Australian XI then gave the tourists an indication of the task facing them. However, nothing could have prepared them for the brutality of day one of the first Test at Sydney. If ever the tone for a series was set on the first day then this was it as the googlies of Schwarz, Vogler and Faulkner were smashed around the ground to the tune of 494-6 at stumps. Could it have been that those taunts of cowardice thrown at Australia back in 1908 by Abe Bailey were being avenged? This was a team in transition but for the unfortunate South Africans the old guard of Hill and Trumper were seemingly as brilliant as ever while the new recruits, Bardsley and Macartney, showed every sign of being as good as their illustrious predecessors. On the second day, Tibby Cotter's pace ripped out the heart of the South African batting and despite a grim and commendable rearguard action by Schwarz, Faulkner and Nourse an innings defeat was duly recorded.

The first lesson had been learnt; never tour Australia without a fast bowler. The googly quartet that had comprised the attack on the damp English wickets of 1907 before humbling all bar Hobbs on the matting in 1909-10 was now a shadow of its former self. White was missing and Vogler, who had been proclaimed the world's best bowler only two years earlier, was apparently a spent force. Former player Murray Bisset described Vogler's form as 'utterly useless', blaming his lack of 'determination and thoroughness'. With the loss of the reliable Hathorn to serious injury, the cupboard looked decidedly bare as the tourists travelled to Melbourne for the New Year Test.

Against all expectations the South Africans prospered. Aubrey Faulkner hit a double-century to establish a first innings lead of 158 and then Reggie Schwarz made immediate inroads in the second innings. Victor Trumper, however, came to the rescue, having, by his own admission, been given a life by umpire Crockett. The South Africans required just 170 runs on a blameless wicket to record a famous victory before collapsing for 80 to Whitty and Cotter. A mere three days later the two teams once again took to the field and once again the South Africans showed enormous resolve to put their disappointments behind them. Sherwell was struggling both on and off the pitch not least with the boisterous behaviour of his team who, according to baggage man/scorer WH Ferguson, 'were a high-spirited bunch often indulging in crazy competitions, like throwing pint glasses of beer through a dumb waiter'. Despite one of Victor Trumper's greatest innings, a chanceless and brilliant double-century, the visitors scraped a first-innings lead. In the second Test the South Africans had fallen apart with victory in sight but this time they maintained their composure to the end as Faulkner compiled a century to set a daunting 378 to win on a pitch finally showing some signs of wear. The hosts took the game well into the sixth day before finally succumbing by 39 runs.

Sadly the rest of the series was an anti-climax as Australia bolstered their attack by introducing Dr Herbert Hordern who proceeded to show exactly what could be achieved by googly bowlers on Australian wickets. The fourth Test was won by 530 runs amid a welter of dropped catches (Vogler alone put down four in the first innings) and a bowling attack described as 'at times a mere laughing stock'. Any Australian celebrations were muted by the death of the grand old man WL Murdoch on the ground during the lunch interval on the second day. The fifth Test was less one-sided but always looked like resulting in a home victory and so the series ended 4-1.

The South Africans had fought hard and were popular opponents both on and off the field attracting healthy crowds for all bar the last Test, but in the end they had been outclassed despite the 700 runs of Aubrey Faulkner and 25 wickets of Reggie Schwarz. Victor Trumper averaged a lordly 94 while Hill, Bardsley and Armstrong all managed an artisan's 50. Even more damaging was Bill Whitty's 37 wickets at 17.08. The South African team-manager RP Fitzgerald was able to celebrate the fact that the tour had helped 'to bring the people of the great dominions of the Empire into closer touch' but he also recognised that his was a team on the wane and players such as Sinclair and Vogler were no longer the forces of old. With Sinclair it was a question of age but with Vogler the reasons were more contentious. Abe Bailey had 'convinced' Vogler to stay in South Africa after he had considered signing for Middlesex in 1906 but the benefactor's patience was now wearing thin. The two had argued before the tour and then afterwards Bailey claimed that alcohol had played a large part in the deterioration in Vogler's form and on this basis he withheld the tour fee of £475. Vogler was a fighter and got busy for his date in court by collecting character references from players such as Clem Hill, asking him to confirm his sobriety during the course of the series.

Of equal seriousness for future prospects was a report emanating from Johannesburg in October 1911 that Percy Sherwell was concerned that his business would not allow him sufficient time to practise and, that being the case, he was unlikely to travel to England in 1912. The South Africans now quickly postponed a visit from Australia that had been proposed to follow the Triangular Tournament and Reggie Schwarz confidently backed Australia to give England a beating next time they met. James Pegler, chairman of SACA, was gloomy in his prognosis and wondered whether South African cricket wouldn't have been better suited by a further three years to prepare for the Triangular:

'In the natural order of things many players upon whom South Africa has relied have fallen out of the ranks, and it will be a difficult matter to fill the vacancies.'

At the 2 November annual SACA meeting, Pegler issued a call to arms:

'I take this opportunity of appealing to those players who contemplate retiring from the game….to turn out once more, and help us to maintain our position in the cricket world.'

He seemed to have missed the Agincourt mood when the reports from South Africa just before Christmas indicated that Sherwell was out, Sinclair, Mitchell and Tancred probably out and even Schwarz and Llewellyn doubtful. Trial games were called for the week after Christmas in Johannesburg to find suitable replacements and confirm form and fitness.

For the oddsmakers there remained plenty of unknowns. Was the Australian victory in the first Test of the 1911-12 tour really a continuation of five years of dominance? Did the brilliance of Barnes on the first morning of the second Test really indicate a shift in fortunes? Would Sherwell be returning, had Vogler found his form again and would the trial games reveal new talent? If so, wouldn't both England and Australia find South Africa and the mighty Aubrey Faulkner earnest opponents? What would 1912 bring? The bookies chalked up their Triangular prices.

AUSTRALIA 4/5   **ENGLAND** 11/8   **SOUTH AFRICA** 7/1

PART II

1912

JANUARY

Mo	Tu	We	Th	Fr	Sa	Su
1	2	3	4	5	6	7
8	9	10	11	12	13	14
15	16	17	18	19	20	21
22	23	24	25	26	27	28
29	30	31				

1912

Jan
Mo	Tu	We	Th	Fr	Sa	Su
1	2	3	4	5	6	7
8	9	10	11	12	13	14
15	16	17	18	19	20	21
22	23	24	25	26	27	28
29	30	31				

Feb
Mo	Tu	We	Th	Fr	Sa	Su
			1	2	3	4
5	6	7	8	9	10	11
12	13	14	15	16	17	18
19	20	21	22	23	24	25
26	27	28	29			

Mar
Mo	Tu	We	Th	Fr	Sa	Su
				1	2	3
4	5	6	7	8	9	10
11	12	13	14	15	16	17
18	19	20	21	22	23	24
25	26	27	28	29	30	31

Apr
Mo	Tu	We	Th	Fr	Sa	Su
1	2	3	4	5	6	7
8	9	10	11	12	13	14
15	16	17	18	19	20	21
22	23	24	25	26	27	28
29	30					

May
Mo	Tu	We	Th	Fr	Sa	Su
		1	2	3	4	5
6	7	8	9	10	11	12
13	14	15	16	17	18	19
20	21	22	23	24	25	26
27	28	29	30	31		

Jun
Mo	Tu	We	Th	Fr	Sa	Su
					1	2
3	4	5	6	7	8	9
10	11	12	13	14	15	16
17	18	19	20	21	22	23
24	25	26	27	28	29	30

Jul
Mo	Tu	We	Th	Fr	Sa	Su
1	2	3	4	5	6	7
8	9	10	11	12	13	14
15	16	17	18	19	20	21
22	23	24	25	26	27	28
29	30	31				

Aug
Mo	Tu	We	Th	Fr	Sa	Su
		1	2	3	4	
5	6	7	8	9	10	11
12	13	14	15	16	17	18
19	20	21	22	23	24	25
26	27	28	29	30	31	

Sep
Mo	Tu	We	Th	Fr	Sa	Su
						1
2	3	4	5	6	7	8
9	10	11	12	13	14	15
16	17	18	19	20	21	22
23	24	25	26	27	28	29
30						

Oct
Mo	Tu	We	Th	Fr	Sa	Su
1	2	3	4	5	6	
7	8	9	10	11	12	13
14	15	16	17	18	19	20
21	22	23	24	25	26	27
28	29	30	31			

Nov
Mo	Tu	We	Th	Fr	Sa	Su
			1	2	3	
4	5	6	7	8	9	10
11	12	13	14	15	16	17
18	19	20	21	22	23	24
25	26	27	28	29	30	28

Dec
Mo	Tu	We	Th	Fr	Sa	Su
						1
2	3	4	5	6	7	8
9	10	11	12	13	14	15
16	17	18	19	20	21	22
23	24	25	26	27	28	29
30	31					

THE QUESION FOR THE NATION ON NEW YEAR'S DAY 1912

Every one alike, miners, cotton-spinners, railwaymen, suffragettes and right up to Ministers of the Crown, one and all are thinking of some particular object which occupies the foreground in their minds and to the attainment of which they intend to devote all their energies. With the miners it may be a minimum wage: with members of Parliament the retention of their seats at a possibly near General Election: with Mr Lloyd George the Disestablishment of the Church in Wales: with Mr. Asquith Home Rule in Ireland. And probably the last thing any one of them will think about, for they will leave it to others, and yet on it the success of all their schemes depends, is the certainty that during the coming year we, as a nation, of which they are integral parts, shall be able to retain our postion in the world, not merely as a strong and influential Power, but as an independent nation at all; whether, in fact, we shall not by the end of the year have been wiped out of international politics altogether, and have become dependent on the will of others...

It is not the elders only, but the younger manhood that need arousing to what is before us: it is they who need to be convinced that their day has fallen on times when there is something more grave on which to expend their time and work off the exuberance of their physical strength than football, cricket or athletics.

Just now their happiness in the New Year lies first in gaining some trophy of football prowess: then comes the result of the University Boatrace, and finally the superiority of the old country in cricket over South Africa and Australia...what they must be prepared to do is similar to what their ancestors some few centuries ago were called on to do...to appear at the archery butts to employ their leisure hours.

THE KING-EMPEROR IN CALCUTTA
A POPULAR WELCOME   ENTHUSIASTIC SCENES

...this was the first time in the annals of India that the reigning sovereign of Great Britain had come amongst the peoples of the Indian Empire. The visit of their Imperial Majesties had called forth the deepest feeling of loyalty, devotion and rejoicing. It had still more closely cemented the ties of affection which had at all times bound the people of India to their sovereigns, and afforded abundant proof of the abiding interest of their Majesties in the welfare and advancement of their Indian subjects.

THE KING-EMPEROR'S "BAG"

The total "bag"in Nepal was 39 tigers, of which the King-Emperor shot 24. The party also bagged 18 rhinoceros and four bears. His Majesty on one occasion secured a tiger and a bear with his right and left barrels, and shot splendidly throughout.

THE BEST DOCTORS IN THE WORLD

It is worth while to note that the best physicians, whose eminence in their profession is the fruit of the best skill and best experience, smoke State Express Cigarettes, choosing them not only because of their purity and their wholesome soothing influence, but because they are among the best of the good things in life.

LIVERPOOL STEAMER WRECKED

Snow continued to fall heavily in many parts of Northern and Midland England yesterday, the fall in some places being the greatest known for 40 years...

The worst disaster occurred on the Aberdeenshire coast early yesterday morning when, after drifting helplessly, the Liverpool steamer Wistow Hall was driven upon the rocks at a dangerous spot known as the Bullers of Buchan near the village of North Haven and smashed up before much assistance could be rendered.

ANARCHY IN SZECHUAN

THE LABOUR REVOLT

PEACE PROSPECTS IN THE COTTON TRADE

THE MINERS' AGITATION

THE COTTON AND COAL DISPUTES
DEADLOCK IN MANCHESTER
MINERS' BALLOT TODAY

THE GERMAN ELECTIONS
STRENGTH OF THE VARIOUS PARTIES
RADICAL SUPPORT FOR SOCIALISM

INDIAN TEA ON THE CONTINENT

TEA ROOMS ARE OPEN AT

ANTWERP .. .. Rue du Berceau

BRUSSELS .. .. Avenue Louise

BERLIN .. .. Friedrich Strasse

HAMBURG .. .. Grosser Burstan

ROME .. .. Piazza Di Spagna

MILAN .. .. Via Carlo Alberto

THE GERMAN ELECTION CAMPAIGN
AN OBSCURE OUTLOOK

As the bells rang out and glasses clinked to welcome in the new year in the more prosperous quarters of Manchester, Pretoria and Adelaide, the cricket lovers of the three nations had plenty to ponder. In Australia, the old year had been ushered out by Syd Barnes putting a whole new complexion on the Test series through his decimation of the cream of Australian batting, thus placing England in a position to level the series. In South Africa, the majority of the country's best players had assembled in Johannesburg to play a series of trial matches that would, hopefully, reveal a body of men capable of winning the Triangular Tournament scheduled to begin in May. In England the cables arriving from Australia were being hurriedly transcribed to fill the hungry newspaper columns in order to satisfy an audience eager for the warmth that the genius of Barnes could provide.

The South Africans had returned from their tour of Australia nine months earlier proud but chastened having performed gallantly in defeat against a powerful side determined to show who was top dog in the imperial league. It was clear that some of the older players were now past their best while the younger players had, by and large, failed to fill the widening gaps. The team had been too reliant on the batting of Faulkner, the bowling of Schwarz and the captaincy and wicket-keeping of Sherwell. So now the cream of South African cricket, most of it at least, had been welcomed to the trials at Johannesburg between Christmas and New Year by Sir Abe Bailey who took the opportunity to remind them that there could be no finer honour in the game than being one of the 33 players representing the Empire in England that coming summer. Then, in company with the selection committee and the governor-general Lord Gladstone, he sat down to see who could do what and identify the men to carry the Springbok colours to England.

Triangular trials in Johannesburg – Some of the players collected for the three matches. Back: JL Cox, GPD Hartigan, CP Carter, DJ Meintjes, HW Taylor; front: F Le Roux, T Ward, PT Lewis, LG Tapscott, DK Pearse, BG Melle. Only five of this group actually made the final party.

Transvaal had nominated no less than 36 players, dwarfing the representation from other associations. Natal sent nine, Western Province five, Border two and Eastern Province and Griqualand West one apiece. The first game between Transvaal and the Rest saw Gerald Hartigan strike a fluent century, Dave Nourse and Billy Zulch reminded selectors of their skills with the bat and Rolland Beaumont impressed as a talented new stroke-maker. The bowling honours went to relative unknowns Le Roux, Cox and Carter. The failure of veteran Jimmy Sinclair saw him omitted from the second game which, like the first, ended in a draw. Once again Fred Le Roux prodded the selectors, this time with both bat and ball, and Tapscott dominated the Rest's batting with a century and a fifty.

The teams were tweaked for the final match with the supposed best young batsmen being pitted against the best bowlers. The youngsters were no match for a re-invigorated Ernie Vogler who took 10 wickets; only Hartigan and Herby Taylor appeared able to fathom the veteran googly bowler. On the other side the old lags made hay against the young bowlers as Le Roux, Cox and Carter (the pick of the first two matches) toiled against Zulch, Tancred, Nourse and Snooke. Now the selectors could retire to consider the evidence and attempt to find a group capable of winning the Triangular Tournament.

Without further ado the five-man committee set about quickly producing a squad for the approval of the South African Cricket Association (president, Sir Abe Bailey). The names were handed over on 2 January. Despite only 24 hours being required to rubber-stamp the list, the newspapers were still the quickest to the draw, a combination of guesswork, common sense and loose talk enabled them to correctly surmise most of the players. Even so, when the official announcement was made there was still plenty to discuss, so much so that the *Sporting Star* immediately convened a panel of experts for that very purpose. The reality was that this announcement was the first of many, the selection saga would drag on for another two months.

The first question mark concerned the captain and selection-committee member, Percy Sherwell. Along with Aubrey Faulkner, he was one of only two South Africans worthy of a place in a 'World XI' but it was no secret that business commitments and his recent marriage were likely to prove a barrier to his travelling. Ernie Vogler was another over whom serious doubts hovered although for very different reasons. He had been described by RE Foster only four years earlier as 'the greatest bowler playing cricket in either hemisphere' but his form had begun to slip through his fingers, culminating in a disastrous tour of Australia. Vogler blamed a thumb injury but the authorities were more inclined to explain events with reference to alcoholic refreshment on a tour that was notable for excessive consumption and *joie de vivre*. Vogler's fee had been withheld and on 9 January the *South African* News reported his 'standing grievance' against the Cricket Union. Furthermore his wife was unwell and he was loath to leave her for six months.

As to the fast bowling, apparently it was veteran JJ Kotze or nobody. Attending his ailing father had prevented his participation in the trials so the selectors kindly left a place open for 'a fast bowler or Cox' in order to give him time to get fit and prove his worth. For his part, Kotze planned to travel from his farm near Cape Town to Johannesburg at the end of the month in order to secure his place. Amongst those not selected, there was sadness though no great surprise that Jimmy Sinclair was to be denied one final charge and Louis Tapscott could feel somewhat aggrieved at his omission. The supposed certainty, Louis Stricker, was not included, a decision that seemed to baffle most experts; the *Natal Advertiser* was one of many to express itself dumbfounded despite the fact that Stricker had yet to pass 50 in 17 Test innings. A bout of pneumonia had scuppered the chances of William Shalders and another player disappointed to be ignored was Ormy Pearse. He had toured Australia with the national side and scored runs in the trial matches but his refusal to play in the fourth Test in Australia, after being excluded from the third, certainly counted against him.

With all the huffing, puffing and rumours flying around, the news coming from faraway Old Buckenham in Norfolk was a distraction but a very unwelcome one. Benefactor Lionel Robinson had organised a jolly New Year's Day football match to be refereed by Archie MacLaren. Amongst the players were two of South Africa's finest, and automatic selections, Reggie Schwarz and Aubrey Faulkner, the latter having been resident in Nottingham for over a year since his marriage. The following day, reports of the game led with the news that Faulkner, the world's best all-rounder, had broken his leg.

Fortunately, only a week later, better tidings arrived and the injury was now classified as a fracture of small bones in his ankle. Good news also for Gerald Hartigan on the same day; Bussey & Co had elected him outstanding uncapped triallist and awarded him the prize of a complete new cricket kit.

There was nothing to be done but wait on the decisions of Sherwell, Vogler and Kotze but cricket stayed in the news with publications such as the *Rand Daily Mail* running optimistic editorials:

> 'In some quarters there has been a disposition to think that South Africa will be outclassed. It is argued that cricket in this country is not quite up to the standard it reached a few years ago. The giants of those days are naturally older now, and the younger players, it is asserted, do not quite come up to the level of the past. But many distant experts do not hold this view and Mr. Sewell, the well-known writer on sport, holds that if Vogler and Faulkner regain their best form, the South Africans will make Australia and England "fight their hardest for victory". Indeed, we see no reason for pessimism. Given fairly favourable weather conditions, it would not be surprising to find the South Africans rise to the occasion and give a display such as will surprise even their warmest admirers in this country.'

Writing in the *Daily Express*, the aforementioned Sewell was seemingly slightly less convinced, fearing that if Kotze shouldn't play the lack of a fast bowler would be crucial in diminishing the chances of South Africa. He also treated readers of the London *Evening Standard* to an extensive introduction to the South African players. As a supporter of Cape cricket he was pulling strings in the hope of attracting decent crowds during the summer.

Most baffling of all at this time was a report in the Johannesburg *Star* that Sherwell would refuse the captaincy and Yorkshireman Frank Mitchell had been approached to replace him.

'But Mitchell took the broad view, South Africa must stand or fall as much as possible on South African born and bred thew and sinew. So he refused a very tempting invitation.'

Time alone would tell whether some or any of these rumours would turn out to be based on fact but judging by reports in English newspapers it appeared very unlikely that Percy Sherwell would be part of the summer's entertainment.

Over in Melbourne the Australians were fighting back in the second Test. Despite Barnes' bowling and then the batting of Rhodes and Hearne almost overhauling the Australian score with one wicket down, the game was suddenly finely balanced after three days. Firstly England collapsed and then Warwick Armstrong, supported by the tail, combined to set a tricky 219 to win in a low-scoring game. But then up stepped Jack Hobbs to make light of the target with an assured unbeaten century and the visitors coasted home by eight wickets.

In terms of its effect on Australian cricket this defeat was a mere bagatelle compared to the ominous rumbling behind the scenes and the constant reports of the latest gambits in the increasingly acrimonious battle between the Board and the players. MCC captain Warner 'declined to discuss local misunderstandings' when approached during the game but was prepared to say that "Nothing should be allowed to stand in the way of Australia and South Africa being represented by their very best players".

With the details of the Board meeting of 30 December now in the public domain, a conflict broke out in a slightly more private sphere as the selectors attempted to find a combination capable of turning the tide in the third Test due to start at Adelaide on 12 January. As 'luck' would have it, only Clem Hill of the three men was in Adelaide as the match approached and he wished to delay the final selection for as long as possible due to the chance of rain changing the condition of the pitch. In that event, Hill favoured the claims of Charlie Macartney's left-arm spin and cabled fellow selectors Iredale and McAlister his suggestion that he, together with senior players Trumper and Armstrong, should make the final decision, based on Macartney's fitness and the weather. McAlister, unsurprisingly, disagreed. Hill's next cable read:

'Macartney all right. Think must have left arm bowler. Suggest Macartney and Matthews in place of Whitty and Minnett. Minnett twelfth.'

McAlister's response was immediate and unequivocal particularly as Roy Minnett, the suggested twelfth man, was a great personal favourite and had batted exceptionally well in the first Test.

'My team as forwarded yesterday. Still oppose Macartney's inclusion. If Iredale agrees with you [as to Macartney's inclusion] favour yourself standing down not Minnett.'

The antagonism in this suggestion was plain. Clem Hill was not only captain of the team but also its most reliable batsman. The petulance of McAlister's proposal would not be forgiven or forgotten. In the event, a compromise of sorts was reached as Matthews replaced Whitty, Minnett was retained and Macartney excluded.

The changes made not a jot of difference as England won easily by seven wickets amid a welter of dropped catches and despite needing 150 overs to dismiss the Australians in the second innings. Once again Hobbs, Barnes and Foster were too much for the home side whose poor performance was understandable given the distraction of angry team meetings taking place during the game. The subject was how to respond to the Board's appointment of their representative in England that summer which would nullify the need for the players to choose a manager. Warren Bardsley, a player with strong Board contacts, was excluded from these meetings whilst the others agreed that any protest should be made only by players absolutely certain to be selected for the tour on merit; lesser players could simply be excluded should they complain about the Board's actions. So the certainties agreed to a joint response and the 'Big Six' came into being: Clem Hill, Victor Trumper, Warwick Armstrong, Tibby Cotter, Hanson Carter and Vernon Ransford.

On 17 January, the final day of the Adelaide Test, a letter signed by these six players was sent to Sydney Smith, secretary of the Board of Control.

> '....We respectfully contend that the players are entitled to appoint their manager, and that, as was done last time, fourteen players should be first selected, and they should then select a player-manager who should rank equally with the other players in respect to the remuneration for the tour. If this be done....such of us that may be selected will be prepared and will be glad to make the trip; but failing compliance with our request, we have to inform you with much regret that none of us will be available for selection, or to play if selected....'

Confusingly for English followers of the dispute, the *Sportsman* reported on the same day that the situation had now eased:

> 'The players have learnt that the forty applications received by the Board of Control for the post [of manager] do not include certain men who would be objectionable to them.'

Not for the first, or last, time the English press had either misunderstood the issues at hand or been fed erroneous information.

In reality the chips were down and the players could hardly be accused of keeping aces up their sleeves. 'Either Laver comes as manager or we don't go' was the message. The Board were quite ready for such a response and didn't delay in replying, not even bothering to call a Board meeting to discuss it. Sydney Smith wrote on 22 January (presumably under McElhone's guidance):

> '....the team which is being sent to England by the Board, as the governing body

of cricket in Australia, in accordance with the agreement entered into with the MCC, has nothing whatever to do with the arrangements….the Board….has only expressed its opinion that as a representative of the Board will accompany the team the appointment of a manager is unnecessary…. Whilst the Board is anxious at all times to send the best team possible, still at the same time it will not permit any number of cricketers to dictate the terms and conditions on which a visit is to be made or if a manager is appointed the terms and nature of his engagement.'

These exchanges soon became public knowledge and the press entered the fray. On 24 January the *Sydney Daily Telegraph* backed the officials:

'The Board doubtless sees, as it has consistently done, its duty to stand firm against any attempt to curtail its powers even if the immediate prospects of the game seemed to be dimmed by its action. There has been too much of this niggling at authority.'

Other members of the Board were less resolute (or confrontational) and one approached the invalided Pelham Warner to arbitrate. Although still determined to remain impartial he was driven by fear of the repercussions for the Triangular Tournament to contact McElhone. The reply Warner received supported the letter from Smith to the 'Big Six', going so far as to name Frank Laver as the stumbling block. The Board would not endorse Laver as manager or countenance him as representative (an idea floated by Hill) because they considered the performance of his duties in 1909 as displaying disloyalty to the Board. The press continued to report on and analyse the dispute, feeding a public craving news and opinions on what was rapidly becoming something of a national crisis.

One feature of the entire saga was the openness with which it was played out; players and officials alike could hardly wait to rush to their favourite newspaperman and so even something as private as the 'exchange of telegrams' between selectors Hill and McAlister swiftly became common knowledge. Rumours flashed here and there even in the sterner quarters of the press with the *Manchester Guardian* reporting on 18 January that:

'The threatened trouble….will not come about. Mr Clem Hill denies the rumour current in Sydney that he will not go to England for the Triangular Tests. On the contrary, he states that he has reserved berths for his wife and family.'

When the idea of Monty Noble's return was mooted after the third Test he refused to count himself out, despite having retired from big cricket two years before. The *Australasian* reported him as saying:

'I would like Australia to win the rubber and would like to help towards that end if it is thought that my services would be of assistance.'

In the event he found his business commitments too great and in all likelihood realised he would be rushing to join a sinking ship. Anything and everything seemed possible but was anyone really playing with a straight bat? As the days passed, the situation became simultaneously more dire and clearer as talk moved on to the Triangular touring party, the manager and the inevitable resurrection of disputes that had lain dormant for years.

Mercifully the old enemies also managed to have a few spats relating to activities on the field. Jack Hobbs, rather ill-advisedly, gave his opinion to the *Evening News* concerning barracking, particularly in Sydney. The Australian public had welcomed and recognised Hobbs as a batsman and fielder of outstanding ability but they could also recognise a whingeing pom when they saw one and anyway it hardly seemed to have affected either Hobbs or the rest of the team. Clem Hill pointed out that the Australian team, even the venerable Victor Trumper, were just as likely to be the targets of what was good-humoured mockery and nothing worse. Then after the third Test the England captain, Johnny Douglas, made a complaint about Hordern and Kelleway using resin on the ball to aid their grip. The latter denied the accusation but Hordern was happy to admit it, his reasoning being that it helped him grip the ball rather than get break (one could argue that the two are related). Monty Noble and Bert Hopkins claimed that it had been common practice for 20 years and anyway neither bowler had exactly prospered during the match in question. But if there was bickering there was sportsmanship too. When Tibby Cotter dismissed Tiger Smith in the Adelaide Test it was an English player, Joe Vine, fielding as Australian substitute, who took the catch.

The travails of the dominions were not replicated in London. True, the weather was foul causing floods in the Thames Valley and the capital was suffering under an excess of soot deposits but the cricket authorities could sit back, toast their toes and read of MCC triumphs down under. The *Daily Express* reported that Ranjitsinhji was returning to England for the summer and harboured ambitions of participating in the Triangular Tournament; imaginative journalism in action. In reality Ranji was 'forty and plump', fancying some months of easy runs at Hove accompanied by some easy socialising with old pals at the Test venues. In some minds, however, the idea was surely forming that with South Africa possibly losing at least two of its best and Australia likely to suffer even greater damage, wasn't there a major danger that this much heralded Tournament might become a trifle one-sided?

No such worries for Lord Hawke and Archie MacLaren however, as they and their colleagues were seen off at Waterloo by friends and family before boarding the steamship *Asturias* at Southampton bound for Buenos Aires – MCC on tour in Argentina!

FEBRUARY

Mo	Tu	We	Th	Fr	Sa	Su
			1	2	3	4
5	6	7	8	9	10	11
12	13	14	15	16	17	18
19	20	21	22	23	24	25
26	27	28	29			

1912

Jan
Mo	Tu	We	Th	Fr	Sa	Su
1	2	3	4	5	6	7
8	9	10	11	12	13	14
15	16	17	18	19	20	21
22	23	24	25	26	27	28
29	30	31				

Feb
Mo	Tu	We	Th	Fr	Sa	Su
			1	2	3	4
5	6	7	8	9	10	11
12	13	14	15	16	17	18
19	20	21	22	23	24	25
26	27	28	29			

Mar
Mo	Tu	We	Th	Fr	Sa	Su
				1	2	3
4	5	6	7	8	9	10
11	12	13	14	15	16	17
18	19	20	21	22	23	24
25	26	27	28	29	30	31

Apr
Mo	Tu	We	Th	Fr	Sa	Su
1	2	3	4	5	6	7
8	9	10	11	12	13	14
15	16	17	18	19	20	21
22	23	24	25	26	27	28
29	30					

May
Mo	Tu	We	Th	Fr	Sa	Su
		1	2	3	4	5
6	7	8	9	10	11	12
13	14	15	16	17	18	19
20	21	22	23	24	25	26
27	28	29	30	31		

Jun
Mo	Tu	We	Th	Fr	Sa	Su
					1	2
3	4	5	6	7	8	9
10	11	12	13	14	15	16
17	18	19	20	21	22	23
24	25	26	27	28	29	30

Jul
Mo	Tu	We	Th	Fr	Sa	Su
1	2	3	4	5	6	7
8	9	10	11	12	13	14
15	16	17	18	19	20	21
22	23	24	25	26	27	28
29	30	31				

Aug
Mo	Tu	We	Th	Fr	Sa	Su
		1	2	3	4	
5	6	7	8	9	10	11
12	13	14	15	16	17	18
19	20	21	22	23	24	25
26	27	28	29	30	31	

Sep
Mo	Tu	We	Th	Fr	Sa	Su
						1
2	3	4	5	6	7	8
9	10	11	12	13	14	15
16	17	18	19	20	21	22
23	24	25	26	27	28	29
30						

Oct
Mo	Tu	We	Th	Fr	Sa	Su
1	2	3	4	5	6	
7	8	9	10	11	12	13
14	15	16	17	18	19	20
21	22	23	24	25	26	27
28	29	30	31			

Nov
Mo	Tu	We	Th	Fr	Sa	Su
			1	2	3	
4	5	6	7	8	9	10
11	12	13	14	15	16	17
18	19	20	21	22	23	24
25	26	27	28	29	30	

Dec
Mo	Tu	We	Th	Fr	Sa	Su
						1
2	3	4	5	6	7	8
9	10	11	12	13	14	15
16	17	18	19	20	21	22
23	24	25	26	27	28	29
30	31					

Race Distinction in South Africa

In many parts of the world, and nowhere more than in some of our colonies, there is going on a struggle between different races - the assertion in various ways of supremacy by people of European descent, and claims to equality by those belonging to races of a very different type.

THE FIGHT WITH FRENCH RAILWAY THIEVES

At the Orleans railway station in the early hours this morning two men were seen in the booking office. On being approached by the station officials they fired their revolvers, wounding two of the officials, and then escaped into a train which was just leaving for Paris. Telegrams were immediately sent to all the stations along the up line at which the train stopped. At Angerville, the first stop from Orleans, a man hurriedly left the train on the side away from the platform and shot dead a gendarme who attempted to arrest him. A second gendarme discharged his carbine after the fugitive, who was ultimately arrested. At the next station, Etampes, the train was at once boarded, and a suspicious looking individual who was questioned promptly drew his revolver and blew his brains out. Another man who escaped from the train at Etampes was pursued across country and finally, like his associate, avoided capture by shooting himself.

ALARMING INCREASE IN CRIMES OF VIOLENCE

The fight with railway thieves reported yesterday proves to have been a bigger affair than was at first supposed. The two thieves... left the train together at Angerville and made off along the road to Etampes, pursued by a gendarme and a police sergeant on bicycles. The pursuers missed the criminals and took up their stand in a village on the Etampes road. Soon two men were heard approaching through the darkness. The sergeant stepped forward and ordered them to stop. An electric lamp was flashed on him by one of the thieves while the other shot him through the heart. Both men then made off and a hue and cry was raised. More policemen came up and the fugitives were ultimately overtaken and surrounded in a marsh. A fusilade took place without effect on either side. The police gradually drew nearer and one of the criminals thereupon turned the revolver on himself... the second thief jumped over a brook into some rushes and disappeared. He was ultimately captured in a small inn at Etrechy by a local policemen whose suspicions had been roused by the man's tattered appearance...This man, who first gave the name Oscar Wilde, has now been identified as Joesph Renard, an Anarchist...

The passenger in the train who shortly after being questioned by the police at Etampes shot himself through the head does not appear to have had anything to do with the two train thieves. He had entered the train at Limoges in the neighbourhood of which a murder had recently been committed, and it is supposed that this man was the perpetrator of this crime.

Although there can be no doubt of the improvement in the general attitude of the German public regarding relations with England there are already some unsatisfactory signs of a reaction, at any rate in the Press, against the cordial views expressed last week.

HARROW – THE CENTRE OF ITS PRACTICAL AND INDUSTRIAL DEVELOPMENT

THE FUTURE OF AVIATION IN ENGLAND

THE COAL CRISIS
MINERS' STRIKE NOTICES
FUNDS OF THE UNIONS

THE SUPREMACY OF THE NAVY
MR. CHURCHILL ON NAVAL RIVALRIES

BLACK FEVER
DEVELOPMENT OF PARASITE DISCOVERED

THE CRISIS IN THE COAL TRADE
PROSPECT OF GOVERNMENT ACTION

The Jungfrau railway

The Jungfrau railway tunnel was pierced as far as Jungfraujoch at 5.45 this morning. This is the last station on the railway, and is at a height of 12,070ft.

STRIKE BEGUN BY DERBY MINERS
NO COMPROMISE IN SOUTH WALES

"THE MINERS NEXT STEP"
ELIMINATION OF COLLIERY OWNERS

WOMAN SUFFRAGE
TO-NIGHT'S ALBERT HALL MEETING

January had seen more questions than answers in both Australia and South Africa. It would now need some considerable compromises to clear the air. Early in February it became apparent that this was not on the agenda in Australia. The next Board of Control meeting was scheduled for 2 February and on that morning the *Sydney Morning Herald* wrote:

> 'We urge the Board to set itself towards compromise, to let bygones be bygones, to rest the new order not upon the wreck of the old but by the merging of one with the other....We think the letter of the players ill considered in its threat [but] the eminent players of Australia cannot be ignored in their insistence upon the spirit of the Board's constitution.'

The Big Six letter was read into the minutes and Smith's reply to the players was endorsed even though not everyone was in agreement, four members recording their refusal to participate in the appointment of a Board nominee as representative. But this was only a token protest. McElhone's iron will was always going to carry the day. Clem Hill offered to show Laver's 1909 tour books but this apparent climb-down was rejected out of hand by a Board that was now out for blood. Even a discussion of the infamous telegraphic interchange between McAlister and Hill failed to elicit any sympathy for the standing captain of the national team. The other main business of the evening was how to fill the controversial post of Board representative for the forthcoming tour. Many applications had been received for this poisoned chalice and the debate was lively. Associations combined and then withdrew support and for once Ernie Bean and Billy McElhone were in disagreement and then, emerging through the ensuing confusion, there was one George Crouch, a player of modest talents and with no experience of cricket management. Priceless. For McElhone's candidate, Ernest Hume, the story would take a tragic twist only five months later. The Board's next move came eight days later, but those intervening eight days gave the press and public alike time to absorb the most notorious incident of all.

Once again the three selectors were faced with the dilemma of producing a winning team from the ravages of a savage defeat at the hands of an English team that had now added confidence to its evident talent. This time, on 3 February at Bull's Chambers in Sydney, Iredale, McAlister and Hill at least managed to convene in the same room, with Sydney Smith overseeing the meeting. The atmosphere was prickly from the outset with the cables exchanged before the previous Test match still very much in the memory.

Peter McAlister wasted no time in criticising Clem Hill's captaincy in the first three Tests and Hill responded by questioning McAlister's credentials to make such judgements. The 'discussion' soon degenerated into a trading of insults as McAlister called Hill the worst captain he had ever seen. Hill was an essentially calm man but this was one provocation too many, causing him to thunder:

> "You've been looking for a bloody punch in the jaw all night and I'll give you one."

And thereupon he did so. Hill claimed a 'gentle slap', Smith saw 'a violent blow' and

Iredale witnessed 'a back-handed clip' later amended to 'a severe blow'. The ensuing brawl lasted either 10 or 20 minutes, depending on the source, but the severity of the fisticuffs was not in doubt and, best of all, a blow-by-blow account was soon available for all and sundry via the daily 'papers. The *Australasian's* version was the most graphic:

> 'Whether the first blow was struck with the open or shut fist, it roused McAlister to retaliation, and he rushed round the table and grappled with Hill. They fought fiercely, and, locked in each other's arms, swayed round the room, crashing against the table and walls. The two spectators, Frank Iredale and Syd Smith, were powerless to interfere, and in spite of their efforts to separate the combatants, the struggle proceeded. At the end of the bout McAlister was on his back on the floor, and Hill was standing over him. McAlister got to his feet, and as they struggled dangerously close to the window, Syd Smith leaned forward and grabbed Hill's coat tails and pulled him off, Iredale leaning across and holding McAlister.'

Was there a tone of a light amusement or even satisfaction? Frank Iredale's version was equally explicit:

> '….they went at it hammer and tongs. Very few blows were struck; it was more like a wrestling match. Smith and I did our best to part them, but they were all over the place, and when the big table was upset I was pinned in the corner. I strained my side, and still feel the effects….it all occurred as quick as lightning. They were both game and determined.'

Eventually Hill was led from the room and the remaining combatant and witnesses could attend to injuries and bloodstained clothing. Incredibly enough the three then calmly sat down and picked not only an unchanged team for the fourth Test but also the first ten names for the tour of England. Hill, Trumper, Armstrong, Ransford, Cotter, Carter, Minnett, Bardsley, Carkeek and Hordern were, in due course, to receive invitations to play for Australia in the Triangular Tournament. The *Sportsman* lived up to its name in reporting:

> 'That the quarrel should have come to blows is not so very serious but that Hill should have resigned from the Selection Committee is very regrettable for Australia.'

The three selectors took the train to Melbourne following this fracas and were met by a throng of reporters who gleefully noted the bountiful evidence of the brawl on the bruised and battered face of Peter McAlister. When the game began, on 9 February, the Australians were soon under the cosh. Twice skittled by Barnes, Foster and Douglas and thumped by a record first-innings stand of 323 in 268 minutes between Rhodes and Hobbs, they subsided to defeat by an innings and 225 runs in three days. The English team was good and playing brilliantly, the Australians good and playing terribly. Clem Hill, who had resigned from the selection committee, was cheered to the echo as he came out to bat, umpire Crockett reporting that Hill had tears in his eyes as he took guard. A large section of the public had spoken. Back in England, AO Jones had his own views:

> 'Fancy going into the field without a left-arm bowler! I cannot understand why Macartney was not in the side. I am astonished at the weakness of the Australian batting and fielding. We all know that a little friction might upset the side, but whether that accounts for the Colonials' poor show, or whether it is due to our exceptional bowling one cannot say.'

The Australian team at Melbourne, 9 February – Hill, Ransford, Kelleway, Hordern, Armstrong, Cotter, Carter, Trumper, Minnett, Matthews, Bardsley. By this time it was becoming clear that the majority of this side would not be travelling to England for the Triangular Tournament.

The state teams were equally unsuccessful. Despite the efforts of Warwick Armstrong with the bat (food poisoning prevented him from bowling) Victoria were brushed aside and a certain EA McDonald managed just two wickets. This pair would make ample reparations a decade later. New South Wales were saved from humiliation, but not defeat, by Syd Gregory's 186, an innings that all but guaranteed his selection for the Triangular party, probably as captain if Hill declined – MCC's most successful bowler was Jack Hobbs!

It was, however, the parallel, but inextricably linked, events off the field that filled most column inches. The continuing dismantling of Australian cricketing tradition as the selectors, literally, and the Board and players, metaphorically, continued to trade punches. The *Times* of 14 February reported

> 'that Mr Warner and Mr Foster are endeavouring to act as mediators [and] it is hoped that a settlement will be effected.'

The *Pall Mall Gazette* even quoted 'a prominent official of the MCC' fearing the possibility of two teams touring simultaneously as had been the case in Australia in 1887-88. He went on to hope that there would be 'no bickerings, no heartburnings, no jealousies' the following summer.

The fourth Test at Melbourne, 9 February – Frank Foster bowling left-arm round to Victor Trumper with a strong leg-side field. Tiger Smith is standing back!

Clearly the majority of the Australian team were mightily distracted, particularly as the Board had chosen the first day of the fourth Test match as a suitable date to issue those 10 invitations to tour England. The conversations taking place in the Australian dressing room as the game progressed are not difficult to imagine. The moment of crisis was careering into view and the Board had contributed to the pace of events by giving the 10 players just 10 days in which to decide whether to accept or decline. The press was fed stories from interested parties, Armstrong for one indicating that though they could accept Crouch they would not back down over Frank Laver.

Events in the meantime had treated Frank Laver the player in an unkindly fashion. He had represented his state, Victoria, against the tourists earlier in the season and despite his veteran status he had completed 63 overs and taken six wickets. His reward was to be unceremoniously dropped, thereby effectively disqualifying him from consideration for the national side. It is not hard to hear the voice of Billy McElhone whispering into the ears of friends and colleagues at the VCA, one of whom was none other than state selector Peter McAlister!

As the 10-day deadline passed, only four replies had been received. Bardsley, Minnett and Carkeek accepted while Herbert Hordern regretfully declined due to the pressure of work at his dental surgery. Hordern had played in England with a degree of success in two previous summers while studying and it is highly surprising that he resisted the temptation of one more visit especially as he had vaulted to the position of number-one bowler in Australia. Unfortunately his reminiscences throw no light at all on events although it is difficult to believe that the general turmoil did not influence his decision to decline.

That left the Big Six. The deadline had been extended and their reply to the invitations was finally received on 22 February, the day before the fifth Test match was due to commence. There were no surprises and no backing-down. They accepted on condition that the appointment of the manager would be made by a majority decision of the full selected touring party which, according to clause 9, the players were totally entitled to do. The fact that they attached conditions to their acceptance was taken as tantamount to a refusal to accept the Board's conditions and thus a refusal to tour.

Frank Laver had, in a belated attempt to rescue the situation, already sent a cable asking the players to ignore him as a potential manager and even Pelham Warner had re-entered the dispute. On 20 February he had attended a meeting between four of the Big Six and Lord Chelmsford, governor of New South Wales, in which both men pleaded with the players to search for a compromise. It was all in vain, they were adamant that there was no going back. On the same day the *Sydney Daily Telegraph* had applauded the Board's stance:

> 'Any temporary disadvantage that Australian cricket is put under.....will, it is hoped, be more than compensated for by the clearing of the atmosphere of the game.'

Another Sydney newspaper argued for a different, and more subtle, approach from the players:

> 'Clearly, therefore, they should have accepted unconditionally the Board's invitation to join the tour. Then, if the combined vote of the Australian side had been cast for Mr Laver as manager, the onus of the next move would have been upon the Board of Control.'

The somewhat inflammatory weekly, the *Bulletin*, was having a field day. The Big Six were now the 'Insurgent Six' and on 22 February it printed an outline of the powers bestowed on the Board's representative in England by Billy McElhone who, the journalist imagined, sitting in some candlelit stygian gloom wearing a wrestling singlet and sweating profusely. This Dantesque vision proclaimed that any player could be sacked or suspended for misbehaviour or repeating the 'scandalous treatment meted out to McAlister during the last tour'. The subject of expenses was also raised and dashingly paraphrased:

> 'Players who wish to indulge in fire-water, smokes, picture expeditions with chamber-maids and so forth will part up out of their own pockets.'

'Fire-water' and 'picture expeditions' would feature strongly during the summer of 1912. The *Sydney Mail*, while no less pro-Board, was considerably more sober:

> 'The cleavage between the amateur and professional in Australia is becoming too great to be longer hidden, and the position is acute on account of the lack of backbone of the English authorities, who accepted cricketers from Australia as

amateurs when they were getting "presents" of large sums of money for playing for the honour and Joys of the Commonwealth.'

Everybody was now rushing into print. Fred Spofforth, the Demon of yesteryear, threw in his twopenny worth, sounding for all the world like Geoffrey Boycott:

'The controlling body wants more playing members on it; otherwise it gets at loggerheads with the active players in some way or other....it is no good trying to pick teams from the pavilion – you want players to pick players.'

And in the middle of all this rhetoric and advice the players took the field for the fifth, and final, Test. The Australian team was much changed and even one of the Big Six, Tibby Cotter, had been dropped. The new men, McLaren, Hazlitt, Macartney and Gregory, were to do little better than their predecessors and MCC won easily enough by 70 runs thanks to a century from Frank Woolley and more brilliance from Syd Barnes. Macartney was lucky to be playing at all having narrowly avoided serious injury when a net post blew down and inflicted 'a severe wound, marking him for life'.

The series was over and England had won 4-1 largely thanks to the efforts of Douglas, Barnes and Foster who between them took 81 of a possible 100 wickets. Hobbs hit 662 at an average of 82.75, his opening partner Rhodes was also prolific with youngsters Jack Hearne and Frank Woolley both hitting match-winning centuries. Behind the wicket, Smith had taken advantage of Strudwick's rheumatism and his understanding with county colleague Foster was a consistent feature of play. Much later it emerged that Foster had helped engineer the change by giving Strudwick misleading instructions in the first Test. The one bright spark in the home side was Herbert Hordern's 32 wickets but he would not be travelling to England. The *Sportsman* renamed **J**ohnny **W**ont **H**it **T**oday Douglas. He was now **J**ohnny **W**ent **H**ome **T**riumphant and was pictured being congratulated by Plum Warner with a kangaroo weeping in the background.

On 23 February the *Times* reported from Sydney that the game was up:

'Messers Armstrong, Ransford, Carter, Cotter and Trumper have notified the Board of Control that they will only accept the invitation to join the Australian team in the Triangular Tournament if Mr Laver is appointed manager. The Board has, however, refused these conditional acceptances, and has cancelled the invitations. Mr Gregory, Mr Maclaren [sic] and Mr Hazlitt have already been selected to fill three places and the other two will be chosen later. Mr C Hill is certain to adopt a similar attitude in which case it is expected that Mr Gregory will be captain. The position appears almost hopeless.'

At least one of the players, Victor Trumper, believed that the matter was now closed and the selectors were instructed to pick 16 players to tour England. Still a war of words raged in the press and rumours briefly circulated that two English-based Australians, Philip le Couteur and Frank Tarrant, might be asked to join the tour. Recently retired captain Monty Noble gave his version of events on 29 February:

'In these six years they [the Board] have not been credited with one single act of conciliation or forbearance. They have held the pistol of coercion at the heads of the players the whole time, and gradually taken away their privileges....Both the spirit and the letter of the constitution have been violated.'

Current captain Clem Hill's verdict was equally damning but more specific:

'If it is considered desirable that control of Australian cricket should be left in the hands of one man, by all means do it openly, but don't pretend to invest the Board with this control when you know an individual controls the Board.'

But these were the last utterances from men who knew that the end of the line had been reached.

South Africa also remained on tenterhooks regarding the fate of some of its leading men. The first news was good; Aubrey Faulkner was recovering well in England and would be walking normally by the end of the month but the possibility of Sherwell leading the team seemed to be fast receding and of the various alternatives suggested Louis Tancred seemed the most acceptable. On 6 February the formal announcement came and the open secret was confirmed that 'Percy Sherwell regrets....'. Then the *South African News* reported that Vogler was still 'holding back till his claim for services in the Australian tour are satisfied'. This was a considerable battle of wills. Sir Abe Bailey could easily have settled the account and thus strengthened his team for a tournament that was his brainchild, but he didn't and he was clearly furious with either what Vogler had done in Australia or what he was doing now. Taking the other side, Vogler could hardly be expected to play for a team that was refusing to pay for services rendered a year previously. To add to the tension, Vogler was interviewed at the Wanderers' on 10 February saying that he had declined the invitation due to 'business commitments' which he hoped would be completed by the end of February.

It was clearly now time for the selection committee to meet again, which they duly did on 15 February. *Cricket* summarised the outcome:

'Mr Sherwell and Mr Vogler will be unable to accompany the team selected to represent South Africa in the Triangular Tournament. Mr Frank Mitchell, the old Cambridge University and Yorkshire cricketer, and Mr J Cox have been chosen to replace them. Mr Mitchell has been elected captain.'

The conclusions were simple but the ramifications considerably less so. Kotze had plainly not been able to get fit so Joe Cox could now pack in earnest and the team would be without a genuine fast bowler. Even this decision was subject to criticism from correspondents Linesman and Free Lance who both considered Fred Le Roux a superior bowler, batsman and fielder.

Then there was, again, the question of Ernie Vogler, always a prickly subject. Newspapers had agreed not to print any references to the Vogler/Bailey feud but once it was confirmed that Vogler would not be going the cat was out of the bag. The 'business commitments' to which he had referred were, in fact, the commencement of his court action against Bailey which was scheduled for the third week of April. He would then be free to travel to England having sued the president of the South African Cricket Association! Funnily enough Vogler's offer was refused and Linesman in the *Star* reported darkly that 'I happen to know he was offered a fairly big inducement to go'. However large, it was clearly not the full amount that Vogler felt he was owed from the Australian tour. Bailey was not short of a few bob but principles were at stake on both sides. The authorities did, however, show remarkable flexibility with other players. Gordon White would travel a month later than the others and Charlie Llewellyn would be playing Lancashire League cricket between Tests, but the case of Ernie Vogler was just a bridge too far. There was little sympathy but much regret in the press, particularly as he was now bowling brilliantly wherever he played.

And what of the selection as captain of Frank Mitchell? Yorkshireman, English Test player, Boer War veteran, leader of 1904 South African tourists and employee of Bailey. He was now 40-years-old and had been out of the Currie Cup for seven years. It is hard not to see the guiding hand of Mitchell's friend and employer Sir Abe Bailey behind what was, despite the rumours, an unexpected decision and the press reaction (at least in that part not owned by Bailey) was predictable. The Durban correspondent of the *Rand Daily Mail* wrote:

> 'The announcement that Frank Mitchell has been chosen captain of the South African cricket team has astounded Natal cricketers. At Lords to-day there was general wonder expressed while it was even suggested that the selection demands an instant protest on the ground that Mitchell is essentially an English player….did not take part in the trials and was not included in the original team selected….It is felt that the selectors have countenanced a policy which it is hoped the Association will not tolerate. Men who claim to know, and evince the greatest possible esteem for Mitchell, deride his inclusion as an egregious error….It is feared that the choice of Mitchell will raise a storm of criticism from oversea, apart from the certainty that the choice will at once attract attention to the poor resources which South Africa has to rely on in the emergency created by the defection of Percy Sherwell.'

The Transvaal press was more even-handed but hardly universal in its praise. The *Star* dedicated column upon column to the decision. According to Free Lance (BW Thwaites) even members of the SACA believed rumours of Mitchell to be 'street corner talk' and

> 'even when it became known that the authorities had abandoned all hope on that score [Sherwell captaining] the appointment of Mitchell was not seriously contemplated.'

Two days later the same journalist expanded on the issue:

> '….in Frank Mitchell the South Africans will have at their head the best captain in South Africa and in this case the question is not one of capacity but of principle. Frank Mitchell keeps out of the side one of those young players who have been

> trying for a place in this team for months, and unless the Selection Committee could not get a captain from among the men already chosen – strange confession of weakness – they ought not to have made the choice they have. It is said that Gordon White was approached to act as captain and that he declined and that it was no use appointing Schwarz as he had intimated he could not play in all the matches. Two questions: to what extent was his responsibility to South African cricket brought to bear on Gordon White and was any suggestion ever made to Schwarz that he should act as captain, and in view of this, was he asked if he would play throughout the tour and what was his answer?'

This was not idle speculation. Both White and Schwarz had indeed declined, which meant that Mitchell was fourth choice. And what precisely was the situation with Sibley Snooke who, in the absence of Sherwell, had led South Africa to victory against England in 1909-10? What had he done wrong or was he another refusenik? Perhaps the selectors remembered his excessive sportsmanship when allowing the injured English wicket-keeper Strudwick to be replaced by his understudy Tufnell. Snooke's reward was to be 'stumped sub'. Or was it simply that a man combining a tour with his honeymoon was in no position to lead the side?

Mitchell graciously agreed to give his answer to the invitation within 10 days and after that time had elapsed he replied in the affirmative. One week later Tommy Ward was announced as second 'keeper and the authorities in Griqualand West gave up an absurd public appeal for £300 to send Dusty Tapscott to England to join the team. Seemingly matters were, for better or for worse, now settled.

Having recovered somewhat from the shock of the naming of Mitchell, the air in Natal was 'full of cricket' as that most 'English' of colonies celebrated the victory of England in Australia and looked forward optimistically to the events in the near future:

> 'There will be enormous interest in Natal in the Triangular Tests especially if South Africa is at all in the running. And she may be; after all, nearly every man chosen can bowl, and if we have no fast bowler we have any amount of variety. If Faulkner, Schwarz and others are in form our men may yet set both England and Australia thinking hard.

Sir Abe Bailey was no less optimistic when buttonholed in Johannesburg:

> 'I predicted that England would win the rubber in Australia this time and now I will venture on another modest prophecy, namely, that England will be at the top in the Triangular Tests, South Africa second and Australia third.'

In England the great deeds of Barnes, Foster, Hobbs, Rhodes and Woolley were duly celebrated but the stream of information from both sides of the Australian dispute attracted almost as much attention. Both the Board and the players made sure that the English press was acquainted with their side of the argument and every expert from Spofforth to Fry was ready and willing to express an opinion. The general consensus was that the Board was, in essence, a force for good but that its behaviour left much to be desired. *Cricket* was forced, unwillingly, to make the connection between events off the field and those on it, fearing that the row 'can hardly have helped the men to show their true mettle, one fancies'.

While most newspapers remained doggedly optimistic that the summer's Test cricket would be successful and exciting there remained plenty of sceptics. Stanley Jackson, who had done so much to calm troubled waters three years earlier, feared that five Test matches in one summer were more than sufficient and that nine would be found excessive. President of MCC, Lord Desborough, speaking at the jubilee dinner of the Incogniti Cricket Club, referred to "the spirit of unrest in this age of insubordination" but hoped that sportsmanship and fair play would draw the three nations together in "heart and spirit".

One man who had epitomised these characteristics over the previous two decades was about to take his leave. Gilbert Jessop had resigned the secretaryship of Gloucestershire in January and it came as no surprise to students of shamateurism when he announced his intention to retire from the game at the end of the 1912 season. The *Press Association* still rated him, along with Frank Foster, as one of the two most popular players in the country.

Meanwhile Lord Hawke's intrepid warriors were struggling in South America; two draws and a defeat at the hands of the Argentine Republic coupled with four successive ducks for Archie MacLaren spoke of tricky wickets.

MARCH

Mo	Tu	We	Th	Fr	Sa	Su
				1	2	3
4	5	6	7	8	9	10
11	12	13	14	15	16	17
18	19	20	21	22	23	24
25	26	27	28	29	30	31

1912

Jan
Mo	Tu	We	Th	Fr	Sa	Su
1	2	3	4	5	6	7
8	9	10	11	12	13	14
15	16	17	18	19	20	21
22	23	24	25	26	27	28
29	30	31				

Feb
Mo	Tu	We	Th	Fr	Sa	Su
			1	2	3	4
5	6	7	8	9	10	11
12	13	14	15	16	17	18
19	20	21	22	23	24	25
26	27	28	29			

Mar
Mo	Tu	We	Th	Fr	Sa	Su
				1	2	3
4	5	6	7	8	9	10
11	12	13	14	15	16	17
18	19	20	21	22	23	24
25	26	27	28	29	30	31

Apr
Mo	Tu	We	Th	Fr	Sa	Su
1	2	3	4	5	6	7
8	9	10	11	12	13	14
15	16	17	18	19	20	21
22	23	24	25	26	27	28
29	30					

May
Mo	Tu	We	Th	Fr	Sa	Su
	1	2	3	4	5	
6	7	8	9	10	11	12
13	14	15	16	17	18	19
20	21	22	23	24	25	26
27	28	29	30	31		

Jun
Mo	Tu	We	Th	Fr	Sa	Su
					1	2
3	4	5	6	7	8	9
10	11	12	13	14	15	16
17	18	19	20	21	22	23
24	25	26	27	28	29	30

Jul
Mo	Tu	We	Th	Fr	Sa	Su
1	2	3	4	5	6	7
8	9	10	11	12	13	14
15	16	17	18	19	20	21
22	23	24	25	26	27	28
29	30	31				

Aug
Mo	Tu	We	Th	Fr	Sa	Su
		1	2	3	4	
5	6	7	8	9	10	11
12	13	14	15	16	17	18
19	20	21	22	23	24	25
26	27	28	29	30	31	

Sep
Mo	Tu	We	Th	Fr	Sa	Su
						1
2	3	4	5	6	7	8
9	10	11	12	13	14	15
16	17	18	19	20	21	22
23	24	25	26	27	28	29
30						

Oct
Mo	Tu	We	Th	Fr	Sa	Su
1	2	3	4	5	6	
7	8	9	10	11	12	13
14	15	16	17	18	19	20
21	22	23	24	25	26	27
28	29	30	31			

Nov
Mo	Tu	We	Th	Fr	Sa	Su
			1	2	3	
4	5	6	7	8	9	10
11	12	13	14	15	16	17
18	19	20	21	22	23	24
25	26	27	28	29	30	

Dec
Mo	Tu	We	Th	Fr	Sa	Su
						1
2	3	4	5	6	7	8
9	10	11	12	13	14	15
16	17	18	19	20	21	22
23	24	25	26	27	28	29
30	31					

COAL INDUSTRY AT A STANDSTILL
800,000 MINERS IDLE
MR. ASQUITH'S APPEAL TO THE MEN

THE POWERS AND THE WAR
Germany and the Mediation Proposals

Although no formal announcement has been published, it is now being made evident that Germany and Austria-Hungary have given a favorable reception to the revived Russian proposals with a view to the restoration of peace between Italy and Turkey.

THE NAVAL SITUATION
British Shipbuilding

A general survey of warship construction at home and abroad during 1911 shows that, although this country has not improved its position relatively to the next strongest powers, it is very far at present from having been overtaken in any department of material naval strength.

SUFFRAGIST OUTRAGES
WHOLE SALE WINDOW SMASHING IN LONDON
ATTACK ON THE PRIME MINISTER'S HOUSE

THE GREAT COAL STRIKE
NEGOTIATIONS SUSPENDED
NO CONCESSIONS BY EITHER PARTY

BUILDING OF BRITISH AND GERMAN BATTLESHIPS
A COMPARATIVE STATEMENT

MR A DE ROTHSCHILD ATTACKED, FOUR SHOTS FIRED IN A CITY STREET

THE CONTINENT AND THE STRIKE

Westphalian Mining Dispute
Diminished Traffic at French Ports
Demands of Bohemian Miners
The Spanish Orange Trade

NEW RAILWAY ACROSS THE ANDES
LAYING OF THE LINE COMPLETED

THE IMPERIAL WIRELESS SCHEME
SIX STATIONS TO BE ERECTED

A circular issued yesterday by Marconi's Wireless Telegraph Company announces that the Postmaster-General has accepted the company's terms for the construction of all the long-distance wireless stations which will be required within the next few years for the Imperial wireless scheme. The company will proceed immediately with the erection of the six stations (London, Egypt, Aden, Bangalore, Pretoria and Singapore)….

THE SOUTH POLE WON

It is clear from the tidings sent by CAPTAIN AMUNDSEN that he reached the South Pole in the middle of December, and thus secured the last great trophy of Polar exploration. The whole British nation will offer its congratulations... on this dashing achievement... we may be sure that wherever CAPTAIN SCOTT may be…he would be the first to acclaim the success of that truly hardy Norseman…   .

BALLOT PROSPECTS IN THE COALFIELDS
ATTITUDE OF THE MINERS
PITS REOPENING TODAY

THE GRAND NATIONAL
ATTENDANCE DIMINISHED BY THE STRIKE

THE OLYMPIC GAMES AT STOCKHOLM

PROSPECTS AND PROGRESS
OF ARRANGEMENTS

"GERMANY AND THE NEXT WAR"
The gospel of Realpolitik….has just been promulgated in a convenient form in General Bernhardt's new book "Deutschland und der nachste Krieg"…[and] is the most candid expression that has been given in recent years to the doctrine that Germany must, regardless of the rights and interests of other peoples, fight her way to predominance.

The cards were now on the table and the implications could be fully digested. With no late reprieves Australia would travel to England without the Big Six (the 'recalcitrant six' as they were christened by Frank Iredale and now the 'sorry six' in the *Bulletin*), without Herbert Hordern, without Frank Laver and also lacking Monty Noble and Bert Hopkins who continued to hold that big cricket was no longer worth the effort. These ten were surely worth any eleven that Australia could now put onto the field.

A last desperate cable was sent by Pelham Warner asking MCC to intercede and a reply from the president, Lord Desborough, was received on 8 March just as the RMS *Orvieto* was leaving the quay at Adelaide to take the English side home, but it was all too little and too late.

It had been an unpleasant and destructive episode and it's hard to see how it could have been handled worse on both sides. Billy McElhone's avowed intent of being a pilgrim of reform was carried through with a mixture of ruthlessness, bullying and steely skill but the short-term prospects of regaining the Ashes and making the Triangular Tournament a success may well have been sacrificed in the process. The Board had even launched a broadside at its own selectors (McAlister, Iredale and Mayne) at the beginning of the month, making it clear that 'in any circumstances the present trio will not be re-elected'. Quite what they had done wrong or how the election would be rigged against them was not touched upon except for a scathing reference to Edgar Mayne having selected himself for the tour of England in the way McAlister had done in 1909.

The players' loyalty to Frank Laver could be seen as both touching and commendable but it also played into McElhone's hands and enabled him to circumnavigate the contentious clause 9 by scarcely legal means. Laver for his part might have withdrawn his name from consideration at an earlier date.

There can be little doubt that the Board was right in its contention that cricket must be controlled by one central body and the fact that most players saw the logic of this argument makes the steamroller tactics employed by the Board seem both counter-productive and bloody-minded. Pelham Warner's summary was succinct:

> 'As regards the dispute as a whole it may perhaps be said that the Board made a mistake in delaying the publication of their intentions until a few weeks before the selection of the team. What they did then might have been done a year ago, and that would have allowed time to smooth things over. The Board made wounds, and gave them no time to heal. Moreover, each side lacked confidence in the other. If the blinds had been pulled up and all the cards put on the table something might have been done but even then the negotiations would have been anxious and harassing and bristling with difficulties, for Australian cricket of to-day is honeycombed with an amount of personal animosity and bitterness which is almost incredible.'

Tom Horan, in the *Australasian,* branded the Board

> 'neither more nor less than wreckers of Australian cricket....they came apparently bent on destruction, and nothing but destruction would satisfy them....The autocrat touched the button and the players were shunted.'

Even as the depleted Australian team were travelling to England to play their part in the Triangular Tournament, the war of words continued. Pamphlets were issued by the Citizen's Cricket Committee, the Victorian Cricket Association, Frank Laver, Peter McAlister and the Melbourne Cricket Club, although none made an understanding of the previous months any easier. 'Enough red herrings to restock the North Sea were brought in' wrote Ray Robinson and the scars would take decades to heal. When the Board of Control was renamed the Australian Cricket Board some sixty years later the authorities were still trying to distance themselves from the conduct of some of their predecessors.

Cricket repeated its February analysis but now in the knowledge that the worst of outcomes was at hand. Again both sides were castigated for their intransigence but this time 'the best of all fellows', Frank Laver, was marked out for special criticism as probably the only individual who could have doused the fires if only he had acted sooner.

Still the press tried to look on the bright side, in England at least, as even the most forthright or short-sighted journalist could not fail to appreciate how damaging premature criticism of the summer's visitors would be. It was hoped that the vast experience of Syd Gregory would draw the side together and that national pride and even a 'siege mentality' would make the sum of the team far greater than its parts. For better or for worse the list was now complete (abbreviations as in *Playfair Cricket Annual*):

Syd Gregory Captain (NSW) RHB 41. The diminutive Gregory (whose uncle Dave had captained Australia in the first-ever Test), nicknamed 'Little Tich' after vaudeville comedian Harry Relph, had been on no fewer than seven previous tours but must have thought it was all over when omitted from the early stages of the 1911-12 series. But without the Big Six the captaincy reverted to him. He had a marvellous record and could point to an unbeaten 186 for his state against the most recent tourists and two decent innings on his recall in the final Test. As a young man he had been described as a 'blackberry-eyed slip of accomplishment' by CB Fry who later offered further praise: 'No man who ever played cricket could have more usefully been offered a young cricketer as an example for standard strokes'. As if this weren't enough, he was widely reckoned to be the best cover-point produced by Australia. His experience of English wickets and conditions was extensive, a considerable advantage given that only four of his team had been on the previous tour. His personal life had chartered slightly rougher waters; three times betrayed by business partners he filed for bankruptcy in 1905. His popularity was obvious when a benefit game was organised to get him back on his feet.

S.E.GREGORY.

C.B.JENNINGS.

Claude Jennings Vice-Captain (Queensland) RHB 27. The nearest this ex-South Australian had come to Test cricket was as twelfth man against Warner's team of 1903-04. Thereafter he had found his work in a shipping office an impediment and had been forced to move on numerous occasions but he was now reasonably settled in Brisbane. In December 1911 he had written to Clem Hill asking if he was likely to be selected because he would need to delay taking an accountancy course! Despite performing well twice for his state against MCC in the latest tour (and being praised by both Douglas and Foster), he was never seriously considered for national honours. A sound and stylish bat (one MCC player compared him to Reggie Spooner) and excellent slip fielder, his inclusion and sudden promotion to second-in-command was a clear result of other refusals although one pre-tour brochure predicted he would be the 'star' batsman of the tour.

W. BARDSLEY.

Warren Bardsley (NSW) LHB 27. It's doubtful whether a more dedicated cricketer has ever donned the 'baggy green'. As a youngster he would practise before work in order to gain experience of a dewy wet wicket and he was always the first onto the ground, pacing out distances to boundaries and checking slopes and visibility. A non-smoking, teetotal vegetarian of comically gloomy disposition, he came to prominence in 1909 in England when he crowned a fine series by becoming the first player to score two centuries in a Test match and was deservedly recognised as a *Wisden* cricketer. He took the form home for the series against South Africa but flopped badly against Barnes and Foster the following year, being dropped for the final Test. His response was intense work with Bill Whitty to prepare himself for the left-arm round attack of Frank Foster and, on form previously shown in England, he was an automatic selection.

Edgar Mayne (South Australia) RHB 29. He narrowly missed inclusion in the 1909 tour, his moderate fielding counting heavily against him. Replaced Clem Hill as a selector after the infamous brawl in February 1912 and, despite his lack of international experience and a moderate state record, he was soon afterwards included in the squad. This was the path to Test cricket followed by Peter McAlister three years earlier. He was described as a 'cricket book student' who had 'studied the science of batting' rather in the manner of Fry although his slow and sure methods were no match for the brilliant Englishman.

Dave Smith (Victoria) RHB 27. Another uncapped batsman, rushed into the squad to replace the last of the big name defectors, Clem Hill, only after the giant New South Wales leftie Jack Massie had been unable to accept an invitation. 'A sturdily built robust young man of breezy manner and methods' and a capable player but unable to curb his 'reckless hitting', he had a modest record for his state although he did have some success against MCC. Under other circumstances would never have come near the tour.

Charles Kelleway (NSW) RHB/RMF 26. First came to notice as a bowler with a fine high action and the ability to swing the ball but his inability to add the subtle variations of pace and flight led to a change of disciplines. A dour, stiff but reliable opening batsman of 'limitless patience' and a very useful change bowler, he scored consistently if 'rather colourlessly' in his debut series against South Africa. Struggling with an illness, he managed little against Foster and Barnes the following year despite eight attempts but much was expected of his steely defence, 'undisturbable self-confidence' and boundless concentration in England.

R.B.MINNETT.

Roy Minnett (NSW) RHB/RFM 23. A student of medicine at Sydney University and a champion sprinter, he came into the first Test against MCC in 1911 with a lofty reputation and his 90 in 111 minutes, overshadowing even Trumper, backed it up. Although his form declined, along with the rest of the team, during the series, he still scored over 300 runs which was better than most. His hard hitting and stylish batting interwoven with a quiet and unassuming nature made him a popular selection and team-mate but opinions were divided over his bowling; round-arm in style with the ability to make the ball 'fly' but considered 'nothing exceptional' by LOS Poidevin in the *Athletic News* although he hoped that English conditions might help him find some swing if he had fully recovered from a knee problem.

C.G.MACARTNEY.

Charlie Macartney (NSW) RHB/SLA 25. Made his debut in the 1907-08 series against Jones' MCC team and the following year sealed his reputation as a left-arm spinning all-rounder by bowling Australia to victory at Leeds. His form then deserted him in international cricket but a combination of big scores in state matches, the faith of Clem Hill, the prospect of the tour of England and his outstanding talent saw his recall for the final Test of the 1911-12 series. Blessed with a marvellous eye and boundless confidence, his return to form was only a matter of time.

T.J.MATTHEWS.

Jimmy Matthews (Victoria) RHB/LB 28. A wrist spinning bowling all-rounder, he was a 'capable and busy', if rather unpolished, batsman and had come near to Test cricket when three times twelfth man against the South Africans in 1910-11. He finally made the side against MCC the following year but managed only one wicket in two matches. Generally regarded as a real 'scrapper' who liked to be involved in all aspects, his bowling was in some ways reminiscent of Armstrong in that he didn't use the googly but possessed an effective top spinner. The feeling was that the busy schedule of 1912 would suit him well if he could recover from the personal tragedy of losing an infant son early in the year. Like Carkeek and Smith he played rules football in the Victorian League.

Sid Emery (NSW) LBG 25. Undoubtedly the dark horse of the side in more ways than one. On the plus side he bowled leg breaks and googlies at great pace, got a real whip off the pitch and possessed a fine yorker, all delivered with an uncomplicated action. On the other, his length was often awry and his 'nervous and impulsive' character both on and off the field made him something of a liability. LOS Poidevin wrote that 'he owes his selection more to the extraordinary respect in which [his] "good ball" is held rather than the success with which he has exploited it'. Furthermore his absence from the NSW team in 1911-12 was not merely due to a lack of form. The *Hobart Mercury* described him as 'probably the keenest cricketer in Australia' but worried that 'this keenness affects his usefulness at times'. A fascinating prospect on English wickets but if Hordern and Armstrong had been available he would surely not have been risked.

Gerry Hazlitt (NSW) RM OB 23. Slightly-built academic and schoolmaster with a weak heart, he seemed an unlikely sportsman but made his debut for Victoria at 17 and Australia at 19, making him his country's third-youngest player ever. In his first Test he ensured victory in a ninth-wicket partnership and in his second he failed to secure a tie by poor fielding. He paid less attention to cricket in the following years but his flighted medium pace and off-break continued to be effective, returning for the last Test against England as the selectors looked at touring possibles. He had proved his stamina with a marathon spell for NSW against MCC and had gained the respect of Wilfred Rhodes but there was some confusion over exactly what he bowled! His captain described him as 'a little above medium in pace' while others referred to a 'slow yorker', 'medium paced swerving off breaks' and a 'peculiar jerky action'. Spin was his main weapon but swing and change of pace, by cutting his hand under the ball, were also liberally employed.

J.W.Mc LAREN.

Jack McLaren (Queensland) RFM 25. He had impressed the South African tourists in 1911 without getting a call-up and it was only in the last Test of the 1911-1912 series that he was finally recognised as a replacement for Tibby Cotter, having acted as twelfth man in the previous game. Even then his name was announced very late and it was surrounded by controversy as rumours abounded that he had taken part in strike-breaking as a special constable in Brisbane and for this reason he had not been selected in the fourth Test. Not noted for his stamina and suffering from diabetes, he was something of a risky proposition despite his undoubted pace and it seemed that the best hope was that 'he is bound to have his days' when his 'two distinct swerves' and yorker would meet with success.

W. J. WHITTY.

Bill Whitty (South Australia) LFM 25. A left-arm swing bowler in the manner of George Hirst, he visited England in 1909, after only six first-class matches, but with no great success. He came to the fore with an astounding series against South Africa the following year in which he garnered no less than 37 wickets. When not in the best of health after two operations for appendicitis he found English batsmen a different proposition and was dropped after taking only three wickets in the first two Tests. Plum Warner was in no doubt of the error: 'Whitty bowled well in the second innings of the second Test and was dropped too soon. He will be the best bowler in the next series….in England'. With a fine open-chested action and an appetite for work, he looked a natural leader of the bowling attack.

Barlow Carkeek (Victoria) WK 33. The long-standing understudy to Hanson Carter but yet to make his Test debut, he had few pretensions to greatness ('sound rather than brilliant' according to *Wisden* and 'belongs to a very moderate order' wrote the *Morning Leader*) and a reputation for unpopularity.

Harold Webster (South Australia) WK 23. A first-class novice with only two seasons of Shield cricket, he had shown enough potential to be not only selected but also to be reckoned a possible first choice behind the wicket even if the *Athletic News* thought him 'very lucky in his promotion'. A twin, whose brother played in Sydney, he was fortunate that his work took him to Adelaide where the state side were in desperate need of a wicket-keeper.

H.W.WEBSTER

At the functions organised to wish the party 'God speed', various luminaries and men who should have known better spoke with wild enthusiasm about the prospects for the summer. At the New South Wales Cricket Association the president, Sir Joseph Carruthers, said that the team was as good as had ever gone abroad from Australia. Two days later the entire squad, except for Mayne and Macartney, found themselves royally entertained at the Vienna Café in Melbourne where the prime minister, Andrew Fisher, was guest of honour. The *Age* reported his speech:

> 'Much had been said by some who should have known better that the team was defeated already. (No No). This was ungenerous; it was not sportsmanlike; it was not Australian….He hoped they would play the game, and would be sportsmen enough to take their licking and congratulate the winners on their success as heartily as they hoped to be congratulated if they won.'

Gregory in reply stressed the need for the team to start the tour as they meant to go on – by winning. He hoped that his team would pull together and may even be better than a team chock full of talented malcontents and that it would prove that Australian cricket was not so hard up that it could be crippled by the withdrawal of half a dozen players. He pointed out that the team was young and young players (Hill and Trumper spring to mind as examples) had been successful in the past. Manager Crouch was equally optimistic and, like the prime minister, aware of the ambassadorial role of his team:

> 'It had been said that the team could not possibly win; but their first achievement was to play the game as sportsmen and to be a credit to Australia. Their second objective was to bring back the ashes.'

In reality Syd Gregory, now embarking on his eighth tour, must have looked back to previous sides. Charles Turner, George Giffen, Ernie Jones, Jack Saunders, Hugh Trumble, Reggie Duff, and Joe Darling; did his side have any players of this calibre? Australia's most respected ex-cricketer/journalist, Tom Horan, certainly didn't think so: 'I do not believe the team strong enough to stand a show against England.' A man of Gregory's experience knew that only Bardsley and maybe Macartney could be included in this exalted company. The hope was that players such as Kelleway or Whitty might rise to the challenge. And what of the diminutive skipper himself? *Cricket* tried to be positive, but failed.

> 'One cannot see the makings of a great strategist like Noble, an iron-willed leader like Darling, in Sydney Gregory; but it is quite possible that he may prove as a good a captain as either Hill or Trumper.'

Faint praise indeed and even as the send-offs were being toasted, new developments in the strife were being reported. On 18 March, the day of the Melbourne reception, the *Age* reported that if Vernon Ransford and Victor Trumper were to be in England during the summer then the Board of Control would have no objection to them making themselves available to play although the final decision would rest with the team itself. By the next day Ransford had made it clear he had no intention of doing any such thing; Trumper was slower to respond.

The send-off offered by the *Australasian* was lacking in optimism:

> 'Whitty is the only bowler with any pretensions to being first class in the team, and the combination is going home without one first class wicket-keeper and without the best batsmen outside Bardsley.'

And what was Leslie Poidevin thinking when he wrote for *Imperial Cricket* on the state of the game in Australia?

> 'Therefore, to the inquirer, with the possibilities of the Imperial Cricket Contests of 1912 in his mind's eye, there is but one answer from Australia – eminently satisfactory.'

At least he was slightly more specific when writing for the *Athletic News* that 'good judges….noted the growing decline of skill….of Australia's recognised champions. It must not be supposed that they are indispensable'.

Cricket might have been rather less than generous to Syd Gregory but it managed to be slightly more enthusiastic about the equally experienced (and old) but considerably more portly Frank Mitchell of South Africa. 'Mitchell should be quite the right man in the right place, firm and judicious' it reported, without reference to his lack of cricket in the last half-decade or the storm that his selection had created in South Africa.

The South African team that had been announced in January (and then again in February once availability was established) was subject to some minor tinkering as Billy Zulch withdrew and was replaced by Louis Stricker who had been surprised to miss out in the first place. Amazingly enough Ernie Vogler chose the same day to now announce his willingness to tour, presumably hoping to fill Zulch's berth. Having been thoroughly outmanoeuvred he was now ignored, 'Vogler Bowled Out' read one headline, and everybody was a loser as a result. Behind the scenes, individual finances were also an issue. Arrangements had been made to pay Charlie Llewellyn a match fee of £20 which, given his professional status was quite reasonable. Less well known was Dave Nourse's position; effectively he was also a professional and was granted a £125 tour fee with his wife also receiving a monthly allowance while he was away. Still more bemusing was the gift of £120 to Louis Tancred to enable him to tour as an amateur!

Sussex cricketer and long-standing coach in South Africa, George Cox, added his words of optimism, giving the South Africans 'a good fighting chance with a little luck, which is always a pregnant quality in big cricket'. So now the English public could mull over a second set of names.

Frank Mitchell Captain (Transvaal) RHB 39. An outstanding amateur for Yorkshire during their golden period around the turn of the century (*Wisden* cricketer in 1902) and an international rugby forward in Queen Victoria's last years. He represented England against South Africa in 1899 and settled there after fighting in the Boer War, becoming secretary to Abe Bailey. He led a South African side to England in 1904 but no Tests were played and he did not gain international recognition for his adopted country until, despite not having played regularly during the previous six years, he was surprisingly asked to lead the team for the Triangular Tournament. Always easy to recognise both due to his habit of holding his bat in mid-air while waiting for the bowler's delivery and his somewhat rotund stature.

Louis Tancred Vice-Captain (Transvaal) RHB 35. A member of a famous cricketing family, he scored 97 on debut against Australia in 1902 and that remained his highest Test score through two more series. Visited England in 1901, 1904 and 1907, the last being spoilt by illness and his only Test appearance resulting in a pair. Absent from the national team since then but a consistent scorer in a dogged manner for his province 'adopting a peculiar crouch when batting suggesting a human note of interrogation'.

Rolland Beaumont (Transvaal) RHB 28. A powerful and elegant striker, he was largely unconsidered until making a chanceless 94 in the first trial match. Selected on the basis of this innings it was hoped that he might score fast runs against tired attacks batting down the order. Very much of the 'amateur' sort; tall, handsome and a dashing all-round sportsman, his father was a senior figure in the South African High Court.

Dave Nourse(Natal) LHB/LM 33. Born in Croydon, he went to South Africa with the army as a 17-year-old and became a permanent fixture in the Test team from 1902 onwards through two Australian series and three English. A tough, obdurate and consistent batsman but still without a Test century and his bowling had become negligible. A real trier, but question marks now hung over his ability at the highest level.

Louis Stricker (Transvaal) RHB 27. An opening bat, highly thought of in South African cricket, he had consistently disappointed in nine Test matches without a half century. Had only appeared three times in Currie Cup cricket and after failing twice in trial matches his chances seemed slim despite newspaper agitation but he was called up late on to replace Billy Zulch. Described as a careful bat but rather slow in the field and between the wickets and had 'not enjoyed the best of health'.

Herby Taylor (Natal) RHB 22. Uncapped, coached by George Cox of Sussex and with a big reputation, despite his age, he batted well in the Currie Cup in 1911 as Natal triumphed for the first time in their history. His good form continued in the trial matches and his selection would have appeared to be a formality without the need of his state bringing pressure to bear and threatening to secede from the SACA if he wasn't selected for the touring party. His father Dan Taylor played a handful of games for Natal and his elder brother was his state team-mate.

Aubrey Faulkner (Transvaal) RHB/LBG 30. Made his Currie Cup debut at 21 as a wrist spinner though only when his batting improved did he graduate to the national side. His golden period began in 1910 and in the 10 consecutive Tests against England and then Australia he scored 1277 runs and took 39 wickets. Clem Hill stated 'no one has ever batted better on our wickets'. Certainly the finest all-rounder in the world, he announced his retirement from domestic South African cricket in 1911 as he was moving to England.

Gerald Hartigan (Border) RHB/RFM 27. Had already made his name in Currie Cup cricket, being far and away Border's outstanding batsman and bowler in the 1911 season despite being hampered by a hand injury. He then made his place certain as one of the brightest young batsmen by scoring heavily in the trial matches. An excellent fielder, all-round sportsman and highly-regarded swing bowler, it was hoped that, if fully recovered, he would fulfil his potential in all areas of the game and become one of the mainstays of the side.

G.C.WHITE.

Gordon White (Transvaal) RHB/LBG 30. Topped the batting averages in his debut series against Warner's England side having already visited England in 1904. He managed nothing with the bat on the soft English wickets in 1907 although he did take 72 cheap wickets on that tour. His reputation as an all-rounder was somewhat over-rated as he was clearly inferior to the other three googly bowlers but he was again successful with the bat on matting against England two years later. In 1910 he had been described by the respected writer EW Ballantine as South Africa's best batsman.

S.J.SNOOKE.

Sibley Snooke (Western Province) RHB/RMF 31. Having made his Currie Cup debut for Border as a teenager he was another player who performed well against two England teams on matting but did little on turf in between times. Against the second of the two touring teams he captained in all five Tests in the absence of Percy Sherwell. The fact that he took 24 wickets in his first series and none in Australia in 1910-11 tells of a shift in priorities as did his failure to appear for his province in domestic cricket in the previous three years. On the Australian tour a century at Adelaide was good but a series total of 259 runs in 10 innings less so. His brother Stanley played one Test for South Africa.

LLEWELLYN.

Charlie Llewellyn (Natal) LHB/SLC 35. Vastly experienced in England after a long spell with Hampshire, he had made his international debut at 19 but only played irregularly thereafter due to other commitments. The 1902 Australians saw the best of him with 24 wickets in three Tests and his bowling against the same opposition in 1910-11 was still worthy of his selection for the Triangular team even though his availability would be limited. In between times he came close to being picked for England, being one of 14 players selected for the 1902 Edgbaston Test. As a coloured player (although this was never officially admitted) his career was not always allowed to run smoothly.

Sidney Pegler (Transvaal) RM LB 23. A bowler of limited experience but some potential, had had little success in five Tests against Australia in 1910-11 and then failed in the trial match. Hope won out and his was one of the last names included, possibly influenced by his experience of English cricket as a teenager at the Granville-Lee Club, his strength and fitness and the presence of his father on the selection committee.

Reggie Schwarz (Transvaal) LBG 36. The man who brought the googly to South Africa, he had topped the Springbok averages in 1904 and 1907 having emigrated from England after failing to get his blue at Cambridge and having a career in the Navy stymied by colour-blindness. His influence can be measured by the words of Abe Bailey: 'Our claim to be first-class in an international sense has dated from the time Schwarz first came amongst us'. He suffered a terrible loss of form for two years before establishing himself as his country's leading bowler with an outstanding series against Australia. With Vogler gone, White an unknown quantity and Faulkner distracted by his batting exploits it was hoped that Schwarz would fill the gaping hole.

Joe Cox (Natal) RFM 25. His performances in helping Natal win its first Currie Cup (especially 8-20 against Transvaal including seven clean bowled) in 1911 brought him to the fore and he performed adequately in the trial matches although how he was preferred to Fred Le Roux as an opening bowler is hard to fathom, particularly as the latter was also a fine bat.

Claude Carter (Transvaal) SLA 30. Made a brilliant debut for Natal at 16 but despite consistent wicket-taking he remained uncapped. He was considered for the 1907 tour and his considerable experience of English conditions, gathered while playing in Cornwall and for Driffield in Yorkshire, spoke in his favour as did a successful season for his new province Transvaal in 1911. There was every reason to believe that English wickets would suit his style.

Tom Campbell (Transvaal) WK 30. A long-standing reserve, he got his chance and acquitted himself well when Percy Sherwell was unavailable to face Leveson Gower's tourists. He returned to the bench when Sherwell came back for the Australia trip but was the obvious choice to take the gloves in the Triangular Tournament.

Tommy Ward (Transvaal) WK 24. Finally got into his state team in the absence of Campbell while touring in Australia and was added to the squad when Sherwell declined. Considered almost the equal of Campbell and a reliable and doughty batsman.

The Natalian squad members gathered in Durban to play in a one-day testimonial match for Dave Nourse in which Herby Taylor's batting was 'the feature of the match'. The three boarded the *Balmoral Castle* on 20 March, which then called at East London, where Gerald Hartigan joined, before sailing on to Cape Town to collect the Transvaal contingent who had travelled down by train after receiving a hearty send-off at Park Street station from, amongst others, Jimmy Sinclair. As the train pulled out the players were regaled with the time honoured war cry of "Are we down hearted? Are we ----?" followed by a last inspiring call of "Ingobolyo Zje". Gordon White, who had permission to stay in South Africa for another month, and Sibley Snooke, who had left a week earlier to enjoy his honeymoon en route to the cricket, were not with the group. Three others, Llewellyn, Schwarz and Faulkner, were already in England, the former having signed to play in the Lancashire League following his acrimonious departure from his county of ten years, Hampshire. Negotiations had been taking place between the South African Cricket Association and Accrington CC for many months, the outcome of which was that Llewellyn would be released to play Test cricket except on Saturdays or Whit Monday. Even though the latter restriction would count him out of the first Test, his experience of English pitches still made him potentially one of the most important members of the team.

The correspondent of the *Star* was dockside in Cape Town and concluded that things were not altogether so black. The lack of a fast bowler was not as serious as all that, particularly as neither England or Australia had one, and the appointment of Frank Mitchell as captain was something to be applauded.

> 'It was essential that the team should be placed under the charge of an experienced and trained player, so much often depends during a match on the captain's judgement, and in addition to having a cool and experienced cricketer it was desirable also to have one who was thoroughly acquainted with the conditions of the English grounds and climate.'

With the last game of their Australian tour cancelled, the MCC side, having metaphorically stowed the Ashes away, boarded the *Orvieto* in Adelaide. On 8 March they sailed away with the pleasant prospect of a long rest followed by receptions and parties that were already being organised by clubs and committees all over England. So joyful was CB Fry that one can imagine him hopping around as he merrily put pen to paper:

> 'Perhaps the pleasantest feature of the success of the team is that it will shut up the rotters who are for ever croaking about the degeneracy of modern cricket in the Old Country and are always holding up the Australians as our proved and patented superiors.'

On 11 March the Board of Control of Test Matches at Home convened at the Junior Carlton Club with Lord Harris in the chair. On the lengthy agenda was the nitty-gritty of the upcoming nine-Test series – umpiring, payment, advertising, the method of selecting the English team, hours and duration of matches and the division of gate receipts. The majority of items were largely uncontroversial. The visiting sides had already been guaranteed half the gross gate money and the English share was to be divided between the first-class counties, Test grounds and second-class counties in a 60/30/10 split. The professionals would receive £20 per match. Amateurs could expect only rail fares plus 30 shillings per day as expenses though county secretaries were 'requested to take the necessary steps to secure comfortable Hotel accommodation for the Amateur players'. More contentious was the question of the umpires. The Australian Board of Control, supported by Pelham Warner, had requested the adoption of the Australian system whereby the captains select the officials but this method was rejected in London. A panel of six (Street, Webb, Richards, West, White and Moss), chosen by the first-class county captains, was appointed with each to officiate in six games to be decided by ballot. A cable was sent to both visiting teams to inform them of the decision, pointing out that any umpire objected to on previous occasions had been omitted from the list. The Australians had more luck with their request that a team-list should be presented to the opposing captain before the toss and that this should not be altered without the consent of that captain. This had come into practice in Australia largely due to Pelham Warner's exploitation of the loophole in Sydney on the 1903-04 tour when an early batting collapse prompted him to alter his side. The locals felt so aggrieved that the scoreboard operatives deliberately put the name of the previously selected player into the frame to ensure that the crowd were aware of the subterfuge. Once again provision was made to avoid a tied series by allowing for a timeless Test. This had not been needed in 1905 or 1909 but the rule was again spelt out.

'Test matches shall be for three days only but if after the second match between any two countries neither side has secured an advantage, the third match shall be played to a finish.'

Still nobody thought to act on MCC secretary Lacey's warning that there was no system to determine an overall winner. What if South Africa beat Australia 1-0, Australia beat England 2-1 and England beat South Africa 1-0? But this was an age when even the competition for the County Championship was considered somewhat sordid and the author of the official history of the Triangular Tournament, EHD Sewell, could describe the Ashes as a 'hideous excrescence of cricket journalese'. The game was the thing.

And then there was the England team and how it would be selected.

'Discussion took place with regard to the composition of the Selection Sub-Committee and the appointment of the Captain of the England sides and Lord Harris undertook to write to Mr. C. B. Fry asking for his views on the subject.'

The letter must have been an interesting one and it is not hard to surmise the gist. Fry had, the previous year, expounded his theories of selection in his own *Fry's Magazine*. The author had, in his own inimitable and analytical style, outlined the difficulties facing any selection committee in finding the best-balanced side to take the field. The most interesting of his conclusions was on the subject of consistency of selection.

'But I certainly think that a team which plays regularly together favours that easy and confident state of mind which is all so much to the good in batsmen - where as a team which is collected for the occasion from the four quarters of England and does not know itself as a team is liable to find its batting disadvantageously affected – a team feels its corporate existence and a team that plays regularly together is more likely to bat up to the true individual form of its members than a virtually scratch team. England teams in England are at a disadvantage in this respect. But the worst disability under which they labour is that the batsmen feel that they are "playing for their places" or are under an obligation to "justify their selection". This induces an introspective frame of mind which is unsettling.'

An early advocate of central contracts, at least for batsmen. The following month Fry had turned his attention to the players selected for the trip to Australia in another wordy piece and when he followed these two articles with an analysis of the Australian team that would defend the Ashes he had covered all the bases, in print at least. Nobody could dispute that he had applied his considerable mind to the problems to be faced and Fry had, quite deliberately, made a cogent case for himself to captain England in the Triangular Tournament and to have a selection committee largely doing his bidding. No wonder then that Lord Harris wanted 'his views on the subject'. What Harris really wanted to know was whether Fry would take on the captaincy of England and what conditions might apply.

The team that Fry intended to lead had stopped off briefly in Perth and current captain Pelham Warner received the news that the last ditch efforts by himself and Lord Desborough, president of MCC, to reconcile the warring parties in Australia had failed. For once Warner was furious.

'I think the action of the board of control in not replying to such a cable [from Desborough] savoured of discourtesy.'

He went on to point out previous examples of both lack of professionalism and rudeness from the authorities in Sydney. He had plainly had enough of the whole business.

The Australians left Melbourne on 20 March and berthed briefly at Adelaide where the mayor expressed the sentiment that all differences would be forgotten now that the team had begun to represent Australia. A selection committee of Gregory, vice-captain Jennings and Bardsley was announced and a few days later the players could feel dry land in Perth where a game against 'Westralia' had been organised and Charlie Kelleway managed a hat-trick. Once again Gregory and Crouch met the press and wheeled out platitudes. The manager reported all players in perfect health and the ship's carpenter busy making 'a slip catching machine'. The captain declared that the team's great strength would lie in its fielding! And then it was full steam ahead to Ceylon, the Suez Canal, Gibraltar and England, the trip being enlivened by deck quoits, whistling tune races, cock fighting and 'slinging the monkey'. In the evenings a fancy-dress ball and a bridge tournament were the major distractions.

Three teams were simultaneously coming home. Meanwhile the MCC team in Argentina had finally mastered the Pampas wickets and Archie MacLaren was in the runs at last.

APRIL

Mo	Tu	We	Th	Fr	Sa	Su
1	2	3	4	5	6	7
8	9	10	11	12	13	14
15	16	17	18	19	20	21
22	23	24	25	26	27	28
29	30					

1912

Jan

Mo	Tu	We	Th	Fr	Sa	Su
1	2	3	4	5	6	7
8	9	10	11	12	13	14
15	16	17	18	19	20	21
22	23	24	25	26	27	28
29	30	31				

Feb

Mo	Tu	We	Th	Fr	Sa	Su
			1	2	3	4
5	6	7	8	9	10	11
12	13	14	15	16	17	18
19	20	21	22	23	24	25
26	27	28	29			

Mar

Mo	Tu	We	Th	Fr	Sa	Su
				1	2	3
4	5	6	7	8	9	10
11	12	13	14	15	16	17
18	19	20	21	22	23	24
25	26	27	28	29	30	31

Apr

Mo	Tu	We	Th	Fr	Sa	Su
1	2	3	4	5	6	7
8	9	10	11	12	13	14
15	16	17	18	19	20	21
22	23	24	25	26	27	28
29	30					

May

Mo	Tu	We	Th	Fr	Sa	Su
	1	2	3	4	5	
6	7	8	9	10	11	12
13	14	15	16	17	18	19
20	21	22	23	24	25	26
27	28	29	30	31		

Jun

Mo	Tu	We	Th	Fr	Sa	Su
					1	2
3	4	5	6	7	8	9
10	11	12	13	14	15	16
17	18	19	20	21	22	23
24	25	26	27	28	29	30

Jul

Mo	Tu	We	Th	Fr	Sa	Su
1	2	3	4	5	6	7
8	9	10	11	12	13	14
15	16	17	18	19	20	21
22	23	24	25	26	27	28
29	30	31				

Aug

Mo	Tu	We	Th	Fr	Sa	Su
			1	2	3	4
5	6	7	8	9	10	11
12	13	14	15	16	17	18
19	20	21	22	23	24	25
26	27	28	29	30	31	

Sep

Mo	Tu	We	Th	Fr	Sa	Su
						1
2	3	4	5	6	7	8
9	10	11	12	13	14	15
16	17	18	19	20	21	22
23	24	25	26	27	28	29
30						

Oct

Mo	Tu	We	Th	Fr	Sa	Su
1	2	3	4	5	6	
7	8	9	10	11	12	13
14	15	16	17	18	19	20
21	22	23	24	25	26	27
28	29	30	31			

Nov

Mo	Tu	We	Th	Fr	Sa	Su
			1	2	3	
4	5	6	7	8	9	10
11	12	13	14	15	16	17
18	19	20	21	22	23	24
25	26	27	28	29	30	

Dec

Mo	Tu	We	Th	Fr	Sa	Su
						1
2	3	4	5	6	7	8
9	10	11	12	13	14	15
16	17	18	19	20	21	22
23	24	25	26	27	28	29
30	31					

TITANIC DISASTER
SUNK AFTER COLLISION WITH ICEBERG
LOSS OF LIFE

WIRELESS CALLS FOR AID

UNDERWRITERS' ANXIETY
HULL OF THE VESSEL VALUED AT A MILLION POUNDS

NAMES OF SURVIVORS
DEMAND FOR INQUIRY

BOAT ACCOMMODATION FOR 1200 PERSONS
THE OFFICIAL REQUIREMENTS

SURVIVORS STORIES
THE SCENE WHEN THE VESSEL WENT DOWN

LOSS OF THE TITANIC
MANSION HOUSE RELIEF FUND

THE BENGALS AND ASSAM AFTER LORD CURZON'S PARTITION

TITANIC INQUIRY
MR MARCONI AND HIS SYSTEM

'HEROISM BELOW DECKS'

THE DEATH
ROLL OF WOMEN

CONAN DOYLE
CREATES A NEW CHARACTER
In His Latest Story

"THE LOST WORLD"

UNIVERSITY BOAT RACE
SINKING OF BOTH CREWS IN TURN

AEROPLANES IN WAR
THE GOVERNMENT'S SCHEME

THE FIRST VOYAGE OF THE LARGEST VESSEL IN THE WORLD

NEW BIBLE MANUSCRIPT A COPTIC VERSION OF THE SCRIPTURES

A BRAHMS FESTIVAL IN NEW YORK

NEWS OF CAPTAIN SCOTT
TERRA NOVA'S RETURN
EXPEDITION TO REMAIN ANOTHER YEAR

The Terra Nova, the vessel of the British Antarctic Expedition, was sighted off this port [Akaroa NZ] early this morning and anchored shortly after daybreak. Contrary to expectation, she does not bring back with her Captain Scott and his Antarctic party. Her commander was entrusted with the following brief message from Captain Scott which he had sent back to the base before the Terra Nova left. "I am remaining in the Antarctic for another winter in order to continue and complete my work"

THE HOME RULE BILL

ECLIPSE OF THE SUN
SOME INTERESTING PHENOMENA

TASMANIA'S HYDRO-ELECTRIC DEVELOPMENT

DETECTIVE SHOT DEAD IN PARIS
ANOTHER CRIME BY MOTOR-CAR GANG

It would be another 10 years before TS Eliot was to brand April 'the cruelest month' and in 1912 it could better have been described as glorious. Spring had advanced so quickly that it seemed summer had sprouted straight from a dank winter with rainfall being virtually absent for all 30 days. With so many teams bound for England the reception committees were busy and the newspapers were full of prospects and predictions for the coming season. Could it be that all the rows and rancour had been left in the southern hemisphere?

On 2 April the *Manchester Guardian* published a detailed and even-handed account of the Australians from 'a correspondent' in Sydney. Gregory was praised as a batsman and fielder but doubts remained 'whether he can stand the strain of captaining the young team on a strenuous tour'. He would turn 42 only 12 days later. Great things were expected of Warren Bardsley's batting despite his indifferent recent form and the same held for Bill Whitty's bowling especially as he was now fully fit again. Roy Minnett was heralded as the 'most brilliant bat Australia has produced since Trumper' while Emery would be revealed as 'the "worst-best" bowler in the world for he alternates almost unplayable deliveries with the merest "piffle"'. The writer was no fan of wicket-keeper Carkeek, having meticulously counted no fewer than 54 missed chances during the 1909 tour when he only played 12 times. The bowling was perceived as the major problem. Two days later the same newspaper analysed the prospects for the new season, beginning with the Gregory's side.

> '....perhaps there is some danger, because so many of them are untried in international cricket, of holding them a little too cheap. At the same time one cannot forget that they are not the team that would have been chosen if peace had prevailed....'

South Africa were given pretty short shrift. 'Interesting' and 'full of sporting qualities' was the limit of the praise offered. In the *Pall Mall Gazette* it was a similar story:

> 'Never perhaps in the history of the grand old game has the interest in cricket been so keen as it is at present. And this is saying much....the agitation which has disturbed the peace and harmony of Australian affairs during the past months may have done good rather than harm....it is doubtful whether South Africa possesses quite the same amount of young blood as Australia.'

And then there was the English side. The selectors would have longer to prepare for the Test series than their opponents and could happily await early-season county form before concentrating on two specially arranged trial matches. After the success of the tour to Australia it was reasonable to assume that at least seven places were spoken for, barring injury or catastrophic loss of form.

Jack Hobbs (Surrey) RHB 29. From the moment he made his Test debut in 1908 it was clear that he had easily made the jump from county cricket. Eight half-centuries in his first 11 Tests were followed by four centuries in the next five and a handsome 662 runs at 82.75 in Australia. An aggressive and elegant fast scorer and seemingly the master of hard, soft and matting wickets. Certainly the best batsman in the world and probably the best cover-point.

Wilfred Rhodes (Yorkshire) RHB/SLA 34. The country's best spinner and a number 11 bat when he first represented England in 1899, he gradually moved up the order as his interest began to move from bowling to batting. By 1908 he was at six or seven and two years later he was opening with Hobbs. Melbourne 1912 saw them set a new first-wicket record of 323. The downside was that Rhodes only bowled 18 overs in the whole of that series. A competitive and intelligent cricketer, seemingly immune to pressure, his unflappable reliability and speed between the wickets made him an ideal partner for Hobbs.

Frank Woolley (Kent) LHB/SLA 24. Hugely influential since first appearing for Kent in 1906 and ushering in their golden period. His Test career was a little slower starting, showing little on debut and then disappointing in South Africa before gradually becoming more confident in Australia in 1911-12. The last Test was a triumph with an unbeaten century, three useful wickets and six catches. His bowling showed much of the skill of his Kent mentor Colin Blythe, especially on wet wickets, and his batting was one of the cricketing beauties of the age.

J.W.H.T. DOUGLAS.

Johnny Douglas (Essex) RHB/RMF 29. A supremely fit amateur (and winner of a boxing gold medal at the 1908 Olympics) he had been a slightly surprising selection as vice-captain to Warner in Australia. Through Warner's illness he ascended to captaincy and, after a rocky start, led and bowled well in the 4-1 victory. He returned home with an enhanced reputation in all areas; a popular captain, an obstinate and useful batsman and really talented trier with the ball.

F.R. FOSTER.

Frank Foster (Warwickshire) RHB/LFM 23. Burst onto the county scene in 1910 and the following year captained Warwickshire to the championship. He took his supreme talent and 'inexhaustible vitality' to Australia that winter and, with Barnes, destroyed the hosts. Even off a short run he generated genuine pace with a quick arm and prospered on hard wickets with a short-pitched leg-stump attack that illustrated his adaptability and versatility; he had relied largely on swing in England.

BARNES.

Sydney Barnes (Staffordshire) RMOB 38. Largely unknown when Archie MacLaren took him to Australia in 1901, he had consistently been England's best bowler since then despite his search for the best pay leading him to play only league and minor-county cricket. His belief in his own ability gave him the confidence to back himself against authority, although this did sometimes cost him his England place. His height and high arm enabled him to generate ample pace and uncomfortable bounce, his long fingers allowed him to either cut or spin the ball seemingly at will and his length and line were unrelenting. The best bowler in the world.

Tiger Smith (Warwickshire) WK 26. Went to Australia as understudy to Strudwick but was promoted after the first Test. Standing-up to both Barnes and the quickish left-arm round of county colleague Foster, he did some remarkable things including stumping Clem Hill for a duck down the leg side. His presence in the side seemed to give Frank Foster added confidence and zip.

With these seven players apparent certainties, the core of the team was established but the selectors still faced some ticklish decisions. Men such as Hearne (at 20 England's youngest Test centurion until Compton) and Gunn had done well in Australia but 'room could be found with advantage for one or two batsmen'. Spooner was the first on the list and Fry, if he 'should start the season in his best run-getting form….would seem an almost inevitable addition', not to mention Gilbert Jessop despite, or maybe because of, this being his last season. Newspaper letters' columns were full of persuasive arguments supporting the claims of Hayward, Fry and Rhodes to partner Jack Hobbs. Walter Brearley, one of the few fast bowlers in the country, announced that he would not be playing for Lancashire during the summer but would be in strict training in case his services should be required in the Tests. Early county form and the trial matches would be crucial in deciding the final line-up for England's first appearance in the Triangular Tournament, against South Africa on 10 June at Lord's.

The issue of the captaincy was, however, the one that attracted most attention. Warner had led MCC to Australia and they had won easily which would normally be a cast-iron recommendation, but not in this case. He had originally been second choice behind Fry, he had been ill all tour, there was no guarantee that he was fully recovered and anyway he had been replaced once before, by Jackson, after returning triumphant from Australia. Then there was the man who had stepped in for the stricken Warner, Johnny Douglas. He had led the team well in Warner's absence and was more than worth his place as a player. And finally there was Charles Burgess Fry. For the heaviest run scorer of his generation he had been strangely ineffective in Test cricket, with only two centuries in 20 games, but he was still revered by many as the finest amateur batsman and a tactician of rare subtlety. In March Lord Harris had written to him to ask 'for his views on the subject' and those views would become public knowledge after the meeting at Lord's on 30 April.

There was concern also over mechanics of the season and its financial implications. Just as Stanley Jackson had done in February, the *Manchester Guardian* warned against the quantity of cricket to be played.

'....probably by the close of the season the public appetite for cricket on the grand scale will have been more than satisfied.'

The *Daily Chronicle* was even more gloomy in its prediction of financial disaster for the counties arising from the amount of Test cricket and poor quality of two of the teams.

The first of the travellers to arrive attracted little notice. The MCC team lately active in Argentina docked on the sixth of the month and related tales of derring-do, heat and 'a big fillip' to the game in Buenos Aires. The next day they were followed by their big brothers who had travelled overland from Toulon thus surprising all but a few who, led by ex-Kent captain and local resident Jack Mason, were ready to meet them at the Admiralty Pier, Dover. A considerably larger crowd gathered at Charing Cross to greet them off the train and all were relieved to see that Pelham Warner, who only four months earlier had been critically ill, appeared in the best of health and pronounced himself as such. This verdict was endorsed by a specialist the following day, giving him the all-clear to buckle on his pads again. There was no sign of Frank Foster who was staying with his father in Paris and only a brief glimpse of Rhodes and Barnes who were eager to rush to Euston and King's Cross in order to travel home. Jack Hobbs and Tiger Smith were clearly more than a little under the weather after the long journey but they had a busy schedule in front of them. Invitations were pouring in and Hobbs was feted as 'one of the greatest batsmen and the finest cover-point the world has ever seen' at a reception in his home town of Cambridge two weeks later. The team-manager, Tom Pawley, proudly showed off his memento of the tour, a hollow gold cricket ball containing the ashes of a stump used in the fourth Test.

Johnny Douglas, speaking to the *Pall Mall Gazette,* attributed the MCC success in Australia, rather unoriginally, to 'good fellowship and good cricket'. He was clearly disappointed with the hosts, describing their batting as below expectations and bowling as weak, but stressed the 'splendid possibilities' of the younger players. Wilfred Rhodes, a reasonable judge, was especially keen on the talents of Roy Minnett but also exclaimed "we shall sadly miss the players left behind". Any talking up of the opposition was too much for *Wisden* editor Sydney Pardon who let fly to the *Sunday Times* proclaiming that the promoters of the summer festival were confronted with the risk of failure and that 'nobody seriously believes Australia has found substitutes for those remaining behind', not to mention the loss of Sherwell and Vogler to South Africa.

But with the coal strike ending and the good weather and the prospect of a fine summer's sport in England and Stockholm there came the news of a tragedy that was to alter the country's mood. On 15 April, reports of the demise of the *Titanic* in the icy waters of the North Atlantic began to filter through. Amongst the 1,513 fatalities (from a total number on board of 2,224), and most mourned in the British press, was WT Stead, former editor of the *Pall Mall Gazette*, founder of the *Review of Reviews*, opponent of war and exposer of child prostitution in London. Curiously he had twice written about shipwrecks in the Atlantic. In the first, the cause was an iceberg and in the second the lack of lifeboats resulted in massive loss of life. Stead had been a passionate follower of cricket as a young man:

> 'People are interested in what they can understand, and while the colonial politics are unintelligible to the public at home, every man and boy, and a considerable number of women, know all about cricket. Sport is one of those things before which frontiers disappear, and the many leagues of rolling ocean are as if they were not.'

With the newspapers still full of the *Titanic* and now looking for explanations and answers, the first of the summer's guests, the South Africans, arrived on board the *Balmoral Castle* on Saturday 20 April. Sibley Snooke, already a week into his honeymoon, joined the crowd dockside in Southampton and took the opportunity for some leg-pulling of the press as to the brilliance of Herby Taylor's wicket-keeping and which arm Joe Cox bowled with. Manager George Allsop, as befitted his position, adopted a more sober attitude, thanking Sir Abe Bailey (who was due to arrive by the next boat) for making the coming spectacle possible and crediting him with bringing South African cricket into the modern age. He went on to contradict the words of Pardon, declaring that the Big Six would not be missed as much as anticipated. The furore in South Africa surrounding the captaincy had not died down and vitriolic articles continued even after the team had left. The *South African News* reported on departure that none of the players 'cared to discuss Mitchell's eligibility' and the Cape Town weekly then launched its broadside:

> 'But the point is this – if Mitchell were a Hobbs and a Foster rolled into one would that make him any more South African? Of course it would not, and one has said this before, and intends to keep saying it until the selectors realise its truth, that the South African cricket team led by Mr Mitchell in the triangular tests, reduces what should have been a great festival to something approaching farce. If we have not amongst us a player who is capable of leading a team in the field….we scarcely have a right to be represented at all.'

As in Australia, inter-state rivalry was alive and kicking in South Africa and coloured many issues with both Griqualand West and Western Province still bitter at their lack of representation. Frank Mitchell expressed himself delighted to be back in England and offered high hopes of the bowling of Pegler, Hartigan and Schwarz who was now fully recovered following surgery on a long-standing elbow injury. He was, however, acutely aware of the absence of Sherwell, Vogler, a fast bowler and the fact that Faulkner's batting prowess had adversely affected his bowling. Aubrey Faulkner's contribution to team unity and morale was curious in that he chose to write for the *Sportsman* expressing somewhat pessimistic views.

> 'There should not be the slightest hesitation in placing England an easy first. After their remarkably triumphant tour in Australia, one wonders what can possibly prevent them from retaining the "Ashes"….The Australians grit is proverbial and it is more than likely that several names will be added to the list of great cricketers

produced from "down under" but I, nevertheless, think it is improbable that the same amount of success will attend their efforts as we saw in the 1909 side....As far as I can ascertain the [South African] team offers great possibilities and I hear from Johannesburg that it is a better combination than our 1907 side but this, of course, remains to be seen.'

Back home, the *Rand Daily Mail* was almost as low key:

'On form England ought to win tests without great difficulty [but] both Australia and South Africa have a reputation for fighting losing battles well, and they may yet surprise their friends.'

With those ringing endorsements the team moved on to their London headquarters, De Keyser's Hotel near Blackfriars Bridge, announcing a selection committee of Mitchell, Tancred and Schwarz and, with the promise of fine weather, practice at Lord's was arranged for Monday. The rest of the weekend was spent sightseeing, buying 'London clothes' and acclimatising to the heavy London traffic.

With the exception of Nourse, White and Llewellyn the entire squad was present under the critical eyes of the press for a week of serious acclimatisation. On hard and fast wickets Tancred, Stricker and Taylor showed up well, the latter using his feet admirably and showing the advantage of intense back-foot practice in South Africa under the eagle eye of coach George Cox and at home in front of a mirror. Claude Carter, Sibley Snooke and Joe Cox took on plenty of bowling. The first named impressed, the last didn't. Aubrey Faulkner, in the first of his articles entitled *Our Cricketers* for the *Star* in Johannesburg, had plenty to relate. The players were 'hopelessly at sea' on the first day but improved rapidly, with the batting of Mitchell and Tancred being most eye-catching. He did, however, fear for the prospects of Cox and Carter should the summer be dry.

House party at Old Buckenham, 28 April – Sir Lionel Robinson (nephew of the first Australian prime minister, Edmund Barton) was a generous host to both touring teams. Back: Tom Campbell, Louis Stricker, Gerald Hartigan, Herby Taylor, Reggie Schwarz, Claude Carter, unknown; front: Louis Tancred, Frank Mitchell, Robinson, Claude Jennings, Archie MacLaren (secretary).

For some of the team it was then off to Lionel Robinson's country retreat in Norfolk for a weekend of light exercise, practice and socialising with Claude Jennings of Australia who had arrived ahead of his team-mates. Aubrey Faulkner reported to his South African readers that:

> '....it is little wonder that those of us who had not seen anything of English country high life were very much impressed with everything that was done for us. Our host has a fine ground laid down a stone's throw from the house....'

Good news from the north was that Charlie Llewellyn had started his career at Accrington in top form by single-handedly destroying Bacup on his debut.

The Australian team had managed a brief stop in Ceylon where a game had been arranged against All Ceylon on 11 April. It was won by Australia who fielded an interesting guest in the form of Dick Arnst, the New Zealand sculler, who was travelling on the same ship in order to meet his old rival Ernest Barry on the Thames in July in defence of his title of World Champion.

The Australian tourists on board the *Otway* en route to England – Back: Gerry Hazlitt, Bill Whitty, Jimmy Matthews, Ernest Hume (visitor), Dave Smith, Harold Webster, Charles Kelleway, Edgar Mayne; middle: Syd Gregory (captain), Bill Carkeek, Jack McLaren; front: Warren Bardsley, Charlie Macartney, Sid Emery, Roy Minnett. Absent: Claude Jennings and manager George Crouch had already disembarked and were travelling overland from Toulon in company with the journalist EW Ballantine.

Thereafter there was a stopover and mosque visit in Port Said followed by afternoons spent walking the streets in Naples and Toulon where Jennings and Crouch disembarked to continue the journey overland. The *Otway* finally arrived in Plymouth on 26 April, where Charlie Macartney left in order to proceed by train, thereby gaining an extra day in London. A reporter from the *Evening Standard and St. James's Gazette* managed to grab some hurried words from the Syd Gregory.

'Our side this time is composed chiefly of new men. There are eleven men making the trip for the first time but they are all triers and hard workers. I am sure they will give a good account of themselves. In the first match or two the English wickets may affect them, but once they find their form all should go well with us.'

A reception committee at Paddington was rather disappointed to find Macartney the only player to emerge from the Plymouth boat train and he then 'would not commit himself to any statement as to the prospects of the tour'. The rest of the party then continued onto their final destination of Tilbury which was reached the following day. Even as they stepped on to dry land the newspapers were still occupied with 'the others'. A vote of no confidence in the Board was easily quashed in Sydney, and in Melbourne the Victoria Cricket Association overwhelmingly endorsed the Board's actions concerning Frank Laver and the famous 'account books' from the 1909 tour. *Cricket* was unaccountably still able to report that:

> 'It is quite on the cards that Australia will have the invaluable services of Victor Trumper in some, at least, of the test matches. He will be in England on business during the summer, and the Board will raise no objection to his playing if he consents and the team want him.'

That such an influential magazine and its editor, JN Pentelow, could be so deceived and have understood so little of the arguments in Australia beggars belief. Clearly the team, and especially the captain, would not want Trumper, whatever his reputation and ability, a fact of which the Board of Control was well aware. And what of the notion that Trumper would suddenly change into his kit and turn out in a Test match? He was a better man than that and anyway if he had done so Warwick Armstrong would certainly have wrung his neck on his return to Australia. But the fact remained that most of the talk was still about the players left behind rather than the ones who would be seen at Derby and Taunton and Leyton during the summer.

So when the questions were posed at Tilbury, it was a mixture of what had happened and what might happen. This time Gregory alighted on Hazlitt, Emery, McLaren, Jennings and Minnett as the men to watch, while regretting the absence, in particular, of Armstrong. George Crouch was also besieged by pressmen and, like Gregory, he praised most of the team as 'the best available under the circumstances'. A telegram from Plum Warner was duly delivered: 'Best wishes to all for a happy and successful tour'. From Tilbury they travelled up to St Pancras and then onto their London hotel, The Howard on Norfolk Street.

With the big set-piece practice at Lord's for both sides on 29 April being a major attraction, an admission fee was charged and there were some complaints that it was hard to get near to the players. South African readers could at least picture the scene as set by the correspondent of the *Star*.

> 'Beautiful spring weather prevailed yesterday as both the Australian and South African teams practised at Lord's in the presence of hundreds of spectators

privileged to be present. The novelty of the season is occasioning phenomenal interest in the national summer pastime and there can now be little doubt that the public support will justify the great cricketing festival, the near approach of which is causing a wave of enthusiasm throughout the country, the like of which has not been experienced for years.

Great interest is being taken in the form of the young Colonials and the critics who on such occasions have for so long been accustomed to the well-known abilities of Trumper, Hill, Carter, Cotter and Ransford are greatly impressed with the new Australian school in which they discern very able understudies to the "recalcitrant six". The form of the new members of the South African team is also favourably discussed, and the critics at this stage are wisely refraining from making any statement which they recognise might easily commit them subsequently.'

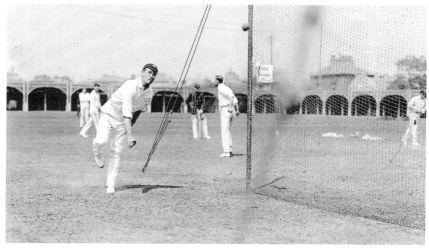

Sid Emery in the Lord's nets, 29 April – An unplayable or an unreachable? Note the South African-blazered player in the background, the two touring teams practised in adjoining nets. The notice pinned on the side of the net states: 'For Australian use only'.

Faulkner had a good look at his opponents and approved of what he saw of Bardsley, Whitty and Hazlitt but he also had words of warning:

> Though Syd Gregory is reported in the papers to have said....they are strong at all points of the game, I nevertheless, with due deference, think that it will not be very long before he is wishing he had Victor Trumper, Clem Hill, W. Armstrong and the others they have left behind. From this it must not for one moment be inferred that I think the present combination a weak one. As far as that goes I think they will be second in the tournament but I cannot see that they are so strong as to be in the position to treat the non-inclusion of the players above mentioned as nonchalantly as they appear to be doing.'

It wasn't all practice and interviews however. The Australian players made a trip to Hendon and 'inspected some of the big flying machines' and both teams took an

Bill Whitty in the Lord's nets, 29 April – Syd Gregory is to the right of the group observing.

early breakfast in company with cricketer/missionary CT Studd at the new YMCA on Tottenham Court Road. The South Africans dined as guests of the Guildhall Cricket Club and Dave Nourse visited the club of his youth, St George's in South Norwood, for his appointment as vice president. Then there was a banquet at the Hotel Cecil as guests of Sir Thomas Dewar who declared 'the visits of the cricketers were creating history not only in cricket, but politically, in assisting to unify the Empire'. Entertainments included turns from vaudeville legends Harry Lauder and George Robey; the latter became firm friends with Warren Bardsley with whom he shared a facial resemblance based on their 'thick curving eyebrows', and Robey took great pride in the gift of an Australian blazer.

The Australian tourists at Lord's during practice – Back: George Crouch (manager), Roy Minnett, Ernest Hume (visitor), Charles Kelleway, Edgar Mayne, Sid Emery, Dave Smith, Bill Whitty, Harold Webster, Gerry Hazlitt; middle: Warren Bardsley, Jack McLaren, Jimmy Matthews, Syd Gregory, Claude Jennings, Charlie Macartney, Bill Carkeek.

The South African tourists at Lord's during practice – Back: Louis Stricker, Reggie Schwarz, Rolland Beaumont, Tom Campbell, Gerald Hartigan, Joe Cox; middle: Sid Pegler, Louis Tancred, Frank Mitchell, Aubrey Faulkner, Sibley Snooke, Dave Nourse; front: Herby Taylor, Tom Ward, Claude Carter.

With all the visitors now safely in London, a meeting of the Board of Control of Test Matches at Home was convened followed closely by the Imperial Cricket Conference. Both took place on the afternoon of 30 April and once again Lord Harris was in the respective chairs. The first meeting was short and sweet. At the previous gathering in March, Harris had offered to write to Fry to glean his views on the captaincy and selection committee. At this 30 April meeting the minutes recorded:

> 'Harris stated that he had, in accordance with his undertaking to the Board at the last meeting, written to Mr. Fry offering him the captaincy of the England side in the first Test Match and Test Trial Match, and asking for his views with regard to the selection sub-committee. He read letters and a memorandum from Mr. Fry embodying his views….and proposed that he should be asked to act as Captain of the England XI for 1912 on the confidential understanding that such appointment is subject to the terms proposed in the memorandum.'

In fact the March minutes show that Harris had undertaken to write to Fry 'asking for his views on the subject'. No objections to this discrepancy, between what he undertook to do and what he actually did, were expected and none were recorded but it was hardly a beacon of transparent democracy. At Fry's instigation John Shuter and HK Foster (the former a substitute for the unavailable Jack Mason) were appointed as his 'assessors' on the selection committee making Fry the only active player, a state of affairs he had actively criticised in writing the previous year. This was a complete coup for Charles Burgess Fry. He was back in the team without hitting a ball in anger, he had vaulted over not one but two Ashes-winning captains in Warner and Douglas, he had secured his tenure for an entire season comprising six Test matches, he had received approval for his preferred system of a small squad for the Tests come what may and he had the men he wanted to back his judgement as to the final team. Not a bad afternoon's work even for a man of Fry's stature both on and off the field. In fact it looked like being a good year; a fawning biography just published, a marble sculpture by Albert Bruce-Joy, his own book on batsmanship on the way, the return of his old friend Ranji and even a lucrative contract to advertise Hartley's Tobacco in South Africa.

The three captains – Frank Mitchell, Charles Fry and Syd Gregory.

Recalling events nearly 30 years later in *Life Worth Living*, Fry remembered everything with astounding clarity. He considered that his only rivals for the captaincy had been Reggie Spooner, who disliked the responsibility, and Plum Warner, who 'was ailing and a doubtful starter'. No mention of JWHT Douglas. The initial letter from Harris had indeed been an offer of the captaincy but only for the first Test and Fry rejected this out of hand. He insisted on the full season and his 'own' selection committee. According to Fry, when Harris read these conditions to the Board he prefaced it with "I think this fellow Fry is right"; a particularly unlikely exclamation. As far as team selection was concerned, Fry then claimed:

'So Foster, Shuter and I met once in May, chose a definite team with definite substitutes if required for the whole series of six matches, and we never met again.'

This plan may have tarried with Fry's beliefs, as outlined in 1911, but the reality was that changes were made for each Test and if Fry really did not meet his fellow selectors again then he had performed an elaborate coup and become, for the summer of 1912, the king of English cricket.

With the captaincy and some matters of finance cleared up within 80 minutes, the representatives of Australia and South Africa were ushered in for the ICC discussion relating to the Triangular Tournament. The umpiring question had effectively been decided at the previous meeting and Australian manager Crouch accepted the principle of the panel of officials already chosen although he managed to insert the caveat that a joint objection by both captains could see any umpire removed from the list. The ballot then took place and the two men to stand in each of the nine Tests decided upon. The Australians undertook to write to each county asking that the hours of play be reduced by 30 minutes starting at midday rather than 11.30. The gate money division had been amicably agreed with the exception of certain counties, most notably Yorkshire, who intended keeping all money collected as transfers from the 6d to 1s enclosures. Both managers strongly objected and proposed writing to Yorkshire; the ICC issued the 'hope this may be remedied'.

At last the talking was over. After both teams had been entertained by Lord Kinnaird at the new YMCA buildings, the Australian team could enjoy the last evening of April at Daly's Theatre watching 'The Count of Luxembourg'. The first day of May would see bat on ball at both Lord's and The Oval and the prospect of witnessing men such as Faulkner, Fry, Gunn and Hobbs in action.

MAY

Mo	Tu	We	Th	Fr	Sa	Su
		1	2	3	4	5
6	7	8	9	10	11	12
13	14	15	16	17	18	19
20	21	22	23	24	25	26
27	28	29	30	31		

1912

Jan
Mo	Tu	We	Th	Fr	Sa	Su
1	2	3	4	5	6	7
8	9	10	11	12	13	14
15	16	17	18	19	20	21
22	23	24	25	26	27	28
29	30	31				

Feb
Mo	Tu	We	Th	Fr	Sa	Su
			1	2	3	4
5	6	7	8	9	10	11
12	13	14	15	16	17	18
19	20	21	22	23	24	25
26	27	28	29			

Mar
Mo	Tu	We	Th	Fr	Sa	Su
				1	2	3
4	5	6	7	8	9	10
11	12	13	14	15	16	17
18	19	20	21	22	23	24
25	26	27	28	29	30	31

Apr
Mo	Tu	We	Th	Fr	Sa	Su
1	2	3	4	5	6	7
8	9	10	11	12	13	14
15	16	17	18	19	20	21
22	23	24	25	26	27	28
29	30					

May
Mo	Tu	We	Th	Fr	Sa	Su
		1	2	3	4	5
6	7	8	9	10	11	12
13	14	15	16	17	18	19
20	21	22	23	24	25	26
27	28	29	30	31		

Jun
Mo	Tu	We	Th	Fr	Sa	Su
					1	2
3	4	5	6	7	8	9
10	11	12	13	14	15	16
17	18	19	20	21	22	23
24	25	26	27	28	29	30

Jul
Mo	Tu	We	Th	Fr	Sa	Su
1	2	3	4	5	6	7
8	9	10	11	12	13	14
15	16	17	18	19	20	21
22	23	24	25	26	27	28
29	30	31				

Aug
Mo	Tu	We	Th	Fr	Sa	Su
			1	2	3	4
5	6	7	8	9	10	11
12	13	14	15	16	17	18
19	20	21	22	23	24	25
26	27	28	29	30	31	

Sep
Mo	Tu	We	Th	Fr	Sa	Su
						1
2	3	4	5	6	7	8
9	10	11	12	13	14	15
16	17	18	19	20	21	22
23	24	25	26	27	28	29
30						

Oct
Mo	Tu	We	Th	Fr	Sa	Su
1	2	3	4	5	6	
7	8	9	10	11	12	13
14	15	16	17	18	19	20
21	22	23	24	25	26	27
28	29	30	31			

Nov
Mo	Tu	We	Th	Fr	Sa	Su
			1	2	3	
4	5	6	7	8	9	10
11	12	13	14	15	16	17
18	19	20	21	22	23	24
25	26	27	28	29	30	

Dec
Mo	Tu	We	Th	Fr	Sa	Su
						1
2	3	4	5	6	7	8
9	10	11	12	13	14	15
16	17	18	19	20	21	22
23	24	25	26	27	28	29
30	31					

JOSEPH CONRAD on
THE TITANIC DISASTER

THE JEWS AND THE "BLOOD ACCUSATION"

Sir, -All Jews must have experienced a thrill of satisfaction upon reading in your columns to-day the generous protest of British Christians against the hideous "Blood Accusation". The high and noble terms in which the protest is framed do justice to the intention of its signatories. I feel sure that Jews throughout the world will deeply appreciate this action. The fact that at this date such a protest should become necessary gives food for painful reflection.

Duelling In Germany
Statement By The War Minister

The Driest April

PETER PAN IN KENSINGTON GARDENS

Children For Canada Lord Grey On A Neglected Opportunity

WRECK OF THE TITANIC - RECOVERY OF SEVENTEEN MORE BODIES

A NEW ANTI-TYPHOID SERUM THE METCHINKOFF SYSTEM

FEDERALISM AND THE HOME RULE BILL

SPEAKING CINEMATOGRAPHY

At the Royal Institution last night, Professor W. Stirling of Manchester, aided by the inventor, gave a demonstration of the Gaumont Cinematograph films before a large audience. The Lecturer explained that the problem was how to obtain at the same time records from a cinematograph and from a phonograph, gramophone or talking machine and how, these being obtained, to reproduce and present them simultaneously.

DIET IN SCHOOLS
THE GUILDHALL CONFERENCE

DETECTION OF ICEBERGS
EXPERIMENTS WITH A PERFECTED MICRO-THERMOMETER

TRIAL OF SUFFRAGIST LEADERS

The trial of the suffragist leaders, Mrs. Pankhurst and Mr. And Mrs. Pethick Lawrence, for conspiracy began yesterday...There was an eager demand for accommodation, chiefly by women, outside the building, and inside the Court itself women formed a conspicuously large majority of those present.

THE LABOUR OUTLOOK

FURTHER DECISIONS AS TO MINERS' PAY

TAILORS RETURNING TO WORK

THE FRENCH MOTOR-CAR BANDITS
ANOTHER SIEGE NEAR PARIS
DYNAMITE EMPLOYED

SURRENDER OF THE TURKISH GARRISON IN RHODES

MR ROOSEVELT'S TRIUMPH IN OHIO

INTERNATIONAL FLOWER SHOW   PRINCIPAL NEW ORCHIDS   DOMINIONS' EXHIBITS

THE FINDING OF A TITANIC LIFE RAFT

At about 12.30 on Tuesday [May 15] we were playing shuffleboard on deck when we noticed our boat making a sharp turning movement. We could not make it out and thought at first a derelict was in front, but after a few minutes we sighted the lifeboat in the water on our starboard. We passed within 50 yards of it. By then the engines had been stopped, so we could plainly see the three men. It was the most pathetic sight I have ever witnessed. One man was lying under the bow and the other two were in the stern. Their legs were under the thwarts, and this no doubt held them in the boat. They all had lifebelts on and we could see their faces were black.

TRANSPORT STRIKE

The strike of transport workers in London continues, and appears to be spreading though estimates of the number of men who have left work vary considerably from 120,000 downwards. Instructions have been issued at Aldershot.

THE NEGRO RISING IN CUBA
American Naval Preparations

May began with yet more socialising. The 125th annual MCC dinner celebrated the arrival of two touring teams for the first time ever, the victory of their team in Australia and also the accession to the presidency of the Duke of Devonshire. A right sumptuous affair it was too, a French-orientated menu being complemented by a Mouton Rothschild '96 and a charming Bollinger '04. After such intense banqueting and practising, the South African players were eager for some match play before commencing the official programme at Derby on Saturday 4 May. With this in mind, Taylor, Mitchell, Schwarz and Hartigan all turned out for Selwood at Esher on the first of the month. Tommy Ward managed to locate a couple of club fixtures, finding the variety and bounce of turf wickets a far cry from the matting of Transvaal under match conditions – but he was gaining valuable experience. Pegler was laid low by a cold but three men, Faulkner, Tancred and Snooke, had the good fortune to receive an invitation to Lord's to represent MCC against Nottinghamshire under the captaincy of none other than Charles Fry. Both Tancred and Faulkner prospered with the bat, causing one newspaper to eulogise that when Fry and Faulkner were in partnership, adding 191 in 150 minutes, 'the world's greatest batsmen were together'.

MCC dinner for South Africans, Australians and their own Ashes-winning side, 1 May – King Cricket accepts the Ashes from Johnny Douglas. Artist George Hillyard Swinstead has managed to squeeze in countless jokes and references, for example the duck's head protruding from Barnes' wicket's bag.

On Friday evening the South African squad took the train to Derby for their first match but disappointment was in store in the form of torrential rain and by early Saturday afternoon it was clear that no play at all would be possible on what should have been the most lucrative of the three days. The captains conferred and agreed that, in view of both teams being free on the Wednesday, the three-day game could start on Monday instead. In terms of gate receipts this would be little compensation but the guests would at least salvage more much needed match practice. Monday morning dawned rather grey and gloomy and even though the pitch remained damp and dead, play was possible. Considering the unfamiliar conditions (even the Lord's practice wickets had been hard and fast) it was a good bowling and fielding performance to put Derbyshire out twice for less than 300. The bowling of Faulkner and Carter attracted particular praise, with both managing to extract plenty of turn. The batting was less than impressive as all players struggled to come to terms with both the pace and bounce but in the second innings Faulkner, Nourse and Snooke all played better and a comfortable seven-wicket win was achieved on the morning of the third day. This didn't stop one reporter sniping that the 'batting was unconvincing and the timing faulty' although the *Westminster Gazette* was more generous, marking the South Africans as the dark horse (if such a thing can exist in a three-runner race). Worry was still expressed as to their bowling on good wickets especially as Reggie Schwarz's elbow, despite his recent operation, was still 'troublesome'. Derbyshire were not a strong side but a win was a win and the team left for London in good heart for the tougher challenge of Surrey.

Frank Mitchell and Sibley Snooke at The Oval, 9 May – Mitchell, solidly cheerful, and Snooke, more pensive, emerge after lunch on the first day of the game against Surrey.

Conditions at The Oval were considerably more conducive to bright cricket. The pitch was fast and true and with a batting line-up boasting Hobbs, Hayward and Hayes it seemed probable that the South African bowlers were in for a severe test. The batsmen could expect an easier time against an uneven attack, although Bill Hitch would be keen to make a good impression given the disputed position of fast bowler in the national side. The game did not, however, produce the expected batting bonanza. Over the three days there was precious little to enjoy beyond the efforts of Reggie Schwarz in the first innings and Dave Nourse in the second. No other player gave any impression of permanence which, given the conditions and the opposition, was a worry. The swinging ball created uncertainties amongst the visitors, especially those with no English experience, and many fell to poor deliveries. On the positive side, the bowling more than compensated for the flaws in the batting and victory was achieved by 52 runs. The only two men that had prospered with the bat also collected 13 wickets between them but reactions to their respective performances were very different. Dave Nourse had supposedly 'gone' as a bowler but this was patently not true of a man who could twice clean bowl Jack Hobbs. Reggie Schwarz, of whom so much was expected, managed seven wickets but most critics commented on his lack of 'nip' compared to 1907 rather than his success. Sid Pegler did attract praise for his accuracy and change of pace on a wicket that would never be helpful to his methods. Considering that Aubrey Faulkner had succumbed to a bad back mid-way through the game, there was plenty of encouragement to be taken from the victory. Faulkner himself was pleasantly surprised by the way his countrymen had acquitted themselves, reserving particular praise for the batting of Schwarz and the bowling of Pegler and Carter. A big century from Tancred, Snooke or Stricker would have crowned a good first week but at least the newspapers at home could call the bowling 'a feature of the season' after just two games.

The XIIIth Australian touring team had begun their tour on Monday 6 May only 30 miles away from where the South African's delayed game was being played. Conditions at Trent Bridge were very similar to those at Derby but the opposition was not. Two Gunns and a Hardstaff spoke of formidable batting, all-rounder James Iremonger had just returned from the Australian tour, Ted Alletson had played 'that innings' at Hove the previous year and Topsy Wass was still snarling at all-comers. This would be no easy introduction to the summer and, in truth, the Australians weren't ready for such a tough fixture and were beaten by six wickets. Having gained a first-innings lead of 46, due largely to the efforts of Charlie Macartney, the second knock was very disappointing especially as Claude Jennings, batting at six, showed what could be done before being run out for 51. In a low-scoring game the Notts. target of 212 was no formality. The pitch rolled out flawlessly on the last day and, with the loss of Whitty to a side strain, George and John Gunn made short work of the matter. The general verdict was reasonably kind to the tourists. They hadn't had the best of the pitch and there was much to like in the bowling of Hazlitt (luckless), Matthews (plenty of spin), Whitty (three short-legs) and McLaren (accurate). In Australia the press reaction was mixed. The *Sydney Telegraph* was not at all impressed and wrote of the team that 'opinion with regard to them is naturally pessimistic'. The *Bulletin* took a more colourful and bright view, declaring such views as 'semi-stinking fish yelp' before lambasting whisky magnate Sir Thomas Dewar!

> '….just before [three days] their long train journey to their first engagement [London to Nottingham] a swagger banquet was "tendered" them, not with any idea of retention of any form they had acquired but to advertise a certain brand of liquid that needs no bush. The Board of Control and Marylebone should agree to bar all banquets until the Tests are over.'

But it was still a defeat and under the murky conditions it was no great surprise that the crowd never rose above 3,000. With the receipts of the South African game at

Derby amounting to a princely £20 it was evident that, although the national coal strike had finished, the scars were still plainly visible in one of the central mining areas and money was in short supply. One bright point for the turf enthusiasts amongst the party was a trip to Welbeck Abbey, the home of the Duke of Portland, to see Carbine, winner of numerous races in Australia including the Melbourne Cup, who had been purchased for 13,000 guineas for stud duty. He shared a nickname, 'Black Jack', with the redoubtable wicket-keeper Jack Blackham, his blood lines prospered and his skeleton is still on display in Melbourne.

The *Daily Graphic* continued its campaign of doom and gloom by reporting that 'cricket officials view the financial outlook of the tournament with concern'. The Australians would now travel to Northampton to face, and presumably prosper against, traditionally one of the weakest teams in the Championship.

They took full advantage from the first day, or at least some of them did. Gregory and Macartney put on 240 in 160 minutes in an aggressive, if not faultless, partnership that was gleefully described by one reporter as an alliance of 'midgets'. The 42-year-old captain proved his stamina and the younger man showed again that he was a far better batsmen than he had been in 1909 and even if there was no great elegance in his play (to English eyes at least) there was power and talent that would garner a lot of runs over the coming months. Although no other batsmen succeeded, the bowlers had a fine time in twice dismissing the hosts cheaply to win by an innings and 64. Sid Emery, with his baffling mixture of the unplayable and the unreachable, collected 12-110 although these figures were considered flattering; this verdict was invariably the fate of such an inconsistent bowler. Again the crowd was a huge disappointment, never rising above 2,000, and with the game being over in two days the Saturday takings were lost as well.

With the two touring teams busy shaking off the stiffness of the long journeys, it was high time for the home nation to start preparing and for selectors Fry, Shuter and Foster to observe the form of 22 likely men in The Oval Test trial between England and the Rest. One section of the press was already harking back to 1905 when Warner and many of his team had been ignored for the home series against Australia after recapturing the Ashes the previous year and not everyone was sure that Fry was the right choice to lead. *Cricket* had no misgivings and lambasted all those who criticised either his Test record or accusations of nervousness. At least there was certain to be stiff competition for places which augured well for the overall strength of the side.

The selection of the teams as much as the match itself gave clues as to how Fry and his assistants (for that is what they were) intended to construct the England team. The backbone would be the men that had reclaimed the Ashes three months earlier. To this the names of four amateurs were added: Fry, Spooner, Warner and Brearley. Warner had not played since a ruptured duodenal ulcer had struck him down in Australia the previous November and Walter Brearley had now ended his association with county cricket so both had plenty to prove. Ashes-winning captain Johnny Douglas had been demoted to the Rest for the game but would surely return to the first team for the main event. Another interesting inclusion was young Irish googly bowler Peter Clarke. He had learnt his art from none other than Ernie Vogler at Woodbrook in Dublin in 1909 where Vogler was coaching as guest of Sir Stanley Cochrane, the soft-drinks millionaire. Fry was nothing if not methodical in his approach to the coming tournament. The South Africans had three googly bowlers and the Australians one; many English batsmen, including Fry himself, had been unsure against this form of attack and here was a golden opportunity to get some practice. Clarke was given plenty of work in the nets as well as in the game itself. All this brought the name of Vogler back into the news and there was something new to report.

> 'The case in which AEE Vogler the cricketer was plaintiff and Sir Abe Bailey KCMG defendant had been set down for to-day in the Rand division of the Supreme Court. It was settled out of court at the last moment in the following terms. The parties abovenamed hereby consent to the withdrawal of the action by the plaintiff, each party to pay his own costs.
> Plaintiff undertakes further to take no further action against the defendant in respect of the causes of action or matters in dispute referred to in the pleadings.'

It transpired that Vogler had signed a three-year contract for £300 pa in 1909 but Bailey had cancelled it while Vogler was on tour because 'the agreement implied that Vogler had to keep himself fit, which he didn't do in Australia'. Still this was not the end of the affair.

Back at The Oval, on a pitch with a little bite but largely well behaved, England made short work of the Rest. Spooner and Jack Hearne seemed to have sealed their places with centuries and Brearley's six wickets put him at, or very near, the front of the queue should a quick bowler be needed. For the Rest, only Harry Dean bowled well and Phil Mead missed the chance to line himself up for a middle-order position if a professional's services were required. In a sense the selectors learnt everything and nothing – Warner was the obvious weak link and Douglas could replace him in a team thick with all-rounders. The second trial match would probably be more conclusive. It would have to be.

With a free Sunday to take stock, both touring teams could reflect on their first two matches with a certain amount of satisfaction but also in the knowledge that they now had two weeks and four matches each before they would meet one another at Old Trafford in the first of the summer's nine Tests. For South Africa, the bowling omens were good. Schwarz and Faulkner had both showed that the googly continued to be an effective weapon on English pitches. Nourse had proved he could still bowl and new men Carter and Pegler had taken to turf wickets well. They had conceded a mere two half-centuries in the two games but, and it was a big but, they had only scored one and that from an all-rounder batting at seven. Tancred, Stricker, Snooke, Faulkner, Nourse and Mitchell (the likely top six) had played some nice shots but time in the middle was lacking. Australia could revel in the excellent form of Macartney with support from Gregory and Jennings. Bardsley, Minnett and Mayne had unfortunately done next to nothing. All the bowlers had acquitted themselves well enough and there was every reason to hope that, with more match practice, Whitty, Emery, Hazlitt, Matthews and McLaren would become a fearsome proposition. The first week was rounded off in style with a grand reception for the two touring teams as guests of Surrey CCC at the Savoy. Amongst the many guests representing all aspects of English and Colonial cricket enjoying the company and entertainment were Fry, Bailey, Ranjitsinhji and Grace. The South African players were left with the conviction

'that if we were to have more dinners on the tour as jolly as this one then a good time was in store for us.'

Next day there was more jollity for the South Africans as they travelled down to Reading to the country estate of Solly Joel, the diamond magnate, to look over his stud farm, meet legendary trainer John Porter and be guests of honour at a banquet for 100.

Back to work and the second week commenced with Australia taking the field at Leyton and South Africa facing MCC and Ground at Lord's. Two very different propositions. The home of MCC would be at its finest after a major spring clean and the application of a £1,000's worth of green and white paint. 'Burrowings under St John's Wood Road' had resulted in the installation of a kitchen in which were to be found 'a stove that can cook 120 fowls at once and a machine that bakes cakes by electricity'. The MCC side was captained by Fry and, in addition to England likelies Spooner and JW Hearne (both centurions in the trial match), the team also boasted fringe players Fielder, Hardstaff and Relf as well as in-form ex-Australian Frank Tarrant. South Africa's opponents Essex, captained by Johnny Douglas, were altogether less inspiring despite the presence of Fane and Perrin. The first day's play reflected the strength of the respective opposition. At Lord's, MCC rattled up 293 and then dismissed South Africa's top four for 84. At Leyton, Essex were put out for 192 on a good pitch before Gregory and Mayne replied with an undefeated partnership of 68 by stumps.

The weather remained fine with both games continuing in much the same vein over the next two days. Macartney and Bardsley put on 362 in 200 minutes, relenting only when faced by the sterling efforts of Douglas, before Essex were quickly dismissed again to complete an Australian victory by an innings and 132. Not the strongest county side but by no means the weakest, Essex had finished above Yorkshire the previous season so the margin of victory was very encouraging and for once good weather and a healthy attendance prevailed. Again all the major bowlers were amongst the wickets and this time all-rounder Charlie Kelleway joined in. For Essex, as well as the English selectors, the only bright point was the form of Douglas who added two half-centuries to his combative bowling.

The chief of those selectors, Fry, was meanwhile having a good close look at the South Africans and leading MCC to a 108-run victory in front of a dismal third-day crowd of just 500 paying spectators. Curiously he also gave the South Africans a nice 37-over sighter of Jack Hearne who, on an unsuitable pitch, managed little. With the help of his captain, Hearne went from being a near certainty for the Test team to a 'maybe'. Despite the obvious disappointment of defeat there were two very positive performances from the South Africans. Sibley Snooke hammered 86 in 100 minutes in the second innings and Sid Pegler took 11 wickets, including a remarkable spell of 6-10, which led one reporter to compare him to Hugh Trumble. On the downside, Carter, Nourse and Schwarz all failed to reproduce the promise of the first two games with the ball and Mitchell, Stricker and Tancred all emerged largely runless once again. In addition Tancred was now struck down by rheumatism and would miss at least one week. Reggie Schwarz did manage one purple patch in which he beat Fry four times in a row before bowling him with the fifth; this would be an interesting contest with Fry still carrying the tag of a man who had mastered everything but the googly. The lack of Faulkner (still sidelined by his back) was apparent although the prospect of including Gordon White (just arrived from South Africa) was some compensation. Aubrey Faulkner's report to South Africa was reasonably positive but he was concerned about fielding and he was certainly offering his captain a prompt when he wrote:

> '....we did remarkably well under the circumstances and it was certainly a trifle rough on us having to meet such a formidable combination so early in the tour. Had Tarrant been taken comfortably, as he should have been before he got 40 runs, a quite different result might have been arrived at....it is preferable in every way to fill the last couple of places [in a Test team] with men whose agility in the field would save at least twenty or thirty runs....'

But the cricket would not get much easier. From Lord's to Marylebone Station and then the 6.20 to Huddersfield to face Yorkshire the next day.

With Tancred and Faulkner unfit and staying in London for 'massage treatment' and Stricker out of form, a new opening partnership of youngsters Gerald Hartigan and Herby Taylor was tried. Rain spoilt most of the first day and what was left of it was further spoilt for the South Africans by George Hirst's three cheap wickets in dreadful light. By the end of the second day, Yorkshire led by 126 with two wickets standing. Hirst and Haigh had tormented all but Hartigan and a dashing Gordon White with the ball before themselves adding 93 in 50 minutes for the eighth wicket to leave South Africa in a dire position. Only Pegler, with five wickets including a hat-trick, had really tested a Denton-led total with the best possible outcome now a draw. By batting almost through the final day, this was achieved. The resistance was built around the sturdy figure of captain Frank Mitchell who defied his old team-mates Haigh and Rhodes (Hirst was unable to bowl) for nearly three hours with staunch support being given by Taylor, finally replicating his net form, and Pegler. Snooke was back into the groove of failure after his fine knock at Lord's and Rolland Beaumont had shown little to justify the optimism that had surrounded his selection three months earlier. Again the financial returns were poor, a mere £100, in what should have been one of the best attended games of the summer.

Two victories against soft opposition in the first week had been followed by a defeat and a losing draw in the second. There now seemed less grounds for South African optimism. One good innings each from Hartigan, Taylor, Mitchell and Snooke hardly constituted a strong body of batting form to bring from four matches and the bowling was looking increasingly reliant on the form of Pegler. South Africa had just two more games to find a balanced team and the return of Aubrey Faulkner couldn't come soon enough.

One man who would not be joining the team was Ernie Vogler; at long last the denouement to the saga (or farce) had seemingly been reached. Rumours that Vogler was about to leave South Africa to join his countrymen were circulating in London although team-manager George Allsop had 'no knowledge of such an eventuality'. Vogler had presented himself to the governing body in South Africa and expressed his desire to play a part in the Triangular Tournament but had been firmly rebuffed. Then when he suddenly boarded a British-bound ship with his family, speculation was again rife until the truth eventually emerged that he was making his way back to Dublin to coach the Gentlemen of Ireland for Sir Stanley Cochrane. A case worthy of Holmes himself had finally been solved, or had it? The *Daily Graphic* pointed out that as batting was the problem, maybe they should be sending for Tapscott or Zulch anyway.

South Africa had found themselves on the back foot throughout all three days at Huddersfield but at The Oval the Australians were having a much better time of it. Having reduced Surrey to 33-5 on the first morning, they were on the attack throughout. Surrey then lost the services of Hitch and it was surprising that only two men, Matthews and Macartney (his third consecutive century), could take full advantage. Despite 81 from Hobbs in the second innings, the target set by Surrey was an easy one and Australia won by seven wickets. Once again Sid Emery mixed up the sublime with the ridiculous, however the little matter of another 11 wickets was an indication that his pacy wrist spin could be very effective indeed. Faulkner had taken the opportunity afforded by his injury to watch The Oval match and was duly impressed by Bardsley and Macartney. The latter had now amassed 571 runs in two weeks and was on target to equal Grace's legendary feat of 1,000 runs in May. Faulkner was less impressed by Emery and singled out Hazlitt as the danger bowler, although 'his action is being queried by several critics as they say his slow one is open to suspicion'. The *Sportsman* noted 'every now and again close observations will detect something that suggests a base-ball flick'.

The third week of May would, it was hoped, provide the final clues and evidence as to who would be representing the three countries in the Triangular Tournament. Australia were scheduled to meet MCC and Ground before indulging in a quiet game at Oxford and then on to their first Test, beginning on Bank Holiday Monday 27 May.

The South Africans would, meanwhile, travel to Oxford and then Worcester for two straightforward fixtures that would provide practice and confidence for the players likely to be involved at Old Trafford the following Monday. England's best were to assemble at Lord's on the Thursday for the second trial match between the MCC Australian Team and the Rest of England.

The Australians had an almost perfect week on the field. MCC and Ground decided to put out a team strong in batting and rather weak in bowling; Frank Tarrant, who had destroyed the South Africans the previous week, was diplomatically not asked to face his countrymen. Fry, Spooner, Warner, Mead and Hearne represented a formidable first five, containing two certainties, two possibles and a probable for the England team but they were mown down by Hazlitt and Kelleway on a wicket with no real spite in it. Second time around they fared better but were always fighting a losing battle thanks to the efforts of the same bowlers. In between, Macartney, again, and Warren Bardsley had put on 189 in two hours giving Fry plenty to ponder and also a good sighter of the batting mainstays of his international opponents. Macartney was showing the benefits of his own individual tour preparations on a specially soaked pitch in Victor Trumper's back garden and also the coaching of that famous stonewaller Alick Bannerman, whose methods clearly didn't include the mantra 'do as I do'. In Australia's second innings the striking feature was a dashing 64 by Roy Minnett – this was precisely the kind of innings he had been picked to play – which led to a five-wicket victory. Hazlitt and Kelleway collected 16 wickets between them. Webster, however, did little for his prospects by conceding 31 byes and he 'seldom took the ball cleanly'. For Fry it was an uncomfortable match: his side was easily beaten, he was outshone with the bat by captaincy rivals Douglas and Warner and he was criticised for some eccentric field placing. In Australia the *Bulletin* was getting itself into a patriotic lather, parodying any other publication that crabbed the frail batting.

'COLLAPSE OF THE AUSTRALIANS
Four Men Make Nine Million (more or less)
The Rest, 15 (one short)'

It then rejoiced in the prospect of meeting

> 'a Test failure like Fry and an old "has-been" like Ranji….There's no earthly reason why they should not leather England next month, as they will most likely leather Africa next Monday'.

Fighting talk indeed.

The next match was as simple as expected for Australia, Oxford University being brushed aside by 10 wickets courtesy of Bardsley with the bat and Whitty, Hazlitt and Macartney with the ball. Even the forgotten man, Dave Smith, finally got a game having recovered from an attack of boils and the whole side had time for some relaxing boating on the Isis.

On the Sunday before the first Test, the selection committee of Gregory, Jennings and Bardsley had a relatively straightforward task. The first five picked themselves; Gregory, Jennings, Macartney, Bardsley and Minnett. Kelleway had done less with the bat than hoped but more with the ball. Matthews, by contrast, had done less with ball and more with bat – these were the two obvious all-rounders. Carkeek had conceded a huge amount of extras but then so had his understudy Webster, so he was safe. Then there were the three bowlers who had already taken 73 wickets in six matches – Emery, Whitty and Hazlitt. On paper it was a well-balanced team with two batsmen in blistering form coupled with a good bowling mixture of the reliable and the unexpected.

If everything was now sweetness and light in the Australian dressing room, the same could hardly have been said for the South Africans. A rain-spoiled game at the Magdalen College ground revealed nothing positive. Another damp and dead wicket was never likely to play to the Springbok strengths and they got considerably the worst of a dull draw. Dave Nourse batted well twice and Taylor once but against that Mitchell, Faulkner, Hartigan, Beaumont and White managed scarcely a run. Worse still, the undergraduates were twice able to dominate the visitor's bowling.

Any hopes of a rapid turnaround on the first day at Worcester were washed away with the rain, leaving just two days to play. Remarkably, the South Africans emerged bright and breezy on the 23rd, Empire Day, with Faulkner and Pegler dismissing the county for 50 before Hartigan and Taylor sealed their Test places by putting on 146 in two hours for the first wicket. The rest of the batting fared less well against the lob bowling of Simpson-Hayward, who many knew from the 1909-10 MCC tour. Worcestershire (who fielded a 16 year-old debutant, one Frank Chester) were able to salvage a draw largely thanks to a ninth-wicket partnership of 77. This was cause for concern. Sid Pegler was now bowling consistently well, attracting the plaudits of his team-mate Faulkner.

> 'Now that he is bowling leg breaks for the most part, with his fast one only occasionally, he is a greatly improved trundler....Fortunately this young man has at last begun to use his head, and his success now is I think assured.'

So how did the South African selectors, Mitchell, Tancred and Schwarz, approach their ruminations? Taylor and Hartigan were now the openers for sure. Faulkner and Mitchell were guaranteed selection and Tancred remained unfit. Snooke, White and Nourse had all made some runs, the latter was also bowling quite well. Campbell was, in theory, the senior 'keeper but Ward had impressed in two games. All of which left three places. Reggie Schwarz and Sid Pegler must play and under other circumstances Accrington professional Charlie Llewellyn would have completed the line-up. However, the contract allowing Llewellyn to appear for his country excluded Saturdays and Whit Monday, as 'luck' would have it the first Test was to start on precisely that spectator-friendly day. No-one else really merited selection on recent form so the most likely inclusion seemed to be Claude Carter who had taken a dozen wickets in the first couple of games.

While the two touring teams were putting the final touches to their preparations, 22 of England's finest were trialling at Lord's. The unlucky man was Warwickshire veteran Frank Field whose telegram of invitation went astray and with it his only ever chance of an England cap. Walter Brearley was again in the Rest of England team, seemingly being lined up for a Test recall. DW Carr of Kent was invited, just as Clarke had been in the first trial, to provide googly practice for the England batsmen. On a wicket described by EHD Sewell as 'one of the easiest-paced wickets ever seen at Lord's', the captains agreed that whatever the toss the MCC Australian Team would bat first. The game showed the selectors mostly what they already knew but also one or two things they were pleased to learn. The pleasures of batting first were fully explored and, led by centuries from Warner and Woolley, the MCC team reached 509. Brearley and Dean toiled honestly but the real bowling stars were both on the other side, SF Barnes and FR Foster, and both of them were in fine form. The leg-theory of Frank Foster's left-arm round to four short-legs combined with the bounce, spit and length of Syd Barnes proved too much twice over. But even here the selectors could be happy because the only batsmen that ever looked comfortable were Fry, Spooner and Gilbert Jessop who, batting at seven, clumped a pair of half-centuries off the best two bowlers in the world. His first innings had begun with a first-ball six, good length on middle stump, pulled flat into the Mound stand off Hitch. Lord Harris is said to have exclaimed: "That's the best stroke I've ever seen or ever will see". It would be hard to keep such a man out of any team. It was an amateur bonanza and largely cleared any selectorial conundrums, which was just as well because, even though England's first Test, against South Africa at Lord's was still two weeks away, Fry wished to announce his twelve immediately.

During the game an article by Plum Warner appeared in the *Westminster Gazette* in which he hoped that a game could be arranged between the winners of the Triangular Tournament and the best of the beaten two. He also promoted the idea of a World XI versus the Rest game and, in an endearingly schoolboy fashion, picked his team: Fry, Hobbs, Faulkner, Spooner, Armstrong, Macartney, Foster, Sherwell, King, Hordern and Barnes.

Back in the real world, Hobbs, Rhodes, Fry and Spooner would be the first four in the England team. Woolley, Douglas, Foster, Barnes and Smith were all certainties although the latter did not see himself as such. That left two places: Brearley or Hitch on a quick wicket even though neither was in great form, leaving one from Hearne, Jessop and Warner, or two if no fast bowler was required. Simple; this was a powerful batting team from Hobbs at one to Foster at nine with a strong, if not very deep, bowling attack led by two masters. For now these men could return to county cricket and leave Test match play to the visitors as, for the first time in the history of the game, international cricket was to be played on a neutral ground.

The South African press was cautiously optimistic, but was forced to pin its hopes largely on one man, 'GA Faulkner, who, if fit and well, many people here believe quite capable of winning a test by his own efforts'. The *Star* found:

> 'The Africans are, one repeats, in the groping stage. They are slower than their opponents in finding their form. But nothing has occurred to show they will not find it.'

There was certainly no lack of enthusiasm. The latest scores would be available in Johannesburg by calling 4437 or visiting the The Welsh Harp on the corner of Market and Joubert Streets. The *Rand Daily Mail* warned that it would not be giving cricket information over the telephone.

On the first day of the Test the *Daily Graphic* printed a long and diplomatic letter from Syd Gregory which smacks of being the work of many hands. After praising all three triangular teams he proceeded to make some rather optimistic, bombastic and patriotic claims concerning the action about to unfold:

'When that history is written it will certainly be found that the year 1912 was the most important year in the history of the greatest summer game the world has ever seen….it was this year that forged a chain out of healthy sport to bind the Mother Country and the Colonies of South Africa and Australia closer together in a bond of mutual understanding.'

On a more everyday level, if betting men are held to be the most disinterested judges of the prospects then the odds quoted by journalist EW Ballantine were revealing. A £10 bet on Australia would earn a profit of a mere £3. 6s. 6d. – odds of one to three.

The First Test
South Africa vs. Australia
Old Trafford 27 May

Day One

'With the glass backing and the wind freshening' the two captains prepared to toss, having announced teams that were largely as predicted. The Australian team was as it had to be with Mayne, Smith, McLaren and Webster the four players omitted. The South African case was more complex. Ward had leapfrogged from understudy to replace Campbell behind the wicket and Rolland Beaumont was included to bolster the batting and sharpen the fielding, a policy previously advocated by Faulkner. A specialist bat listed at number nine with just 75 runs to his name on the tour so far, this did not read well. With Nourse, Schwarz, Faulkner, White, Pegler and Hartigan in the team it was clearly felt that another bowler was unnecessary.

Gregory called correctly and unhesitatingly elected to bat on a pitch that was slow enough to allow the batsmen to counter any unexpected bounce or turn without undue difficulty. However, this slowness and a damp outfield meant that quick scoring was likely to be difficult and with the forecast somewhat unsettled a draw seemed the most likely result as Jennings and Kelleway walked out to open the Australian innings. First Jennings and then, following his departure, Macartney went all out to push the score along but both fell in the first hour. The score continued moving rapidly in spite of these reverses, with only Pegler causing any great difficulty. Once Bardsley joined Kelleway the rate slowed slightly as both men looked ominously determined to stay for a long time. They succeeded, and the longer they were in the more wayward the bowling became. Plenty of comment was passed on the contrast between the elegant Bardsley and the plebeian Kelleway who one reporter called 'the most ungraceful batsman who ever called Australia home'. When lunch was taken he revived himself with three gooseberries, a piece of bread and half a glass of water and then carried on regardless. Schwarz could find nothing in the pitch and his length collapsed (Bardsley hit him for 19 in one over) while Nourse and Faulkner seemed to lack any semblance of either consistency or penetration. Ward missed chances off both batsmen and by the time they were separated each had reached three figures and the score was 293. The rest of the batting didn't shine but 37 from Gregory followed by a last-wicket partnership of 63 between Matthews and Whitty meant that the innings closed at 448 after only five hours and ten minutes play. The run-rate may appear extraordinary but in fact it was only 3.6 per over – decent, but testimony to a rapid over-rate as much as anything. To add to the South African woes, White had injured his hand in dropping Matthews early in his innings and the resulting stitches would severely restrict him. They were left with 37 minutes to survive and it was somehow inevitable that they would fail; Herby Taylor dismissed for a duck in the first over on his Test debut by Bill Whitty. Nourse and Hartigan remained at the close.

Frank Mitchell and Syd Gregory toss at Old Trafford,
27 May – Gregory called correctly and his batsmen took
due advantage in the first of the summer's nine Tests.

The first-day crowd had been reasonable with 8,609 paying for admission (not including officers from two warships anchored in 'the ship canal') and a total crowd of 12,000, but given the fine weather and the fact it was Whit Monday many more would have attended a roses match and the second-day crowd would probably be considerably smaller. That said, they had been well entertained and there was no doubt who had had the best of the day. Centuries by Bardsley and Kelleway and who knows what Macartney might have done if he had played with just a little more restraint. Archie MacLaren remonstrated with the 'Governor General' over his

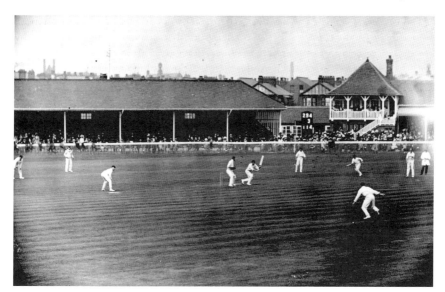

Warren Bardsley pulls at Old Trafford, 27 May – As the Manchester smoke-stacks belch, Bardsley moves onto 115 off Sid Pegler. Syd Gregory is evidently keen on the quick single.

dismissal (bowled when pulling a good length ball from Pegler) to which Macartney replied "I've seen you do the same thing yourself". "Not when the ball is breaking" retorted Archie. Australia were now in an impregnable position but still had to force a win in the remaining two days. The South Africans had, with the honourable exception of Pegler who showed great skill and stamina through 45 overs, bowled pretty appallingly on a pitch that offered little help but was made for stifling batsmen with a good line and length. At least five missed chances proved costly but, by and large, the ground fielding was good and surely on such an easy wicket surviving the follow-on would mean saving the match? For that 298 runs would be needed.

That evening a banquet was held for the touring sides hosted by Lancashire CCC which was clearly a roaring success with luminaries of past and present such as John Tyldesley and Richard Barlow mixing with the visitors. The former, rather mischievously, showed Edgar Mayne an anti-Board letter he had received hoping that the Australian players would return 'stone-broke and without winning a test match'. Barlow would certainly have enjoyed the cricket and recognised, in Kelleway, a man after his own impregnable heart.

Day Two

The weather for the second day was patchily bright and breezy with the pitch easy; the South African batting did not reflect the conditions. Nourse went quickly, followed soon afterwards by Snooke and Hartigan. It was only when White (batting almost without the use of his injured right hand) joined Faulkner that the regular clatter of wickets stopped, though runs remained very hard to come by for both men. White's natural attacking game was curtailed by his injury and Faulkner was acutely aware that the outcome of the game probably rested on his shoulders, so much so that it took him half an hour to get off the mark. The two put on nearly 100, albeit at a crawl, and with Faulkner well-set, despite being dropped by Whitty on 36, it seemed that another 155 to make Australia bat again was quite possible. With news of a fight-back the crowd had risen to 6,000 after lunch and, after White's dismissal, Faulkner, first with Mitchell and then with Schwarz, put on another painstaking 57. Now exactly 98 runs were needed with three wickets to fall. Perhaps picking specialist batsman Beaumont at number nine was not such a bad idea after all. Immediately the runs began to come more quickly as both men cut and drove a tiring attack. Faulkner completed his century and suddenly a mere 33 more was needed when disaster struck. Jimmy Matthews' best chance of a wicket seemed to be to have Beaumont caught in the deep but instead he obligingly swished over a straight ball and was bowled. Now the pressure was on Pegler who promptly departed lbw first ball having probably snicked it onto his pad. Then Test-debutant Tommy Ward walked out; after just one ball he walked straight back again, plumb in front. A hat-trick, and at the other end a distraught Aubrey Faulkner was left high and dry on 122, an innings of skill, patience and resilience in equal measure. Despite the fact that his men were tired (Bill Whitty had bowled 54 overs already) Syd Gregory didn't hesitate to enforce the follow-on. Stumps was only 90 minutes away and even two wickets before the close would leave South Africa in a very difficult position on the final day.

Crowds at Old Trafford, 28 May – The scorers seem bemused by the South African second-innings collapse. The behatted crowd has already witnessed one hat-trick and there is more to come.

To the general bemusement of all and sundry, Gerald Hartigan walked out to open not with Herby Taylor but with Aubrey Faulkner who had been batting virtually the whole day under extreme pressure when still not fully fit. That he was tired was clear.

So why did Frank Mitchell accede to his request to open? Utter folly and rewarded by a second-ball duck. How would that affect morale in the dressing room, bearing in mind he had just carried the first innings? The response from South Africa was to melt away in the face of the accurate but relatively innocuous Charles Kelleway. Only Herby Taylor showed any appetite for the fight but when he was joined by his captain Frank Mitchell at 70-5, a remarkable thing happened. Jimmy Matthews had been given the new ball on the back of his first-innings performance but had not met with any success. However, on being recalled he dismissed Taylor, then removed Reggie Schwarz first ball and, for the second time that afternoon, found himself on a hat-trick. The next man in on the scorecard was Rolland Beaumont but promotion was bestowed on debutant Tommy Ward who had been Matthews' third victim just 90 minutes earlier. Bravery, bravado, a joke maybe? The *Manchester Guardian* related the subsequent events:

> 'It was clear that Matthews intended to go for the third wicket from the fastidious care with which he brought the fielders round the batsman. Ward played his first ball exactly as Schwarz had done, and cocked it up. The ball, however, was hit so gently that for an instant no one thought of a catch. Then one saw a nimble little figure flying up the pitch and making a frantic dive with both hands for the ball. Matthews went tumbling over, and it was not until he had flung the ball wildly in the air that the onlookers could believe that he had made the catch. His colleagues showered their congratulations on him, and the crowd, when they had recovered from their astonishment, gave him a splendid cheer.'

Two hat-tricks in 90 minutes and a 'king-pair' on debut for Ward. Sadly there were not that many witnesses. Spectators had started to leave once Faulkner was out, but those that remained tried to comprehend what they had just seen. Forty years of Test cricket had produced just seven hat-tricks and then two come along in one afternoon at Old Trafford. Jimmy Matthews joined Hugh Trumble as the only dual exponent in international history and what's more it was done without the assistance of a team-mate. His total haul for the match was….six!

Frank Mitchell, having watched this mayhem from the non-striker's end, then recorded his own duck. The innings closed soon after at 95 and the game was over in two days.

Australia 448 (Bardsley 121, Kelleway 114, Pegler 6-105)
South Africa 265 (Faulkner 122*, Whitty 5-55)
South Africa 95 (Kelleway 5-33)
Australia won by an innings and 88 runs (Full card, Cricinfo Test # 121)

Cricket celebrates Jimmy Matthews's great achievment in
the first Test.

The recriminations and the excuses were soon flying. Archie MacLaren in the *Daily
Mail* was in the minority in defending the South African first-day bowling, fielding
and 'keeping on a pitch that was 'one of the easiest imaginable'. His praise of
Faulkner for a 'supreme effort' was easier to understand. Jack Hobbs was of the
opinion (or claimed to be) that the South Africans had not yet adapted and would
'turn the tables before the summer is out'. It was generally agreed that the second day
was one to forget, the *Sportsman* reporting:

> 'Never has been witnessed such an extraordinary debacle in ideal batting conditions.
> The only judgement possible is that the majority of the South Africans do not
> possess the Test match temperament.'

The *Sporting Life* commented on the 'feebleness' of the South African batting and
even saw fit to criticise Faulkner for 'cautioness and hesitancy….he did not play the
innings of a great batsman'. Harsh and completely inaccurate. His was the innings of
a great batsman and he brought the team to within an inch of safety before having to
watch helplessly as Matthews performed his first hat-trick. His error was in choosing
to open the batting second time around and for foolishly agreeing to this request

Mitchell had to take even greater responsibility. The South African press was equally appalled at how events had unfolded. The *Rand Daily Mail* admitted to having had 'gloomy forebodings' even before the match but hoped that they 'could look forward to better displays later on'. Linesman of the *Star* was horribly pessimistic:

> 'It was but reasonable to expect defeat – the most sanguine could scarcely have hoped for more than a draw, it is the crushing nature of that defeat and the fact that there is not particularly much to condone it that calls for rather pessimistic views with regard to the capabilities of the South African team on other than South African wickets.'

Aubrey Faulkner spread his criticism across the whole team. The batting was inconsistent (the inclination of Taylor 'to lose his head' for example), the bowling reliant on one man, the fielding heavy and slow and the absence of Sherwell behind the wickets apparent.

In Australia, the *Age* seemed to be revelling in South African discomfort:

> 'South Africa could not on their record be regarded as stronger than a county team….the Springboks may achieve distinctions that will restore at least some of the prestige they are now so quickly losing.'

In truth, neither the toss nor the injury to White had materially affected the outcome. If Pegler had not been given out first ball the follow-on might have been saved and with it the game but that would have been a travesty. Faulkner and Pegler played well, the other nine did not. Nonetheless, the *Daily Chronicle* was fulsome in its praise of Faulkner as 'the great man of the match', unimpressed by Matthews despite his hat-tricks, surprised at the harmlessness of Emery and certain that the Australian win 'has proved next to nothing'. A remarkably blunt autopsy.

EHD Sewell's summary was both thoughtful and accurate. He rightly assessed the pitch as one that required tight bowling, something that the South Africans had patently failed to provide. On matting wickets the bowlers would seek spin above everything, believing that extravagant movement would mask any deficiencies in length. On a slow English pitch these tactics were apt to be punished as the Australians had just shown. Sewell feared that unless new methods were found South Africa would have 'no Test eleven at all in a very few years time'. Having analysed the failure he then waltzed into an optimistic wonderland by predicting that South Africa would turn the tables on Australia and then go on to beat England. He was writing for a Johannesburg newspaper.

The Australians could feel well pleased with what amounted to a two day cake-walk and fully deserved the message sent by Board secretary Smith to manager Crouch.

> 'Hearty congratulations on a magnificent victory.'

They had scored well, even without the help of Charlie Macartney, albeit on an easy pitch and against a one-toothed attack. The bowling had been disciplined and thorough although it was disappointing that Hazlitt and Emery managed just two wickets between them. All in all a better start could hardly have been wished for and they could travel to Birmingham in good spirits for an encounter with one Frank Foster and his side. The South Africans would try to repair their shattered morale at Northampton where Australia had already given the county side a good hiding. Due to the early finish, both sides took advantage of an unexpected day of leisure; Kelleway, Hazlitt, Minnett, Crouch, Snooke and Schwarz adjourned to the North Manchester Golf Club while the rest of the Australians had a day, and a profitable one at that, at the races.

During the course of the first day of the Test, England had chosen to announce their team for the game at Lord's beginning two weeks later. The timing is hard to fathom, but Fry had expressed his desire to have a settled group of players even if he could have no idea on what kind of pitch they would be playing. Most of the selections were as expected but the presence of Warner, Jessop and Brearley, all amateurs, was interesting. More interesting still was the exclusion of two men who had performed well in Australia. Jack Hearne, who had scored a century in one of the trial games, and Johnny Douglas were the two notable omissions. What precisely had Douglas done wrong? In Australia his bowling had been a perfect support to Barnes and Foster, he had batted adequately and he had captained the team to a 4-1 victory in the absence of Warner. Furthermore, he was fit and healthy and had shown respectable form in both trial games and for his county against Australia. On paper his was one of the first names that should have appeared on the team list but it was absent. Perhaps it is less surprising when seen in light of what Warner had written earlier in the year.

> 'On this form shown in Australia he will be very near the England Eleven this summer if matches are played on hard true wickets. He has improved immensely.'

The patronising voice of a vastly inferior cricketer. It is hard to escape the feeling that Douglas, despite his amateur status, did not fit in, even though there was no doubting his popularity amongst his Ashes-winning team; 'He treated us like men…. there was no "side" to Johnny' recalled his gloveman Smith.

Instead Gilbert Jessop was selected on the back of two half-centuries in the second trial match and Warner's century in the same game saw him included. Walter Brearley was a reasonable pick should the wicket be hard, despite an uninspiring showing in the trial matches, but there was no way of knowing that this would be the case. And the reserve? Ted Humphreys of Kent, a 30-year-old solid county batsman and change bowler. One can only assume that there was more than ability and current form and fitness for Fry, Shuter and Foster to consider. Inevitably the announcement provoked plenty of column inches and there were many adverse comments as to the ability of Fry both as selector and captain. Despite his apparent brilliance in all things, Fry was not always a hero of his time. Perhaps his dalliances with journalism made him fair game. Even South African journalists felt obliged to comment on such an absurd selection procedure, pointing out that Walter Brearley might be playing on a pitch on which Charlie Blythe could win a game single-handedly. That said, Free

Lance of the *Star* thought that it 'would be the cricket sensation of the decade' if England should be beaten.

To their credit, the South Africans emerged, on 30 May at Northampton, apparently revived after the disasters of the Test. It was noticeable that eight of the Test team re-appeared which meant Cox and the unfit Tancred were left out again. Dave Nourse belted a merry century and Rolland Beaumont a carefree 75 in a total of 428. The latter also unfortunately aggravated an old football injury that seemed likely to sideline him for a week. By the end of the second day they had reduced Northants to 99-7 and were on their way to an innings victory given a break in the weather.

The Australians were having an altogether more difficult time. Led by Frank Foster and giving a trial to Percy Jeeves, Warwickshire, the reigning champion county, scored 275 on the first day before watching Jennings and Macartney calmly steer Australia to 80-1 at the close. Once these two were parted on a rain-spoilt second day, there was precious little resistance to Frank Foster who picked up six wickets and sent Australia spinning to 208-8, still 67 in arrears.

Leading Averages To 31 May

Batting	Bowling
Macartney 797 @ 79.7	Pegler 42 @ 14.5
Bardsley 645 @ 71.6	Emery 39 @ 15.3
Nourse 522 @ 43.5	Kelleway 22 @ 15.8
Gregory 394 @ 35.8	Whitty 27 @ 16.7
Jennings 244 @ 34.8	Carter 16 @ 18.2
Snooke 323 @ 29.4	Faulkner 18 @ 18.7
Faulkner 230 @ 28.7	Hazlitt 20 @ 19.0
Taylor 243 @ 27.0	Matthews 14 @ 21.6
Hartigan 257 @ 25.7	Hartigan 13 @ 25.1
Mitchell 247 @ 22.4	Schwarz 16 @ 33.0

Australia: Played 7, won 6, lost 1, drew 0
South Africa: Played 7, won 3, lost 2, drew 2
Monthly rainfall 56.6mm

JUNE

Mo	Tu	We	Th	Fr	Sa	Su
					1	2
3	4	5	6	7	8	9
10	11	12	13	14	15	16
17	18	19	20	21	22	23
24	25	26	27	28	29	30

1912

Jan
Mo	Tu	We	Th	Fr	Sa	Su
1	2	3	4	5	6	7
8	9	10	11	12	13	14
15	16	17	18	19	20	21
22	23	24	25	26	27	28
29	30	31				

Feb
Mo	Tu	We	Th	Fr	Sa	Su
			1	2	3	4
5	6	7	8	9	10	11
12	13	14	15	16	17	18
19	20	21	22	23	24	25
26	27	28	29			

Mar
Mo	Tu	We	Th	Fr	Sa	Su
				1	2	3
4	5	6	7	8	9	10
11	12	13	14	15	16	17
18	19	20	21	22	23	24
25	26	27	28	29	30	31

Apr
Mo	Tu	We	Th	Fr	Sa	Su
1	2	3	4	5	6	7
8	9	10	11	12	13	14
15	16	17	18	19	20	21
22	23	24	25	26	27	28
29	30					

May
Mo	Tu	We	Th	Fr	Sa	Su
		1	2	3	4	5
6	7	8	9	10	11	12
13	14	15	16	17	18	19
20	21	22	23	24	25	26
27	28	29	30	31		

Jun
Mo	Tu	We	Th	Fr	Sa	Su
					1	2
3	4	5	6	7	8	9
10	11	12	13	14	15	16
17	18	19	20	21	22	23
24	25	26	27	28	29	30

Jul
Mo	Tu	We	Th	Fr	Sa	Su
1	2	3	4	5	6	7
8	9	10	11	12	13	14
15	16	17	18	19	20	21
22	23	24	25	26	27	28
29	30	31				

Aug
Mo	Tu	We	Th	Fr	Sa	Su
		1	2	3	4	
5	6	7	8	9	10	11
12	13	14	15	16	17	18
19	20	21	22	23	24	25
26	27	28	29	30	31	

Sep
Mo	Tu	We	Th	Fr	Sa	Su
						1
2	3	4	5	6	7	8
9	10	11	12	13	14	15
16	17	18	19	20	21	22
23	24	25	26	27	28	29
30						

Oct
Mo	Tu	We	Th	Fr	Sa	Su
1	2	3	4	5	6	
7	8	9	10	11	12	13
14	15	16	17	18	19	20
21	22	23	24	25	26	27
28	29	30	31			

Nov
Mo	Tu	We	Th	Fr	Sa	Su
			1	2	3	
4	5	6	7	8	9	10
11	12	13	14	15	16	17
18	19	20	21	22	23	24
25	26	27	28	29	30	

Dec
Mo	Tu	We	Th	Fr	Sa	Su
						1
2	3	4	5	6	7	8
9	10	11	12	13	14	15
16	17	18	19	20	21	22
23	24	25	26	27	28	29
30	31					

Theft Of German Gun Designs

A burglary has been committed at the artillery depot at Spandau. It is believed to have been the work of spies, and it is admitted that 100 drawings of the latest gun models and parts of these models have been stolen. The Vossiche Zeitung states thats it is certain that the thief is aware of the value of the drawings and intends to sell them to a foreign power.

MR HARDY ON LITERATURE......................A PLEA FOR PURE ENGLISH

Mr Henry Newbolt and Mr. W.B. Yeats who were staying with him at Max Gate, Dorchester, for the occasion, presented Mr. Thomas Hardy on Sunday, the 72nd anniversary of his birth, with the gold medal of the Royal Society of Literature.

Tranport Dispute
Employers' reply to mens' demands
Intimidation of workers

DERBY DAY - THEIR MAJESTIES AT EPSOM

THE AERIAL "DERBY"
TODAY'S RACE ROUND LONDON

Titanic Inquiry
The Attempt To Avoid the Iceberg

"THE NEXT WAR" - BRITISH AND GERMAN POLICY

Professor Spenser Wilkinson delivered on Saturday at All Souls College, Oxford, the second of two public lectures on "The Next War". He said that in his first lecture he had attempted a general survey of the conflict between British and German Policy, and had reached the conclusion that while a British command of the sea was regarded as the *sine qua non* of any British Policy whatever, the modern German conception was that a British command of the sea was inconsistent with the well-being and the necessary development of the German Empire. The two conceptions were directly contradictory, and if they were both true, a war between the two nations was inevitable...

RAILWAY ACCIDENT
EXPRESS TRAIN WRECKED NEAR HALIFAX

THE TITANIC INQUIRY
BEARING OF THE DISASTER UPON THE FUTURE

SUFFRAGIST SENTENCED
THE INCIDENT IN THE LOBBY OF THE COMMONS

PRISON TREATMENT OF SUFFRAGISTS
CRITICISM IN THE COMMONS

MEETING OF THE TSAR
AND GERMAN EMPEROR
PROBLEMS OF THE WAR

ESPIONAGE CHARGES IN GERMANY
THE ARREST OF RUSSIAN OFFICERS

When Julius Caesar crossed the Alps
He had no medical service corps such as would accompany a modern army upon a campaign. Medicine, science and surgery were only then in the earlier stages of development.

When you cross the Alps
On your holiday in Switzerland you will not require a large medicine chest with you. A box of Cockle's Pills is quite sufficient, as they are most useful in the case of indisposition.

A special issue of the *Politische Correspondenz* announces in the form of a message from St. Petersburg that the meeting between the Emperor William and the Emperor Nicholas in Finnish waters will take place on or about July 3.

Meetings between the German Emperor and the Tsar are never devoid of importance but to judge by the manner in which their forthcoming rendezvous has been announced, it is desired in Berlin that the world should regard this year's meeting as particularly important.

THE PARIS MOTOR-CAR BANDITS
SELF-CONFESSED ACCOMPLICES

GREAT BRITAIN AND THE TRANS-PERSIAN RAILWAY

THE EMPIRE'S COMMERCE
LONDON CONFERENCE OPENED

Total and utter frustration was the mood of the two touring teams as play came to a close on the first day of June. Australia, despite the rain, had engineered a winning position against Warwickshire and with an hour remaining just 73 runs were needed with seven wickets in hand and the promise of a thrilling finish for the bumper crowd of 10,000. Then it hailed and that was that. Over at Northampton, the South Africans were agents of their own misfortune. Having made the hosts follow on, they dropped catches, bowled 109 overs and finally ran out of time to force a victory. During the course of the game there were rumours that Ernie Vogler would be back. Aubrey Faulkner reported 'we hear that Sir Abe Bailey has paid all his expenses so that he can assist us'. Bailey hadn't and Vogler didn't.

After the drubbing suffered in the first Test and with the prospect of facing England at Lord's in a week's time, South Africa were in dire need of some confidence and serious match practice over the course of the first week of June. The *Times* was of the opinion that googly bowling was seemingly a thing of the past that had been mastered by modern batsmen and South Africa were, and would continue, suffering as a result. Monday morning 3 June found them bright and early in the picturesque surroundings of Fenner's preparing to try out a couple of new ruses. Louis Tancred was finally back from injury which gave Frank Mitchell the chance of a rest and a break from the captaincy and, for the first time, Louis Stricker was tried as wicket-keeper. Of the two specialists in that position, Tom Ward had undergone an appalling Test initiation and Tom Campbell was suffering from the weather, the cold and damp leaving rheumatic pain in his hands. The University team proved to be a soft touch and, despite frequent weather interruptions, the game was won easily. Tancred scored attractive runs and Carter and Faulkner shared 18 wickets in the absence of the resting Sid Pegler. Moving on to The Oval for a sterner test against Surrey, who they had beaten the previous month, they were met by three days of rain which gave the county side time to score 169 and nothing else, bar a nasty hand injury for Carter.

In fact, London had been receiving a real drenching for the whole week. While South Africa had been up at Cambridge, the Australians had spent three days in Lord's pavilion watching the rain fall, just 90 minutes of their game against Middlesex was possible. A trip to the National Sporting Club to see Jim Driscoll floor Jean Poesy in round 12 of 20 might have relieved the boredom but there was no trip to Epsom races and plenty of time to count the cost of such unseasonable weather. Then on Wednesday evening, as most of the country discussed the rare victory of a filly, the grey Tagalie, in that afternoon's Derby, the Springboks came back to town for the game against Surrey while the Kangaroos were travelling up to Cambridge for their tangle with the light blues. The weather the next morning was still miserable but at least Jennings and Bardsley led a jolly thrash of 255 in three hours before Whitty, Emery and Hazlitt skittled the callow students. Only heavy rain prevented Cambridge from avoiding a second colonial thumping in a week.

For Australia it had been a grey and rather depressing week but at least they still had two weeks before their date with England at Lord's, South Africa had just a Sunday off to think about how best to improve on their woeful Test display two weeks earlier. What had the matches at Northampton, Fenner's and The Oval taught them that might help salvage a battered reputation? The arrival of Charlie Llewellyn from Accrington was a huge fillip with his complete familiarity with English wickets and genuine all-round skills. Louis Tancred had scored runs on his return and Claude Carter had not wasted his limited opportunities. If Tom Campbell's hands had recovered sufficiently then he could take his position behind the wicket, the experiment with Stricker had not been a great success. This meant at least three of the team at Old Trafford must go: Ward and the injured White were obvious and the third had to be Beaumont who had not made enough runs batting down the order. With the prospect of a wet pitch both England and South Africa looked closely at the idea of a left-arm finger spinner. England already had two in Rhodes and Woolley but summoned Harry Dean of Lancashire to Lord's anyway before telling him that they would stick with Walter Brearley's pace after all. South Africa decided that now Claude Carter was fully fit again, his spin was preferable to Louis Tancred's batting.

There were plenty of predictions flying around in the lead-up to the match. The South African *Sunday Times* raised a number of points:

> '….we are of the opinion that South Africans will be beaten but not by an innings…. Mitchell is said to be sanguine. Well, it is rather his business, as captain of the team, to be optimistic….Given equal conditions and a bit more nerve and "fizz" in South Africa's play and the Englishmen may find their hands are not unoccupied.'

Frank Mitchell was, in fairness, also optimistic:

> 'We ought to do far better than we did at Manchester where we displayed our worst instead of our best form. I am sanguine we shall be seen to far greater advantage next week. The side will include Llewellyn, and he ought greatly to strengthen the side.'

The *News of the World* claimed

> 'It is an open secret that the Australians expect to beat South Africa easily but lose to England while expecting South Africa always to do better against England than against Australia.'

And then out came the old rabbit from the hat – Ernie Vogler. The *Evening News* reported that Mr Cochrane had agreed to waive his claim on Vogler's services so that he would be available for South Africa when required and there was the feeling that he might just be playing at Lord's. It seemed an unlikely scenario and it didn't happen.

The *Pall Mall Gazette* was already ringing the death-knell of the entire tournament after just one of the nine Tests:

> 'It is to be doubted if the experiment of the Triangular Tests will ever be repeated…. it seems at present that the two Colonial teams will not have nearly so successful a time financially as in previous years when they came alone.'

In an interview on the eve of the second Test, Syd Gregory painted a rather dismal but also combative picture of the state of international cricket:

> 'I do not think either country could put a team into the field to equal those from 1898 and 1902. I remember when Stoddart brought a team….which contained such players as Prince Ranjitsinhji, Tom Hayward, Archie MacLaren, Johnny Briggs and Tom Richardson and yet we won four of the five Test Matches played…You have great cricketers in England but I do not think you have so many varieties of bowling as we have, or as you have had yourselves when Lohmann, Richardson, Peel and Briggs were playing. In Australia cricket has been injured by the critics. We have had too much criticism, too much attention to little disagreements and too little encouragement of cricket.'

The *Sportsman* remained sporting and asked the selectors to send for Charlie Blythe to exploit a pitch made for him. The fact that he had long since retired from international cricket seemed unimportant. The *Times* was more analytical:

> 'Whatever the wicket may turn out to be in this match, the chances, unless luck is most unevenly distributed, are in favour of England. There are some who think that the English side is rather devoid of bowling. If the wicket be absolutely dead and easy, Mr. Brearley, and even Barnes, no doubt lose much of their terrors but the South African bowlers are equally handicapped in such conditions. In any other that are likely to obtain in the next few days, the South African batsmen are not to be envied….'

Most were agreed that prediction was difficult given the unknown nature of the pitch.

The Second Test
England vs. South Africa
Lord's 10 June

Day One

The unremitting precipitation of the previous week had left its inevitable mark on the slow-drying Lord's turf and despite the weather being bright and fine it was clear that a prompt start was out of the question. In fact, a start of any kind on the prepared pitch looked highly unlikely so the captains, umpires and groundsman walked up the ridge to the higher and drier ground and found a suitable alternative. But puddles still lay further down and the crowd would have to wait some hours before seeing any action.

The England 13 before the second Test, 10 June – Back: Walter Brearley, Frank Woolley, Syd Barnes, Wilfred Rhodes, Ted Humphreys; middle: Frank Foster, Gilbert Jessop, Charles Fry, Pelham Warner, Reggie Spooner; front: Tiger Smith, Jack Hobbs, Harry Dean. Only the final XI was granted the honour of wearing an England cap in the only known formal team photograph of the summer.

Frank Mitchell had been busy canvassing opinions as to what his decision should be if he won the toss. A wet wicket might be dead to begin with and then difficult later but if the sun came out it could become unplayable within 20 minutes. Mitchell did win the toss and to the surprise of some, including his own team-mates, he elected to bat. Eventually, at three o'clock, the crowd of 12,000 were rewarded for their patience (although some had lost theirs and 'hurled oaths at the slow drying pitch') and the England team entered the field followed by the understandably apprehensive pair of Taylor and Hartigan.

What would the wicket do? Under similar circumstances at Old Trafford it had been clear within 10 minutes that the Australian batsmen could watch any turn or uneven bounce onto the bat. Within 10 minutes here, Barnes had removed both openers and within 90 he and Foster had removed the entire team. They had done it alone, even greedily sharing the three catches that were offered between themselves. Barnes 5-25, Foster 5-16, South Africa all out for a paltry 58. Had Mitchell made a huge blunder? As a Yorkshireman, he maybe should have known that the wicket would almost certainly get worse before it got better having been under tarpaulins, although in his defence Fry would have also chosen to bat. The pitch was not impossible but the low

England take the field at Lord's, 10 June – From left: Fry, Foster, Jessop, Spooner, Warner, Rhodes, Barnes, Smith, Woolley, Hobbs. Brearley out of shot. The five amateurs join the five professionals from their separate dressing rooms. Frank Foster and Sydney Barnes appear to be discussing, or disputing, the choice of ends – presumably Barnes got his way.

bounce and variable pace made it difficult and the South African batsmen were lacking in both confidence and the technical accomplishments required to combat two bowlers extracting every piece of devil that was on offer. It was an unequal struggle and probably the best tactic would have been to hit and hope; Dave Nourse was the only one to try and the only one to reach double figures apart from 'Mr Extras'. Foster's famous swerve was not present but his unrelenting leg-stump attack (complete with a couple of beamers) and the variable bounce with pace made him, in the opinion of Faulkner, the more difficult of the two. The *Times* correspondent was in raptures over Barnes:

> 'A fine figure of a man, whether in rest or action; a run up to the wicket lithe and "springy", in which not a step is wasted; a beautiful action with the arm right over the head, and then the ball is made to go away or come back; and there is always that inexorable length, the life off the pitch and the subtle change of pace. It is the perfection of the bowler's art, and there is no question that Barnes is the greatest bowler of this generation, and is to be classed with the greatest of all time.'

The pitch was drying very slowly. What would the English batsmen now make of conditions that were largely unchanged? Jack Hobbs was out in the first over but from then on Rhodes and Spooner rode their luck to progress to 122-1 at the close. The bowling mainstays, Pegler and Faulkner, were getting plenty of assistance from the pitch but were not harnessing it in the way Foster and Barnes had done. They were moving the ball too much, hence a plethora of played-and-missed but no outside edges. Reggie Spooner described the first hour:

'Paradoxical as it may seem the ball from Faulkner which frequently proved too good for the batsman, was too good to secure his wicket.'

And because of this effort there were loose balls to be hit for four, something the English pair had not served up. Carter was hardly used at all, his spin turning too slowly to be effective, Llewellyn's bowling was hammered and Schwarz again looked a shadow of his former self. As a googly bowler (not a 'leggie' who mixed them up) Schwarz relied on bounce, nip and extravagant spin rather than subterfuge; these qualities were all lacking. Clearly his injured arm was still troubling him.

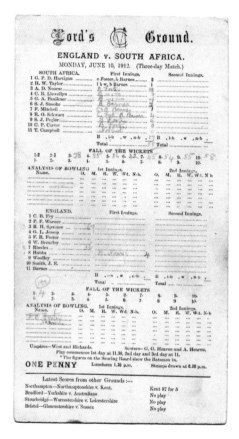

Official scorecard Lord's, 10 June – A disastrous first day for South Africa. The England team is listed in the predictable fashion of the day. The two scorers show the reach of a great cricketing family; Alec and George Hearne were brothers of South African pioneer Frank (the three played together under Lord Harris at Kent) and cousins of 'old Jack' JT and 'young Jack' JW Hearne.

Day Two

England had thoroughly dominated the first day and there was no reason for the crowd of 13,000 on the Tuesday to believe that the course of play would change dramatically. They were right. Reggie Spooner was twice dropped and split a bat before moving on to his first Test century. Then Fry, Warner and Woolley raised the score above 300. The former seemed strangely bemused by the bowling, scratching around for an hour before being dismissed – the irony of his replacement by the ex-captain and Middlesex player Warner was not lost on the Lord's crowd who cheered Plum to the wicket. To say that Fry's captaincy was under some scrutiny would be an understatement. Warner was equally nonplussed by the bowling but, like Fry and unlike the South Africans, he stayed at the wicket despite apparent fatigue after three long recent innings and enjoyed the spectacle of Frank Woolley crashing the ball all over the ground in scoring 73 at a run-a-minute. With England now 250 in the lead and the batsmen under instructions to force the pace, Mitchell tried his best bowler from the Pavilion end for the first time. Pegler's first over was unsuccessful but then the wickets began to fall rapidly, England were all out for 337 and Pegler had taken six wickets for just nine more runs. Why had Mitchell not tried this before? Had senior players such as Faulkner and Schwarz not suggested such a change, and why also was Snooke never tried? True, on his previous visit to Lord's Pegler had excelled at the Nursery end against MCC but that was on a very different pitch and the captain's error was clearly a serious one. One commentator suggested that England would have struggled to make 150 if Pegler had opened from the Pavilion end.

In spite of this English collapse, South Africa found themselves in the impossible position of being 279 behind on the first innings with a day and a half to play. Within 15 minutes of the restart both openers were once again back in the pavilion and Gerald Hartigan had amply demonstrated the difference between the two teams. Playing back to Foster he was surprised by the speed off the pitch and clean bowled; seemingly the previous six weeks had not taught him to get onto the front foot on such a wicket. After these two setbacks, the South Africans finally started to fight back as Llewellyn met fire with fire (after surviving a loud appeal for caught behind when still on nought) knocking Syd Barnes out of the attack. The supporting cast of bowlers was invited on stage. Brearley was tidy but innocuous and Woolley was hit about by Llewellyn in a show of tit for tat for Woolley's manhandling of his bowling that morning. Fry was forced to bring Barnes back on and was rewarded by the crucial dismissal of a listless Faulkner, to leave the score at 114-4 at the close.

ALL WELL WITH ENGLAND AT LORD'S.

The *Daily Graphic* reports from Lord's, 11 June – Top left: Gilbert Jessop nonplussed by Sid Pegler. Top right: Ditto Frank Woolley, left looking anything but elegant after scoring a brilliant 73. Bottom left: South Africa's second innings begins in the worst possible fashion, Gerald Hartigan bowled neck, crop and one-handed by Frank Foster. Bottom right: Reggie Spooner completing his first Test century.

Day Three

The overnight scorecard indicated only one possible result but with the pitch now quite benign and rain clouds forming, time was of the essence. Fortunately for England, Foster and Barnes were much too good for Snooke and Mitchell, and then the Warwickshire trick of a pre-arranged leg-side delivery saw Smith catch Llewellyn off Foster. This was to be Foster's last contribution because soon afterwards he left the field with an injured finger and now Fry needed a partner for Barnes to polish off the resistance. Jack Hobbs was called into the attack in preference to Brearley, Woolley or Rhodes, proceeding to send down 11 tidy overs without ever looking like taking a wicket. At the other end Barnes was picking his way through the stubborn resistance of Schwarz, Pegler and Carter and at 12.40 the game was won amidst a general lack of public enthusiasm. Twenty minutes later the rain came and within an hour the square was a sodden mess.

South Africa 58 (Foster 5-16, Barnes 5-25)
England 337 (Spooner 119, Woolley 73, Pegler 7-65)
South Africa 217 (Llewellyn 75, Barnes 6-85)
England won by an innings and 52 runs (Full card, Cricinfo Test # 122)

Fry had been a lucky man and the questions that had been asked before the match were now repeated with greater urgency. Where do England go if the opening bowlers tire or fail asked the *Times*.

> 'There is a very grave doubt whether there is a sufficient reserve bowling in the English side; indeed, it seems reasonable to suggest that the bowling ought to be strengthened before England meet Australia. Let it be supposed, for instance, that Mr. Macartney and Mr. Jennings were batting and that Barnes should by some unfortunate accident receive an injury....'

This match had provided no answer because the big men had taken all 19 wickets to fall. Charles Fry was not having an easy time as either captain or selector; 'certain incidents in the game....show what view of the matter is taken by the cricket public'. His county form was also under the closest scrutiny; if his place hadn't been guaranteed for the whole summer some sections of the press would already have been calling for his head. Archie MacLaren in the *Daily Mail* was quick to suggest that Douglas, Field and Hearne should immediately be called up in place of Warner, Brearley and Jessop and he went on to throw a wet blanket over the English innings.

> '....despite the overwhelming win, if the performances of Spooner and Woolley were taken away the batting, in my judgement, was appalling.'

On the other hand, England had won easily and the real questions to be asked were in the South African camp. The batting was riven with doubt and disorder. It looked as if the bad old days had returned where England could rout the colonials with just a couple of players being on top of their form. The young batsmen Hartigan and Taylor were helpless and the older hands Faulkner, Snooke and Mitchell were little better. Mitchell was even outed as the weak link in the South African fielding. Hamish Stuart in *Cricket* summed up the first innings:

> 'Other sides have failed before and failed as badly under similar conditions, but few sides have gone down so quickly and so cheaply through the adoption of cautious, indeed timid, methods when the right game was to run risks and go for the bowling.'

The bowling was better but only because Sid Pegler had emerged as one of the finest in England that summer. It was hard to see where they could turn. The return of Tancred and White might help and possibly some batting on hard wickets with the sun on their backs would bring back some much needed confidence but everybody

to make such a trip and was awaiting a reply. Somewhere the old order was having trouble adapting to a new regime of centralised control.

Even though the English team had been announced a week earlier, there was still plenty to say in the days leading up to the first meeting with Australia. *Cricket* had tackled the issue of wicket-keeping and was convinced that Smith was only selected by virtue of his being a better batsman than Strudwick although it did concede that his understanding with Foster was important. Most 'papers were dubious about going into a game on a likely hard wicket without a quick bowler and the *Times* was still of the opinion that the alternatives to Barnes and Foster were not strong enough, doubting England's ability to bowl Australia out twice on anything but a bad wicket despite their recent defeats at the hands of Lancashire and Surrey.

> 'In the past they have always shown that wonderful power of making the big effort for the big occasion. Mr. Jennings has now found himself and of his class there is no doubt. Mr. Macartney….is a batsman who is as dangerous and attractive to watch as almost any one: Mr. Bardsley has never yet mastered Mr. Foster but he is such a fine leg side player that against any bowling he is to be feared.'

Just maybe the two teams were evenly balanced. Now was the time to find out.

The mood in the Australian camp was meanwhile darkened by the death of fellow traveller Ernest Hume just two days before the game was due to begin. He had played for New South Wales, been Billy McElhone's nomination as team-manager, accompanied and assisted the team since the start of the tour and had contracted pneumonia and died shortly after, on 22 June. His exact relationship with the team is impossible to ascertain but it seems to have been cordial enough and there is no reason to think that he was acting as McElhone's 'eyes and ears' in England. The team attended his funeral and he was buried at Kensal Green Cemetery, not far from the final resting place of Billy Murdoch.

The funeral of Ernest Hume – Australian players Macartney, Gregory, Minnett and Kelleway are pictured amongst the mourners.

The Third Test
England vs. Australia
Lord's 24 June

Day One

As expected, Australia made only one change from the first Test. Despite his indiscretions in running between the wickets, Dave Smith was included in the final eleven and Bill Whitty was risked, even though he had told a journalist that he didn't expect to play due to an injured finger on his bowling hand. CB Fry chose to prefer Jack Hearne to Gilbert Jessop, a sensible decision given the extra bowling option that the younger man offered on a potentially dry wicket. Fry won the toss and unhesitatingly chose to bat on a pitch that had benefited in its preparation from the relatively good weather. The Australian team took the field wearing black armbands in memory of Ernest Hume.

Hardly had openers Hobbs and Rhodes taken guard than the heavens opened. The uncovered wicket took a fearful drenching and when play finally re-commenced at 2.15 it was clear that the advantage now lay with the bowlers. The English pair were not downhearted, Rhodes having decided that aggression was the answer and, riding his luck, he rattled up a rapid half-century as he and Hobbs constantly teased the opposition with soft hands and quick singles taken without any apparent calling. After the Yorkshireman's dismissal and a further break for rain, Jack Hobbs strode on to a magnificent century on a tricky pitch that proved much too difficult for both Spooner and Warner. He was finally stopped in his tracks by a leg-break from Sid Emery that Fry described as 'one of the few unplayable balls I have seen, it was a perfect length on the leg stump, came fast off the pitch, and hit the off stump'; vaguely reminiscent of a ball received by Mike Gatting 81 years later. Fry himself struggled to 42 before being run out even though Carkeek appeared not to have gathered the ball cleanly.

More than 200 for just four wickets at the close was a fine result given the change in conditions and one that made defeat a virtual impossibility. The Australian bowling had been good under difficult circumstances, the rain might have made batting tricky but it was equally hard on the fielding side. With the rules not allowing for covering of the bowler's run-ups in addition to a skiddy outfield and damp ball it was a pretty miserable day to be watching Hobbs and Rhodes stealing quick singles. Furthermore they were aggrieved that an early stumping appeal against Hobbs had been turned down. Nonetheless, there was still a feeling that this was an industrious and honest attack but lacking in the two-pronged genius that England had at its disposal. A paying crowd of 14,000 had seen an unforgettable display of batting from Hobbs but the lost three hours made a draw by far the most likely result. In Australia, the *Age* was less than enamoured by the rules which failed to protect the bowler's run-up and also by the three-day restriction:

'Again the complaint comes of the inadequate time allowance for test matches, for it is generally conceded that the comparative merits of teams cannot be well gauged when the normal circumstances of cricket are interrupted.'

SCENES AT LORD'S AT THE CRICKET MATCH OF THE YEAR.

The *Daily Graphic* reports from Lord's, 24 June – Top: The Australians, led by Syd Gregory and Charlie Macartney, take the field on the first morning wearing black armbands in memory of Ernest Hume who had died two days earlier. Bottom left: Wilfred Rhodes cutting one-handed on the front foot in a less than businesslike fashion. Bottom right: The holders of the record Test opening partnership, Rhodes and Hobbs, take the field. They put on 112.

Day Two

If a draw seemed a probability at the end of the first day it had become a virtual certainty by Tuesday evening. In just 20-minutes play England progressed to 241-4 and the rest of the day was spent watching drizzle turn to showers and finally to a torrential downpour before the appearance of late-afternoon sun that was too little too late to save the day. Seven thousand people had paid their shilling for the privilege.

Day Three

At last a clear and bright day with a large and enthusiastic crowd once again descending on St John's Wood in hope of some dramatic conclusion to what should have been a great occasion. Most of the crowd wore an artificial rose to celebrate Alexandra Day in honour of the 50th anniversary of the Queen Mother's arrival in England from Denmark. Her grandson, the Prince of Wales (later King Edward VIII), was due to observe the afternoon's proceedings in company with his tutor, having 'attained his legal majority' three days earlier.

The Prince of Wales at Lord's, 26 June – The future King Edward VIII shows Sir Jeremiah Colman (the mustard magnate) the mid-wicket pull.

Fry decided on a quick slog before attempting the unlikely task of bowling Australia out twice in five hours; just maybe the sun would bring out some demons in the pitch. Fifty minutes batting produced 69 runs before the declaration but if the pitch had had anything to offer then it was squashed out by two applications of the heavy roller and a lack of any real heat from above. By lunch the broad bat of the unflappable Kelleway and the perky genius of Macartney were steering their side to safety. This contrasting pair continued in the same vein well into the afternoon until Macartney fell caught behind, just one short of a well-deserved century. He departed 'swinging his batting glove in an excited manner' before receiving a consolatory pat on the back from Reggie Spooner. There was good reason for him to feel frustrated as many, including Fry, doubted that he had actually touched the ball and there was talk of a missed cash bonus. His innings had many talking of the Victor Trumper who bestrode the wet English wickets of 1902. Archie MacLaren rated it 'as fine an innings as any Australian has played at Lord's'. The introduction of Wilfred Rhodes into the attack saw some late wickets before stumps were drawn with Australia at 282-7, a dead match enlivened by the sparkling skills of Hobbs and Macartney. The crowd had been bemused by Fry's refusal to try the spin of Frank Woolley and 'some of the spectators began to grow facetious' in face of Kelleway's dogged resistance, the value of his contribution was later enhanced when it became known that he had been batting under the effects of 'a nasty strain'.

England 319-7 dec. (Hobbs 107, Rhodes 59)
Australia 282-7 (Macartney 99, Kelleway 61)
Match drawn (Full card, Cricinfo Test # 123)

At the conclusion of the match, 2,000 people assembled in front of the pavilion to witness a presentation of £200 and a silver cup to Syd Gregory to mark his 50th Test appearance. Speeches by Sir George Reid, agent general of the Commonwealth of Australia, and Lord Harris lauded his sportsmanship both on and off the field and his career was praised as 'an honour to his family, to Australia and to all cricketers'.

Although neither side had ever been in any real danger of losing, neither had ever looked like winning and questions would be asked about the bowling of both teams. England had batted on a difficult pitch and scored over 300 but the doubts surrounding the depth of the English bowling had in no way been alleviated. Did this mean that a treacherous wicket would be needed to force a result in three days (as the *Age* had argued) and if this was the case then wouldn't luck play a huge part in deciding the eventual Triangular Champions? And what about a hard wicket? Australia did not have a top-class quick bowler and England's options of Brearley or Hitch seemed lacking in real menace. Even so, Fry was roundly castigated for going into the match without any real pace and also for his eccentric handling of the bowling attack.

The Australians now travelled to Leyton for their second Essex fixture in a good frame of mind. With two months of the tour completed, South Africa had been virtually ousted from the reckoning and nothing at Lord's had indicated that England were as superior to Australia as many had anticipated. Perhaps they relaxed slightly as Minnett, Mayne, Webster and McLaren all returned to the team and they found Essex batsmen in prime form on a good fast surface after Gregory had lost yet another toss. The performance of quick bowler Jack McLaren on a hard Australian-type pitch was poor; Johnny Douglas and Percy Perrin both hit centuries by way of celebrating Charlie Macartney's 26th birthday. After an abysmal showing with the bat the Australians were asked to follow on. Second time around, pride came to the fore with Jennings and Gregory leading them to a safe draw even though the pitch was now quite treacherous. Bill Whitty took advantage of being rested by travelling to Eastbourne to play for 'Shrimp' Leveson Gower's XI where he delivered no fewer than 59 overs. It is hard to imagine either his captain or team-mates being impressed by his appetite for the game. The Essex side also included a man in difficulties through his excessive devotion to cricket; the Reverend FH Gillingham had been strongly criticised by members of his congregation for spending more time playing than attending to the needs of his parishioners in the Birmingham suburb of Bordesley. Gillingham answered in the parish magazine that he saw cricket as 'a means to an end' and that he was taking his six-week annual leave in three-day chunks. He played 14 first-class matches during the season without once ascending to three figures.

It had been a horribly wet June and Felix (Tom Horan) in the *Australasian* was pleased to see the back of it:

> 'It is in the "leafy month of June" that most of the rain has come to our fellows. I hope it won't continue, for, apart from spoiling the cricket the attendances become so moderate that the gate receipts are reduced to such an extent that the probable financial results of the tour assume a decidedly serious aspect. Let us hope that the weather will be much better for cricket during July and August and September. It would be a good thing, not only for the "gates" but for the batting of Minnett who apparently has not cottoned to the condition of wickets at home when the days are wet and gloomy.'

Tourists' Half-Term Report
Australia

Gregory: Clearly not the force of old but still worth his place as a batsman and fielder and an unfussy, if uninspiring, captain.

Jennings: Adapted well to English conditions, continues to play with great style but could do with a really big score.

Macartney: All his latent talent has been revealed during the last two months. Look at his position in both sets of averages.

Bardsley: Not as prolific in June as May but it's a certainty that he will make more big scores. The international opposition fear him as much as Macartney.

Smith: Endured a miserable first month but on returning to full health he quickly found form at The Oval. Promoted to the Test team, he did nothing wrong.

Minnett: Extravagant predictions have proved wide of the mark. He has scored few runs and looked less than convincing on most occasions.

Mayne: Has been a fringe player throughout, letting slip the opportunities that have come his way. Needs a few big scores or injuries to others to be promoted.

Kelleway: A reliable and stubborn all-rounder; line, length and defence are his fortes. It's no coincidence that both his best innings so far have come in the two Tests.

Matthews: After the drama of the double hat-trick, June has been quieter.

Continues to chip in with useful wickets and runs without looking a match winner.

Whitty: Twenty-seven wickets in May but only ten in June tells a tale. Despite this he remains potentially Australia's most dangerous bowler.

Hazlitt: Throughout June the team's best and most reliable bowler although a whispering campaign concerning his action has accompanied his success.

Emery: Prolific in the early matches, only a quarter of his total wickets came in the second month and his accuracy and length are not improving.

McLaren: Unfortunate to find so few fast wickets on which to use his undoubted speed, unless the weather improves will continue to be a bit-part player.

Carkeek: Competent but little more, a limited batsman, he is perhaps fortunate that his understudy is not enjoying a run of form.

Webster: Just five matches and no sign that he is adapting to English pitches or challenging the first choice 'keeper.

South Africa

Mitchell: Some early tour innings were reminiscent of the best form of his younger days playing for Yorkshire. Recent form has been thoroughly ordinary.

Tancred: Hardly played during the first month because of injury and rheumatism. Two fine innings at Cambridge and Nottingham should see him back in the Test team soon.

Taylor: In the nets he continues to impress more than anyone although his form in the middle is patchy. The feeling remains that a major innings is just round the corner.

Hartigan: A highly thought of all-rounder, his early form gave cause for encouragement though latterly a loss of form and debilitating illness have afflicted him.

Snooke: Relatively consistent but his inability to convert good starts to big scores is symptomatic of the whole team's weakness. His bowling is rarely trusted.

Stricker: One or two good innings but each time followed by cheap dismissals culminating in two failures in Scotland. Yet to play a Test on this tour.

Beaumont: Consistently picked as low-order specialist batsman, yet to rise above number six and has not done enough to contradict this vote of no-confidence.

Nourse: Has exceeded expectations in both disciplines but sadly has not produced his best form in either of the Test matches.

White: Arrived three weeks after the others and was then injured in his fourth match. He has shown only glimpses of his skill in limited appearances.

Faulkner: His century in the first Test was magnificent, latterly however his form in major games has declined amid suspicions that he is not fully fit.

Llewellyn: In just one appearance so far top scored against England at Lord's although his bowling looked strangely vulnerable.

Schwarz: Despite taking wickets early on in the tour he did not look the bowler of old. His injured arm has caused further troubles and he feels he cannot do himself or the side justice – he 'may gradually drop out'.

Pegler: The player of the tour so far. Nearly 100 wickets after just two months, has been effective against both the best and worst teams that he has faced.

Carter: With each passing week his control is improving and thoroughly deserved his elevation to the Test team. For some reason was given a mere four overs at Lord's.

Cox: Has had little bowling so far preventing him from coming to terms with the conditions. Omitted from the first four matches and has taken only 12 wickets.

Campbell: Struggling with the climate, he was dropped for the first Test but returned for the second. However, the feeling remains he is only second best now.

Ward: Endured a nightmare Test debut and was dropped for the second. His confidence and form have come flooding back in recent weeks and he looks a fine prospect.

Leading Averages To 30 June

Batting	Bowling
Macartney 1268 @ 57.6	Macartney 21 @ 12.4
Bardsley 828 @ 41.4	Pegler 84 @ 14.5
Nourse 809 @ 38.5	Carter 43 @ 14.6
Jennings 619 @ 34.4	Whitty 37 @ 15.7
Tancred 377 @ 31.4	Faulkner 61 @ 16.8
Gregory 631 @ 30.0	Matthews 35 @ 17.1
Snooke 527 @ 29.3	Hazlitt 47 @ 17.4
Faulkner 469 @ 29.3	Kelleway 35 @ 17.5
Taylor 531 @ 26.5	Emery 52 @ 20.0
Kelleway 343 @ 24.5	McLaren 16 @ 20.0

Australia: Played 16, won 7, lost 3, drew 6
South Africa: Played 16, won 7, lost 3, drew 6
Monthly rainfall 124.4mm – not exceeded until 1980

JULY

Mo	Tu	We	Th	Fr	Sa	Su
1	2	3	4	5	6	7
8	9	10	11	12	13	14
15	16	17	18	19	20	21
22	23	24	25	26	27	28
29	30	31				

1912

Jan
Mo	Tu	We	Th	Fr	Sa	Su
1	2	3	4	5	6	7
8	9	10	11	12	13	14
15	16	17	18	19	20	21
22	23	24	25	26	27	28
29	30	31				

Feb
Mo	Tu	We	Th	Fr	Sa	Su
			1	2	3	4
5	6	7	8	9	10	11
12	13	14	15	16	17	18
19	20	21	22	23	24	25
26	27	28	29			

Mar
Mo	Tu	We	Th	Fr	Sa	Su
				1	2	3
4	5	6	7	8	9	10
11	12	13	14	15	16	17
18	19	20	21	22	23	24
25	26	27	28	29	30	31

Apr
Mo	Tu	We	Th	Fr	Sa	Su
1	2	3	4	5	6	7
8	9	10	11	12	13	14
15	16	17	18	19	20	21
22	23	24	25	26	27	28
29	30					

May
Mo	Tu	We	Th	Fr	Sa	Su
		1	2	3	4	5
6	7	8	9	10	11	12
13	14	15	16	17	18	19
20	21	22	23	24	25	26
27	28	29	30	31		

Jun
Mo	Tu	We	Th	Fr	Sa	Su
					1	2
3	4	5	6	7	8	9
10	11	12	13	14	15	16
17	18	19	20	21	22	23
24	25	26	27	28	29	30

Jul
Mo	Tu	We	Th	Fr	Sa	Su
1	2	3	4	5	6	7
8	9	10	11	12	13	14
15	16	17	18	19	20	21
22	23	24	25	26	27	28
29	30	31				

Aug
Mo	Tu	We	Th	Fr	Sa	Su
			1	2	3	4
5	6	7	8	9	10	11
12	13	14	15	16	17	18
19	20	21	22	23	24	25
26	27	28	29	30	31	

Sep
Mo	Tu	We	Th	Fr	Sa	Su
						1
2	3	4	5	6	7	8
9	10	11	12	13	14	15
16	17	18	19	20	21	22
23	24	25	26	27	28	29
30						

Oct
Mo	Tu	We	Th	Fr	Sa	Su
1	2	3	4	5	6	
7	8	9	10	11	12	13
14	15	16	17	18	19	20
21	22	23	24	25	26	27
28	29	30	31			

Nov
Mo	Tu	We	Th	Fr	Sa	Su
			1	2	3	
4	5	6	7	8	9	10
11	12	13	14	15	16	17
18	19	20	21	22	23	24
25	26	27	28	29	30	

Dec
Mo	Tu	We	Th	Fr	Sa	Su
						1
2	3	4	5	6	7	8
9	10	11	12	13	14	15
16	17	18	19	20	21	22
23	24	25	26	27	28	29
30	31					

THE ESPIONAGE CHARGES IN GERMANY - AN ARREST AT KIEL

A German subject named Ewald has been arrested at Kiel and charged with attempting to obtain the signal book of the navy. He is described in the newspapers as "working for England and France". The German Press is adopting an objectionable tone in dealing with all these so-called espionage cases.

DR. WOODROW WILSON NOMINATED
A BLOW TO MR ROOSEVELT

CLOSE OF THE TITANIC INQUIRY

PROPOSAL FOR INTERNATIONAL CONFERENCE

The court of inquiry into the loss of the Titanic finished its investigation, which has occupied 36 days, yesterday morning. In the course of the inquiry 98 witnesses have been called and over 25,600 questions asked.

UNIVERSITIES OF THE EMPIRE
ADDRESSES BY LORD CURZON AND MR BALFOUR
TRAINING FOR THE PUBLIC SERVICES

THE RUSSO-GERMANY MEETING
THE TWO NAVIES AND THE BALTIC
EXPECTATIONS IN BERLIN

HENLEY REGATTA
THE PRELUDE TO THE ROYAL VISIT
PROSPECTS OF GOOD WEATHER

THE SAILING OF THE FLEET

YESTERDAY'S DISPLAY AT SPITHEAD
MISHAP TO A SUBMARINE

The inspection of the Home Fleets organized by Mr. Winston Churchhill for the members of both houses of Parliament has been a complete success. Too often the brilliancy of these marine pageants is marred by unfavorable weather but to-day the atmospheric conditions if not at all that could be desired, for some rain fell in the afternoon, were at least not inappropriate to such a display.

DOCK STRIKE TO CONTINUE   MEN'S APPEAL TO EMPLOYERS

PLAGUE AT HAVANA
DYNAMITE EXPLOSION IN CHILE
NEW YORK SHIPPING TROUBLE

PIT DISASTER IN YORKSHIRE - GREAT LOSS OF LIFE, MINE INSPECTORS AMONG VICTIMS - THE KING AND QUEEN VISIT THE SCENE

PREVIOUS DISASTERS

1901 Universal 81 dead
1905 Clydach Vale 32
1905 Wattstown 120
1906 Wingate 23
1908 Hamstead 25
1908 Maypole 76
1909 Darran 23
1909 West Stanley 168
1910 Wellington 136
1910 Hulton 344

AUTOMOBILISM ACCIDENTS, NOISE AND RESCUE

Sir.- We have four years in which to set our house in order before the Berlin Olympic Games. Might I suggest that the most pressing change of all is that we should send in a British Empire team instead of merely a British team? The Americans very wisely and properly send Red Indians, negroes and even a Hawaiian amongst their representatives. We, on the contrary, acquiesce in our white fellow subjects from the Colonies contending under separate headings. I am sure that if they were approached with tact they would willingly surrender the occasional local honours they may gain in order to form one united team.

DEATH AT THE PIANO

Mlle Virginie Pavlidi, a talented society favourite, only twenty-two years of age, committed suicide in Bucharest in dramatic circumstances. A reception was being held at her mother's house and she seemed particularly happy. She was a good musician, and, being asked to play, readily consented. After a brilliant rhapsody she went into the next room and returned with a glass, the contents of which she drank off while the guests were still applauding. She then resumed her playing but after a few chords sank dying to the floor.

THE CRISIS IN TURKEY

RIOTING AT THE DOCKS
STRIKERS' PRAYER FOR LORD DEVONPORT'S DEATH
INCITEMENTS TO VIOLENCE

THE SUFFRAGIST OUTRAGES
DISCOVERY OF EXPLOSIVES
FOUR WOMEN CHARGED WITH CONSPIRACY

WHISTLER AT THE TATE GALLERY

CREWE RAILWAY VOTE

The Prime Minister passed through Crewe last night on his way back from Ireland. He was a passenger on the mail train which stops here about 8 o'clock, and Mr Murphy's supporters sent a deputation to greet him. Mr. Asquith was fetched from his dinner to receive the deputation, and, standing on the dining car steps, he exhorted them to do their best to return Mr Murphy. Mrs Asquith shook hands with the deputation, the Master of Elibank smiled on them, and the train resumed its journey.

The season may have been almost half over but the Test series was only just beginning, six of the nine games having been scheduled for July and August. All three sides would meet one another once in each of those two months and all three were fervently hoping that the weather would finally allow competitive cricket in front of large crowds.

The Australians had emerged from June with an enhanced reputation but they still appeared to be strangely vulnerable against county opposition. This was no juggernaut riding roughshod over the smaller teams without any great exertion before pausing to collect itself for the greater challenge of international competition. Yet it was in precisely those international games that the side had shown the mixture of talent, ruthlessness and determination which had long since been the hallmark of Australian tourists. By contrast, the South Africans had taken a fearful beating in both their Tests but were generally faring quite well away from 'big cricket' without ever looking better than a good county side. As for the home nation, the team was largely settled though there was still uncertainty about the best way to support Foster and Barnes. They hadn't needed much help up to now but surely it was too much to ask them to carry the attack four more times. Foster had been showing one or two signs of fatigue, which was hardly surprising given his efforts for Warwickshire the previous season and his workload in Australia that winter. Barnes wasn't without his problems, being prone to knee and ankle trouble in the latter part of competitive games.

On the domestic front the unlikely mid-term leaders of the County Championship were Northamptonshire but they had been lucky to avoid defeat at Bradford towards the end of June and despite still being unbeaten they were being chased hard by Yorkshire. Cricket was attracting its usual space in the newspaper columns – July saw the start of a large debate on the problems confronting the game and the catalyst was undoubtedly the Triangular Tournament. Crowds had been disappointing all summer in all forms of cricket and the inevitable effect was twofold; belt-tightening and solution-seeking. Counties such as Worcestershire were approaching bankruptcy, many were relying on the generosity of one or two wealthy patrons and this would soon be compounded by the lack of money trickling down from Test matches. England and Australia were attracting half of what would normally be expected and games involving South Africa had dismally failed to stimulate the public appetite. The weather was, of course, a major factor but journalists and players alike cast around for others and solutions that might follow. Jack Hobbs, writing in the *Daily Mail*, re-ignited the simmering debate by a call for quicker cricket, less 'off theory' and huge new tarpaulins to protect the whole square keeping the bowler's run-ups dry. The groundsmen at Bramall Lane and Lord's were quick to point out the necessity for a 'framework' on which to place such a protection and wondered if it was really practical. They did, however, ask for greater powers to protect the wicket in the days leading up to a match; freedom rather than restriction. The fact that a professional player such as Jack Hobbs could wield such influence was an interesting illustration of the new age in itself and various suggestions now poured in across all sections of the press. Less time on field changes, punctual starts, two-day county matches, outlawing left-handed batting, better treatment of spectators but never a mention of one-day or limited-over cricket. There was also some talk of reducing Test matches to three per summer, the financial considerations involved meant however that this was one for the purists rather than the pragmatists – this didn't diminish from the general consensus that the nine games of 1912 were way too many. What could hardly be changed was the increasing competition that cricket faced from other leisure activities. As if on cue to remind followers of the game of the glorious recent past was news of the premature death of that great Surrey pace bowler Tom Richardson.

Acutely aware of the financial shortfalls, the Australians left Leyton on the last day of June for a two-week northern tour in preparation for their next Test against South Africa in the middle of the month at Lord's. This fortnight promised to be very much one of two halves. In the first week they would meet two of the strongest counties, both roses, and in the second they would play back-to-back fixtures against a Scottish side that had already had its limitations thoroughly exposed by the South Africans in losing two games by the identical margin of an innings and 97 runs. Meanwhile South Africa had one week and two games in which to prepare for their next Test, against England at Leeds on 8 July.

The prayers for fine weather were, to a degree, answered on the first of the month at Sheffield where Australia spent most of the day compiling 299 against a formidable attack of Hirst, Haigh, Booth and Rhodes. Charlie Kelleway continued in his best stonewalling fashion, managing 39 from 134-1 at lunch and being roundly jeered for his efforts by a crowd that, according to the clichés, should have appreciated his phlegmatic approach. Macartney was again a delight to behold. Alas it was all wasted when the rain washed out the middle day leaving little to play for. At least Roy Minnett, having been dropped for the previous Test, managed to find some form with both bat and ball, unlike poor Alonzo Drake who dropped three catches on the first day and was then run out for a duck on the third! George Hirst: 2-47 from 20 overs followed by a masterly 62, still amongst the best all-rounders in the country even at the age of 40.

In the previous month Australia had followed a fixture at Bradford with one at Old Trafford, this time they made their way straight from Sheffield to Liverpool only to find the opposition again too good. In a low-scoring game on a difficult wicket, Harry Dean took 11-102 and, despite numerous dropped catches, the home side won easily by eight wickets. Reggie Spooner's unbeaten 66 in the last innings, albeit on an improved wicket, made every other player look thoroughly ordinary and once more the brittleness of the Australian team was painfully exposed. During their stay on Merseyside, the Australians were shown around the Cunard liner *Lusitania* which was in dock for a few days before setting off once more for New York. Three years later they would all be painfully reminded of this visit when she was torpedoed by a German submarine.

Australians visit the *Lusitania*, 6 July – Gerry Hazlitt and Edgar Mayne dockside in Liverpool to the left foreground, in boaters.

The following week in Scotland was, as expected, easy by comparison. In the first game Warren Bardsley hit a century and completed his thousand runs for the season (behind Macartney, Hayes, Mead, Spooner and Fry). Roy Minnett was successful with both bat and ball and Bill Whitty's 6-22 in the second innings ensured a comfortable victory. The second game, at Perth, was played in less amiable weather and, with Sid Emery still missing through injury, Edgar Mayne made a bid for one of the few open Test places with two authoritative knocks. Jimmy Matthews' 7-46 ensured that if changes were to be made against South Africa the following week, his name would not be absent.

The Springboks' preparations for their date with England at Leeds had begun falteringly on the first of the month against Middlesex, the game descending slowly but surely into a dank draw. Charlie 'Buck' Llewellyn played, along with Stricker and Ward who were preferred to Beaumont and Campbell in a team that looked likely to be the one to face England the following week. Skipper Frank Mitchell was now to be found batting at number nine, Schwarz and Hartigan were still unavailable. Back home there had been calls for reserves to be sent out, an idea dismissed out of hand by the authorities but at least Louis Tancred had scotched rumours that he was to settle in England directly after the tour was finished. Middlesex had now lost the services of Pelham Warner who was paying for his over exertion during the early part of the season. A diet of 'milk and soda' had not brought him back to full health and following 'an attack of haemorrhage believed to have been brought on by a blow from a ball' he was now confined to bed and unlikely to play again during the summer.

Aubrey Faulkner felt that the persistently bad weather was beginning to wear down his compatriots.

'....we have only played in two matches that have not been interfered with by rain and those of the side who have not visited England before are beginning to wonder how English people manage to exist in such a dreadful climate. Unfortunately the weather is exceptionally cold....and it is no unusual thing to see half the side fielding in sweaters.'

As far as the team was concerned he worried about the form of Schwarz and Snooke but was fulsome in his praise of Ward, 'keeping wicket better than I have ever seen him', and Pegler.

'Our side relies on him to such an extent that should he by any unfortunate chance be placed "hors de combat", I hardly like to imagine what we should do. None of us can compare with him for consistency of length, and he seems to be tireless no matter what the state of the wicket, in fact I feel that I cannot praise him sufficiently.'

Pegler it was who had been the best bowler in the few hours of the Middlesex game before repeating his form at Edgbaston on a nasty wicket where Warwickshire, without the resting Foster, were beaten in a day and a half. The absence of the county captain took away some of the interest but it did prompt Faulkner to write a fairly blunt critique on the bowling methods of his England rival:

'....he plugs away short at the leg stump the whole time, and actually has four short legs between the wicket-keeper, standing back, and the square leg umpire. He bumps them down and relies on the wicket and the short legs doing the rest. It certainly is a type of bowling that has proven wonderfully successful till now, but as bowling pure and simple it can hardly be classed in the same flight as the stuff sent down, say, by Barnes. The latter all the while is trying to bowl one out neck and crop or make one mishit, whereas Foster's main idea seems to be to have a batsman caught out on the leg side in attempting to defend not his wicket, mark you, but his body.'

Douglas Jardine was 11-years-old at the time and presumably an enthusiastic observer. Foster was no Larwood in terms of speed but his success in Australia the previous winter was duly recalled prior to the bodyline series 20 years later.

Victims of their own success, the South Africans had lost the Birmingham Saturday gate, this left a full weekend in Leeds to look at the wicket and the weather before deciding on a team to face England on Monday morning. Of the 17 players originally selected back in February, Hartigan and Schwarz were injured (the former was now recuperating with relatives in Ireland), Cox and Beaumont had hardly played and Faulkner, Tancred, Nourse, Taylor, Llewellyn and Pegler were surely certainties. That meant five places and seven possible players.

England had announced a 12 for the Test at the beginning of the month containing no great surprises. Hamish Stuart in *Cricket* had called for fairly radical changes, wanting to see Hayes for Warner, Douglas for Hearne and Hitch for Foster. He admitted the latter suggestion might be seen as heretical but pointed to an alarming dip in Foster's county form. The Australians remained bemused that Johnny

Douglas was being omitted although it transpired later that, according to Fry, he was in fact selected for this game, a family illness preventing his participation. Fry was considerably less radical than Hamish Stuart in his one change, including fast bowler Bill Hitch in place of Warner. Jessop, twelfth man in the previous Test, was again included and the final selection would be dictated by the state of the wicket on the first morning. The *Times* bemoaned the clash with the varsity match and believed that the tiredness of Foster and the 'better health' of Faulkner might serve to make this Test a closer game than the first had been. The Welsh Harp in Johannesburg had not yet lost its appetite for the fight and was still offering a 'Special Cable Service direct from the field of battle'.

This was another important day for Charles Fry. He had been enjoying great success at Hampshire, and was clear top in the batting averages, but was under sustained pressure in his national role. He had made few runs, his field placing and bowling changes had been widely criticised, team selections were often vilified and there was a general air of unpopularity surrounding him at many grounds. However, these were all things that would surely be swept away by a century.

The Fouth Test
England vs. South Africa
Headingley 8 July

Day One

Despite heavy showers falling over much of Yorkshire, the Headingley ground had remained mostly dry. However, both captains were aware that even in good weather the pitch was apt to give bowlers plenty of assistance; only one half-century had been scored on the ground in the first two months of the season. England made just one change, Gilbert Jessop returning for the bed-ridden Warner, which meant that Bill Hitch was twelfth man and England would be without a fast bowler. South Africa had been rather busier: Frank Mitchell, runless and slow in the field, stood down, to be replaced as captain by Louis Tancred, Ward returned for Campbell behind the wicket with White and Stricker replacing the injured Hartigan and Schwarz.

Misgivings about the pitch following a brief shower did not prevent Fry electing to bat, it was not about to get any easier over the course of the following three days. The game started promptly and off just the second ball Rhodes was fortunate not to be caught and Hobbs was equally lucky not to be run out in the ensuing confusion. Neither man profited greatly from his luck and with the general feeling that England were taking things too easily they subsided to 68-4 within 90 minutes, Pegler and Nourse sharing the wickets. Another failure was marked down to the English captain and he appeared to now be under some pressure: 'Fry's return to the pavilion was a melancholy one....his face was a picture of misery'. For the first time in the series the South Africans now had the upper-hand as Frank Woolley ambled to the wicket to join Jack Hearne. With only four to his name, Hearne snicked the ball to wicket-keeper Ward but the difficult chance was spurned (Archie MacLaren alone thought it impossible) and within two hours the balance of the game had changed. Woolley and Hearne added 111 at better than a run-a-minute and, even though the rest of the side managed little, the final score of 242 was respectable given the poor start and against much improved South African bowling. Fry may have failed again with the bat but he proved his aptitude for detail when invading the field shortly after 1.30, armed with a rule book, to explain to the umpires that lunch was due immediately.

Charles Fry takes to the field, 8 July – Fry, in the raincoat, exhorts the umpires to do their duty.

For the first time Aubrey Faulkner had shown his form of 1907 with the ball and with Dave Nourse and Sid Pegler continuing in their best vein there was precious little room for anyone else, Carter's four overs being the only alternative employed. One or two critics did question Tancred's tactics and felt that Pegler in particular would have been more effective with an occasional rest.

So, shortly before tea, Tancred and Taylor found themselves walking out to the middle aware that, on balance, the first portion of the day had been won. Now was the opportunity to add the remainder and put South Africa in a winning position by the end of play. Once again the South African batsmen failed to rise to the occasion even though Frank Foster appeared listless and Harry Dean was struggling with his length. The great Sydney Barnes was another matter entirely; much too good for the visitors, he took five wickets and by six o'clock they had spiralled to 141-8. Even this paltry score was only reached by some inspired and desperate late hitting by Snooke and Pegler, also described as 'blind defence', when a follow-on still seemed possible. The rest of the side had looked thoroughly miserable with the exception of Herby Taylor who battled bravely for a meagre 31. As if the state of play was not depressing enough, the fact that only 4,000 had paid for admission was further cause for gloom.

Day Two

The last two South African wickets fell quickly on the second morning, perhaps unsurprisingly as Carter didn't bother with a net and last man Ward wasn't even ready to bat during the first over and would have been 'timed-out' had a wicket fallen. This was the same Tom Ward who had recorded a king-pair on his Test debut six weeks earlier.

Once again the English batsmen found Nourse, Pegler and Faulkner a difficult proposition despite the safety net of a first-innings lead of 95. Rhodes fell early (Pegler's 100th of the season, he was the first to the mark) and Fry, Woolley and Jessop all failed. But, as in the first innings, two batsmen stepped forward and carried the day, this time Hobbs and Spooner were the saviours. The latter was particularly watchful and gradually nursed his team to an impregnable lead before falling for 82. He was quick to generously praise the opposition as the most difficult attack he had faced all summer. That said, there were clear signs of tiredness which was hardly surprising given that three men had sent down 150 overs in the two innings. Carter bowled just 54 balls and Llewellyn (who was in fine form for Accrington) was not trusted once. The final total of 238 meant a lead of 333.

Nobody on the ground believed that South Africa had an earthly of reaching such a target but most hoped that a spirited showing under perfect conditions would at least erase the memory of a fairly pitiful first-innings' performance. These hopes were soon dashed on the rock-like countenance of SF Barnes. Even though Foster again appeared below par and Dean continued to bowl too short, only Tancred showed both the skill and aptitude for the fight and by the end of the day South Africa were sunk at 85-7. White and Stricker were picked out as having thrown their wickets away but the whole thing was a sorry sight. EHD Sewell's account of the play was illuminating if not descriptive:

> 'It was perhaps the worst innings in the history of South African Test cricket....so I will leave it at that.'

The weather had been lovely and even though the game was proving to be one-sided a better crowd turned out for the second day – if only the cricket had been more competitive.

Day Three

In an almost deserted Headingley the final rites were duly administered once Carter and Pegler had finished thrashing a carefree 60. Again it was all too little and much too late. The search for Wilfred Rhodes' 100th Test wicket continued with a few late overs, but to no avail.

South Africans observe the last rights, 10 July – On the
third morning of the Headingley Test, a group of players
watch the final exchanges. Mitchell, Beaumont (leaning
forward), Faulkner, White, Ward (standing), Schwarz.

England 242 (Woolley 57, Nourse 4-52)
South Africa 147 (Barnes 6-52)
England 238 (Spooner 82, Faulkner 4-50)
South Africa 159 (Barnes 4-63)
England won by 174 runs (Full card, Cricinfo Test # 124)

It had been an improved performance from the visitors in some ways but the overall
result had been little better and for the *Times* it was clear where the fault lay.

> 'The South African batting was undeniably weak. It is to be regretted that they
> do not make more runs, for they play the most sporting cricket, but it must be
> disheartening for their bowlers after having done good work to get so little help
> towards winning matches from the batsmen.'

Aubrey Faulkner's verdict was much the same with one interesting exception. Every
newspaper had commented on the difficulty of the pitch but Faulkner would have
none of it.

'It could hardly have been better, and was consequently in no way responsible for our failure. Our batting was once again hopeless and none of us played with the slightest degree of confidence. On the other hand our bowling was of such a high order that it should certainly have won the game for us.'

Faulkner went on to praise the bowling of Barnes, emphasise the importance of the missed chance on the first day, admire the 'grit and determination' of Taylor and praise the vastly improved South African fielding. There were words of warning from EW Ballantine to the South African captain:

'Pegler....is used too freely, and if this sort of thing goes on I do not see how he is to last through the season.'

Bearing in mind what Faulkner had said of Pegler's vital importance to the team, it is strange that his energy was deployed in an often cavalier fashion.

There was little solace for either side in terms of crowds and receipts; less than 10,000 paid and the receipts were barely £600. Set against the figures for the 1907 meeting between the same two countries at the same ground, this made depressing counting.

After the first two humiliations of the summer the South Africans had, to their credit, eagerly and successfully bounced back against lesser opposition but this time no such immediate tonic was at hand. They would have four days without cricket (except for Llewellyn who returned to his Accrington contract) before turning out at Lord's the following Monday against Australia. If they had had selection problems before the Leeds game then these were now multiplied many times over. Stricker, White and Snooke had scored a mere 64 between them, Llewellyn had neither scored runs nor bowled and Carter had been entrusted with a mere nine overs. The possible replacements, Schwarz, Mitchell and Beaumont, were hardly likely to fill the Australians with dread. At least there were compensations off the field as they again enjoyed the hospitality of Sir Richard Solomon, the South African high commissioner in London, at the Empire Club and basked in the unlikely one-two in the Stockholm Olympic marathon of their countrymen Kenneth McArthur and Christian Gitsham.

Most of the England team were to be found on the Leeds-London express straight after the game heading for the Gentlemen vs. Players fixture at The Oval. Spooner continued his good run, Fry and Hearne hit centuries and Foster again looked short of his best. On the final day the game was interrupted for 20 minutes as a mark of respect for Tom Richardson's funeral which was taking place in Richmond. Wilfred Rhodes had been given permission by Yorkshire to play at The Oval despite an important Championship game at Tunbridge Wells. Kent were less generous with the services of Frank Woolley, which caused some friction between the two leading counties of the day, nevertheless Yorkshire still won by an innings.

The Australians returned from Scotland on the Sunday before the Lord's Test with a comparatively settled side, Smith and Emery being the only men now vulnerable who had played in the game against England, the latter having missed the last four matches with a strain. The *Times* weighed up the prospects on the morning of the match:

> 'The Australians won the first match, at Manchester, by a single innings, and they will, on all form, be strong favourites. The South African bowling, however, is not all to be despised: Mr Faulkner has been bowling well lately, and Mr. Nourse very steadily, while Mr. Pegler is, of course, first rate. The weather seems settled and it is to be hoped that the match will be played on a really fast wicket, which is the truest test.'

The *Star* thought 'the South African's superiority in bowling will hardly compensate for their weakness in batting' while the *Daily Mail* pointed to the Australians being 'at their very best in these big encounters' and the lack of 'backbone' in their opponent's batting.

The Fifth Test
Australia vs. South Africa
Lord's 15th July

Day One

In many ways this Test match was intended to be the highpoint of the Triangular Tournament. Two colonial teams meeting at the headquarters of English cricket, an Imperial Cricket Conference and the King scheduled to watch play on the afternoon of the second day. The question now was, would the cricket and the crowd match up to the perceived significance of the three days?

The answer to one of these questions soon became apparent. A disappointing attendance was scattered about the terraces as the players prepared to take the field despite the weather being, for once, gloriously hot. Both sides had made two changes from their previous Tests: South Africa brought back Mitchell and Schwarz for Snooke and Carter even though neither man had done anything useful for a month. Possibly Mitchell felt that he should assume the captaincy again for such an auspicious occasion, his form certainly didn't warrant it. As for Schwarz, either he had made a dramatic recovery or this was a last desperate throw of the dice. The Australians decided that the newly in-form Minnett should return for Emery who, though now recovered, was lacking match practice. Edgar Mayne's recent runs also brought him the first cap of his career at the expense of Dave Smith.

Mitchell won the toss and unhesitatingly chose to bat under a glorious blue sky but a re-jigged top order completely failed to do itself justice. The pitch was quick but not totally reliable, the odd ball coming off at an alarming height – a Jezebel pitch, 'both fast and unaccountable' as Raymond Robertson-Glasgow would have termed it. Cotter or Kotze would have been a hairy proposition and the fact that Jack McLaren had been excluded from the Australian team, under perfect conditions for quick bowling, was an indication of how far his stock had sunk since May. Faulkner opened and White batted at three but it was all to no avail as they sank to 74-5 before lunch, Roy Minnett showing that even a part-time pace bowler could be a handful. The only positive of this new batting order was that Herby Taylor would now come in at six and it was from this position that he began to engineer a recovery that lasted well into the afternoon. Supported firstly by Stricker and then by the free-hitting Pegler, he moved the score above 200 and began to close in on a century. When the ninth wicket fell and Tommy Ward entered the field, still searching for his first Test run in his third match, Taylor must have felt time was tight. Ward did finally get off the mark but Taylor was out soon after, caught in the deep for 93. Remembering the innings 13 years later, Taylor wrote: 'Whitty, Hazlitt, Minnett and Kelleway were right on the top of their form, and I can assure my readers I had to fight extremely hard for every run'. The total was decent given the poor start and Taylor had finally shown himself to be the high-class batsman that many had suspected. Just as the South African fortunes had revived during the afternoon, so the crowd steadily increased to a respectable but still disappointing 7,000. The Australians had bowled efficiently and well, Whitty was the chief wicket-taker but it could just as easily have been Matthews, Minnett or Hazlitt (murmurs from the Long Room still accompanied his action). The fielding was, however, far from blameless. At least half-a-dozen catches went to ground and Bill Whitty again advertised his ability to drop absolute sitters as well as suffering from the misdemeanours of others. The Australians now had a difficult two hours to face and within 20 minutes Dave Nourse had turned the game on its head by dismissing Jennings and Macartney for a song. South Africa had had England on the ropes for a brief period at Leeds seven days earlier but were unable to drive home their advantage, it was a depressingly similar story here. Charlie Kelleway was the perfect man for the situation and, together with a watchful Bardsley, he took their team nearer and nearer the refuge of stumps. The stonewaller attracted the usual criticism and 'ironic applause' but surely there was grudging admiration as well?

> 'Mr Kelleway is a batsman whom it is rather painful to watch. He has practically no strokes: the ball is just stopped and stopped and stopped, no matter what the bowling may be.'

Apparently no admiration at all, grudging or otherwise, but in fact Kelleway had scored at almost the same speed as Bardsley. Shortly before the close he gave a difficult chance at the wicket, just as Hearne had done at Leeds, and Ward, once again, put it down. All was not doom and gloom however, with the general feeling that the pitch would crumble on the last day and that Australia would need at least 300 in the first innings to avoid defeat. That evening both teams were entertained at a fine MCC dinner with the Duke of Devonshire in the chair and a glittering array of cricketers and politicians from all parts of the world present. The loudest cheers were reserved for Lord Harris when he stated that he did not doubt for one minute that if the necessity ever arose, the colonies would be found sharing the responsibilities of Empire. Somehow one imagines that Charlie Kelleway remained extremely frugal in his consumption for he had a job of work to do in the morning.

Day Two

As over after over was sent down on the warm and sunny second morning, the South Africans had plenty of time to reflect on, and rue, the missed opportunity of the previous evening. The left- and right-hand combination of Bardsley and Kelleway was driving the fielding side to distraction as the morning wore on. Mitchell seemed to lose sight of the fact that Kelleway preferred to score in singles which were easily accumulated with half the team ringing the boundary. The situation was compounded by the fact that three men, Mitchell himself, Tancred and Stricker, were horribly slow and cumbersome. Bardsley again showed his on-side strength and seven bowlers were tried before the partnership was finally broken. Having added 242 runs, and broken the record partnership for the third-wicket set at the great Melbourne Test by Brown and Ward 17 years earlier, they had brought their side to within just seven of the South African score. Warren Bardsley carried on well into the afternoon and, assisted by Mayne and Minnett, saw his team to a safe and match-winning lead by the time the last wicket fell. Once again Sid Pegler polished off the tail in rapid fashion, 4-16 in 30 minutes. For South Africa the task was simple to assess – bat for an entire day and force a draw.

The pitch was now quite amiable but recent form spoke loudly against any heroics. Stricker was promoted to join Tancred and the pair immediately began to throw their bats at everything in a display born of desperation rather than gay abandon. The partnership was brief and then play was interrupted by the arrival of the King accompanied by the prime minister, Herbert Asquith. He was escorted to the committee room by the Duke of Devonshire and the rest of the reception committee, the first time a reigning monarch had attended a Test match. Shortly after the re-start the second wicket fell and tea was taken at 54-2. After rapid refreshments both teams were presented to King George V and he found time for a chat with captains Mitchell and Gregory. Following the break, Charlie Llewellyn quickly hit a half-century but the wickets were falling regularly enough and by the time the two men capable of a sustained rearguard action were at the wicket there were only five to fall. Faulkner batting at six after delivering 28 gruelling overs was understandable but what on earth was Herby Taylor doing at number seven, especially considering his first innings performance? By the end of the day the game was all but up; 146-8, 19 in front and Taylor three not out. The King departed shortly before the close of play having presumably avoided the 'stale penny buns' that attracted such ire from a correspondent of the *Sportsman*.

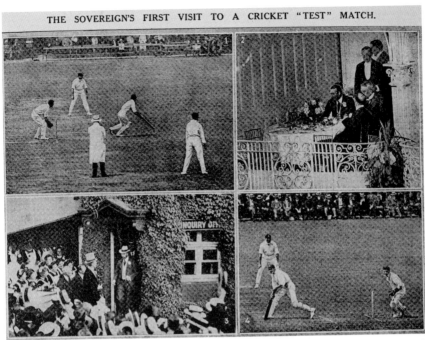

THE SOVEREIGN'S FIRST VISIT TO A CRICKET "TEST" MATCH.

The *Daily Graphic* reports from Lord's, 16 July – Top left: Warren Bardsley pushes the ball to mid-off to complete his century. Top right: The King enjoys tea with the Duke of Devonshire in the 'president's private pavilion'. Bottom left: King George V leaves Lord's to a great reception. Bottom right: Charles Kelleway moves onto 100.

Day Three

There must have been a feeling of *deja vu* for Sid Pegler as he came out to bat on the third morning. Precisely one week earlier, at Leeds against England, he had done exactly the same thing with a Test match all but lost and the ground virtually empty. He responded in the same way with a brief slog and South Africa, with Taylor stranded on 10, left Australia 47 to win. Louis Stricker was given another go behind the stumps and Jennings and Mayne spent a mere 40 minutes completing the formalities.

South Africa 263 (Taylor 93, Whitty 4-68)
Australia 390 (Bardsley 164, Kelleway 102, Pegler 4-79)
South Africa 173 (Llewellyn 59, Matthews 4-29)
Australia 48-0
Australia won by 10 wickets (Full card, Cricinfo Test # 125)

The Australians had won comfortably and at least one of their players was unimpressed with the opposition, telling a journalist "Those fellows want a good shaking up". They had matched England pound-for-pound and together they had been able to kick sand in South African faces with barely a murmur of protest. In fact the *Sporting Life* took it further, reporting:

> 'It is significant that the Australians, though owing much to Kelleway and Bardsley, out-played the South Africans more obviously than did England.'

Taylor had batted well and given the rest a lesson in footwork and Pegler was as good as ever but the other nine were little short of a shambles. Surely this wasn't just a case of poor form? It seemed that a simple lack of ability had now been exposed. They would now have to complete the month in the knowledge that they were, and would stay, firmly at the base of the triangle. In some respects the Australians had merely done what they were expected to do but it must have given the English plenty to ponder. They had won easily without any contribution from Macartney, who one newspaper accused of being 'intoxicated with success', in addition they had hardly been able to call on either Whitty or Minnett in the second innings and had still found enough bowling reserves to skittle their opponents. The *Times* felt that Australia deserved to suffer more for their fielding aberrations on the first day and that the lack of form from the talismanic Faulkner (possibly he was still not fit) was crucial to the travails being suffered by his team. Faulkner himself made no reference to his own form or fitness but there was a tone of despair in his weekly dispatch to South Africa. The batting was 'lamentably weak' and he could hardly envisage a win being achieved in the Tests. His only positive words concerned the batting of Herby Taylor who had finally lived up to his promise. This, however, was scant compensation for the continued poor form of White and the clear evidence that Mitchell and Schwarz no longer had any place in international cricket. The *London Budget* was brutal in its assessment that the South Africans 'looked as though they had been doped with paralytic serum'. *Cricket* was inclined to concentrate on two factors: the lack of big-match temperament and the inability of the older players to inspire the younger ones. Frank Mitchell was generous in defeat:

> 'You're too good for us: and that is the proper view to take even for many who, like myself, still believe the South Africans capable of better things with the bat.'

Shortly before the King's visit on the second afternoon of the match an Imperial Cricket Conference had been convened with two representatives from each of the triangular countries and chaired by Stanley Jackson. The first aim was to establish a scheme of Test cricket for the next five years and there was plenty to say on the subject. The South Africans were insistent that they had no desire to send a team to either Australia or England until 1915 at the earliest. More than likely the beating their team was taking on English turf had prompted the South African Cricket Association into being somewhat cagey concerning the near future. The main demand from the Australian Board was encapsulated in a cable read by George Crouch:

> 'Opinion Board against continuation Triangular Contest. Try to arrange visit English Team 1914. Australia visit England 1915. Can visit Africa any time convenient them.'

This message did not, despite its ambiguous wording, refer to the tour in progress but to the future of the entire concept and this strident 'opinion' was certainly based on the news of a fearful financial shortfall. The Board was aware that, even with two months of the season still to play, their team was not going to earn anything approaching that achieved by their predecessors.

The various requests were accommodated and a schedule was agreed on: 1913-14 England in South Africa, 1914-15 Australia in South Africa, 1915-16 England in Australia, 1916 Australia in England and 1917 South Africa in England. The idea of regular Triangular contests was apparently dead. Finances, guarantees and percentages were discussed, as was the question of time limits. MCC was to approach the Australian Board to fix the duration of Tests in Australia at five and a half days, there was no move to extend the three-day limit in England. Finally there was a brief attempt to agree at a method of deciding the winner of the Triangular Tournament currently in full swing:

> 'It having been pointed out that at the end of the Triangular contest no result might be reached. It was decided that no system of points would be practicable now, but that the decision as to the necessity of a fourth match could be deferred until the result of the third match is known....'

Even this left the situation unclear. What if all three England against Australia games were drawn but Australia beat South Africa three times and England beat them only twice? Would a fourth match between England and Australia still be necessary?

As if the King, the Test and the ICC meeting at Lord's were not enough there was plenty of other cricket activity to fill the newspapers. Lord Harris' address to the Cricketers' Fund was mostly well received but at least one critic felt that he had shirked his duty in not mentioning illegal bowling. In fact, the 'old county player' in the *Daily Mail* was more specific and mentioned the Test match just finished in which case the player in question was Gerry Hazlitt. His action had been under observation from the pavilion all season and the consensus was that he 'chucked' the occasional ball although he was never called, which may well have been a thoroughly diplomatic solution. Perhaps of slightly lesser significance was a report of burglary most foul at the Edgbaston pavilion. The champions Warwickshire were in the process of inflicting a first defeat of the season on current leaders Northants where the game was marred by the intrusion of crime. Players

> 'have had articles belonging to them stolen....several bottles of whiskey and a number of cigars were taken while Mr. Foster lost a large quantity of cigarettes.'

Presumably it was the amateur dressing room that was breached and a revealing insight it gives into the world of county cricket for the unpaid – Raffles it was not.

South Africa once again surprised their critics by bouncing back from Test ignominy against county opposition, this time at Maidstone. Under a sunny sky and on a fast wicket, their 360 in good time was their best batting of the tour with Taylor, Stricker,

Snooke and Beaumont proving themselves capable of scoring runs even against Colin Blythe. The crowd blossomed from an early-morning pittance to a healthy 6,000 by tea; what it would have been if the normal charge of 6d had been levied is anyone's guess. Predictably enough, the weather didn't hold and in the restricted time left Kent's batsmen easily forced a draw with Frank Woolley giving the tourists a further sample of his deft skills. Socialising was this time as guests of Sir Marcus Samuel, the former mayor of London and owner of the Mote Park ground in Maidstone. The entire game baffled Aubrey Faulkner. How could the batting, that had been so lamentable against Australia, be so sparkling against a Kent attack that 'is hardly inferior'? His answer:

> 'As far as I can reason matters out the trouble seems to be that we have somewhat lost the temperament we had for big cricket. Our batting….has been totally spiritless, most of us simply pottering about….before receiving our "conge."'

Of equal concern was the form, or rather fitness, of Sid Pegler. Faulkner reported him, and to a lesser extent Dave Nourse, to be 'dead tired out', lacking 'sting' despite his accuracy and called for 'careful nursing' over the coming weeks.

The Australians were meanwhile completing the third week of the month at Leicester where they welcomed back Sid Emery and gave Charlie Macartney a well-earned rest. Gerry Hazlitt remained in London for a minor operation to relieve an eye condition that had been troubling him for weeks. They were always in command but were eventually denied victory by a total washout on the final day. Their social activities were slightly less refined than those enjoyed by their rivals in Kent. One evening was spent at a music hall and then a visit was organised for the players to see the final destination of some good Australian wool – the Wolsey underwear factory.

Possibly in response to the financial disaster of the Lord's Test and the ICC meeting, articles now started to appear concerning money. The *Age* began by comparing the Australian earnings in 1909 with those they were likely to receive in 1912. Monty Noble's side had garnered an average of £1,090 from each of their five Tests in 1909 but this latest vintage had got just £334 from their first, against South Africa at Old Trafford, and there seemed every likelihood that the pickings from their next two would be similarly slender. It appeared even at this stage that Hazlitt, Macartney and two others had chosen wisely when opting for a £400 flat fee rather than a share of the profits. The same newspaper suggested that, given these figures, the approval of a tour of America on the way home with a guarantee of no less than £1,000 was a sensible idea even though it would be a private venture and not Board sponsored. The proposal of a late-season tour of Scotland was considerably less appealing and had been scrapped; the mere fact that it came under serious consideration indicates the dire straights that had been reached. Obviously the weather was a significant factor but there were also deeper underlying causes to be considered.

The *Pall Mall Gazette* ran a pair of 'special' articles in the middle of the month entitled 'Has the Triangular contest failed?' and their answer was an unequivocal 'yes'. With crowds for both touring sides small it was clear that:

'It has failed to grip the attention of the public. And why? It is not altogether because there are only two sides in the running, for this strange apathy existed before the first match was finished and South Africa were found wanting. It is principally because there is nothing definite in the tournament. No one is yet certain how the scoring for the tournament is to be conducted. What shall happen in a drawn match? Shall the first innings count?'

The views of CB Fry were then summarised the next day:

'He considers that it is not at all a question of deciding which is the "best" team; the idea was merely to play an interesting series of games in England....between three really strong, and approximately even teams.'

There was little that even Fry could do about the weather or the South African team but his hopes for an 'interesting series' were firmly rooted in the past. For better or for worse the British public was now in love with competition, tables, leagues and averages. This may not have suited the traditionalists but it was a fact and the inability of the ICC to decide on any scoring rules was one of many factors undermining the entire enterprise. There were, of course, plenty of others.

It wasn't just international cricket that was suffering, behind the small crowds was the very real danger of the collapse of cricket. In an article entitled 'Cricket "Stars" And Their Methods', the *Age* pointed to the general decline in crowds in face of competition from other sports and also its inability to compete with the speed and excitement of 'the kaleidoscopic changes of a football field'. The conclusion was that 'The outlook is anything but pleasing'. *Pearson's Weekly* decided the time was right to re-launch the old debate about Australian shamateurs by pointing out that the 1909 tourists earned £700 each which compared very favourably with the £300 that an MCC professional tourist could expect or the £150 for a county player. There might just have been a touch of *Schadenfreude* in the suggestion that the current tourists would certainly do less well. Curiously enough the *Australasian* had run a piece a week earlier which identified Bill Whitty and Jimmy Matthews as professionals in the sense that their only income was from cricket, a definition that had long taxed students of different interpretations of the word 'amateur'. At least it seemed that the guns in the 'Board dispute' were finally running out of ammunition. Frank Laver's pamphlet had been dismissed by the *Bulletin* and Billy McElhone believed, rather prematurely, that 'all the bickerings were over' and that 'there would be no more heart-burnings. What had been done had to be done'. There would, however, be some stings still in the tail.

With the Stockholm Olympics now over and the post mortems beginning (Britain only third in the medal table) thoughts were now, hopefully, turning to the England versus Australia game on the last three days of the month. First there was another week of cricket to play. The South Africans spent their 'rest' day travelling from Maidstone to Holyhead and then on to Ireland for two games as guests of Sir Stanley Cochrane at the superbly appointed Bray ground, complete with private railway station, on the outskirts of Dublin. The Australians would spend their week on the south coast of England.

The first game in Ireland saw the South Africans up against a Woodbrook Club and Ground side boasting their professional, none other then Ernie Vogler. Maybe there was a touch of relish in the way Louis Tancred carved him around the ground on his way to a rapid century, Vogler's 21 overs costing 117 runs. At least he could console himself with an offer to manage a new sports ground in Pretoria. Woodbrook responded vigorously until rain intervened and a draw was declared. Clear weather for the next three days enabled the visitors to crush Ireland even without the help of Pegler. Faulkner and Carter shared the wickets in a 'deplorable' batting display and Nourse, Tancred and Snooke scored the runs, Nourse being the first South African to complete his 1,000 for the season. Poor Gerald Hartigan finally returned to the team after a six-week absence only to fracture his arm throwing the ball in from the boundary, the rest of the team clearly hearing the bone break. With 'a silver plate put in the arm' he clearly wouldn't play again on the tour.

Back in England the South Africans' final game of the month was again very low key – against the Minor Counties at Stoke. As if the event were not short enough on glamour, it rained for most of the three days and a total of just four-hours play was possible. Charlie Llewellyn was having troubles of his own with his club, Accrington. He took exception to a caricature of himself that appeared on a town wall after a defeat by local rivals Church CC and asked to be released from his three-year contract. Matters were eventually patched up and he continued to perform successfully.

Down on the south coast, the Australians were being treated to two batting masterclasses within a week. The first was from a prolific young accumulator of runs whose first Test recognition had ended in failure in Australia the previous winter – Phil Mead. The second was provided by a rather portly 40-year-old amateur who had scored one of the most brilliant of all Test centuries against Australia at Old Trafford 13 years previously – HH the Jam Sahib of Nawanagar. The games against Hampshire and Sussex were both played in proper summer weather, the fact that the first game resulted in an ignominious defeat and the second in a high-scoring draw was down to two things. Hampshire possessed the tireless and redoubtable medium-pace swing-bowler Alec Kennedy, who took 11-181 in 55 overs, and Phil Mead, who scored a total of 193 runs without being dismissed. The form of these two men was simply too much for the visitors and there was a 'demonstration of great enthusiasm' after the game to celebrate the county's first victory over Australia. Of great concern to everybody was the attitude of the *Times* to this game and others like it. Having printed four-paragraph reports of two county games involving Surrey, Middlesex, Yorkshire and Warwickshire, it devoted just four lines to the tourists. This was a stark contrast to the enthusiastic coverage that had greeted their arrival three months earlier.

Charlie Macartney returned at Brighton after a two-match rest and immediately showed the benefit of his break. He scored a century in each innings to match the brilliance of Ranji's 125, his 72nd and last in first-class cricket, scored with a bandaged wrist and completing his 1000th run of the season. He showed his pleasure by presenting Syd Gregory with a gold watch and also hosting the entire team at his mansion for the duration of the game. A rather worrying rumour began to appear in print that Macartney intended to marry on his return home and then settle in Colombo; fortunately for Australian cricket this never came to pass.

Charlie Macartney and Warren Bardsley at Brighton, 25 July – After a hearty lunch Macartney completed a 'brilliant and attractive century'.

As far as the selection for the following week's Test was concerned, the main point of interest concerned the possible return of Sid Emery to the side. But at whose expense? Gerry Hazlitt was fit again after his eye operation and the removal of some teeth in Brighton and with three specialist bowlers and three all-rounders, it seemed unlikely that Emery would force his way back in on the form shown in the previous week.

England had once again announced their 12 the previous week and it contained two changes. Harry Dean had not bowled particularly well at Headingley and Schofield Haigh, who had taken plenty of Australian wickets at Bradford, replaced him. *Cricket* felt the change justified in view of the fact that the younger man, Dean, had plenty of Tests in front of him. The other change saw Gilbert Jessop replaced by Ernie Hayes of Surrey. It was quite clear that this signified the end of a long and never dull Test career which included the unforgettable century at The Oval in 1902. Jessop had announced his retirement from the game at the end of the season and there were now reports that he was about to enter the Leeds Anglican Clergy School as a student. This left two places for Haigh, Hitch and Hayes. Haigh in wet, Hitch in dry and Hayes whatever was the general verdict although one or two pointed out that

Hitch was effective on soft surfaces and that if the sun shone the pitch might suit him on the last day. One source of encouragement for England was the return to form of Frank Foster with a bundle of wickets against Middlesex.

Most commentators pointed to the indifferent recent form of the Australians against the counties but they were also not naïve enough to believe that this form would be repeated against England. 'They have come over with the deliberate policy of concentrating all their energy and all they know on the Test matches', 'they are, and always have been, notable test fighters' but 'the odds lean towards the old country'. The *Times* hoped for a fast, sporting wicket at a ground prepared for a large crowd but at the same time expressed a doubt as to whether England would be able to force a result in three days under such conditions.

The afternoon before this much anticipated game was due to begin found the majority of the Australian team and various members of the press at St Pancras station ready to board the Manchester train for a four-hour journey. As the train passed through the midlands the sky began to grow dark and by the time they crossed into Cheshire 'the rain came banging against the carriage windows'. On arrival there was no crowd and no welcoming committee and cabs were hailed as the team made straight for their hotel.

The Sixth Test
England vs. Australia
Old Trafford 29 July

Day One

The rain didn't ease even as the players slept and by the following morning the pitch was under water. Finally it relented and, with a strong south-westerly blowing, the pitch was deemed dry enough for play to commence at 1.50.

England left Hayes as twelfth man which meant a first Test of the summer for both Haigh and Hitch. For the former there was a chance of a bonanza if the sun would only come out; the latter must have blanched at the pudding on which he was supposed to bowl fast. The Australians had decided on the attacking option of replacing the injured Roy Minnett with the dangerous but inaccurate Sid Emery rather than bolstering the batting with the woefully out-of-form Smith. Within 10 minutes it was clear that this was the kind of pitch that suited no-one. Fielders slithered after a wet ball, bowlers struggled with run-ups, sawdust and grip while batsmen found timing improbable and boundaries impossible. One man prospered – Wilfred Rhodes. After being dropped by Hazlitt before scoring, his well-renowned patience and ability to adapt his game to what little was on offer saw him carry his bat through to the close, 92 not out from 185-6. Fry failed again (caught by substitute McLaren who was on for Macartney) and Spooner was unable to reproduce his county form or show the Australians what the Africans had seen. Whitty and Hazlitt had proved hard to get away but there was no Hugh Trumble in the team to really exploit the conditions. In addition a couple of chances went begging, the easiest of which was to Bill Whitty – again. Unless there was a drastic climatic change it was hard to see either side forcing a win and it hardly needed saying that the 4,407 hardy souls that parted with their shillings left the ground as disgruntled as the men they had paid to watch.

Fry and Gregory return from a pitch inspection, 29 July – Nothing positive for the two captains to report at a sodden Old Trafford. Play eventually began at three o'clock.

Considerably more lined the Thames to see Englishman Ernest Barry beat Dick Arnst over the four-mile boat-race course to secure the title of world sculling champion and collect £1,000 for his trouble. Arnst had travelled over with the Australian team and even played for them in Ceylon. His defeat was an expensive one for the players, Gregory had backed him at 6/4, Whitty at 7/4 and Bardsley 'stood to win a tidy sum'. Even as this expensive news was being digested, the players were off up Warwick Road to the recently-completed other Old Trafford to watch a 130-yard sprint, for a 'considerable purse', between Charles Holway of the USA and Jack Donaldson; the two were 'billed as the fastest runners in the world.'

Day Two

Further overnight rain ensured that there was no possibility of any action before lunch and as miserable hour followed miserable hour so all chance of a result melted away. Play finally resumed at five o'clock and, as if to advertise the inadvisability of such an enterprise, Rhodes slipped while playing the second ball and was bowled by Whitty. The remaining three wickets soon fell as the two sides went through the motions of international cricket. Jennings and Kelleway then safely negotiated 13 overs, Fry didn't even give the ball to Barnes, and the players and officials trooped off in the dank gloom of a Manchester evening.

Day Three

The pitch was worse than ever on Wednesday morning but with no rain in the air the covers were removed at 11.00 for a prompt start 30 minutes later. At 11.28 the rain returned, at 1.15 the game was abandoned and by 1.50 CB Fry was safely ensconced in the restaurant car of the London train saying "That's my last Test here, good-bye Manchester". The Australians were moving on to Derby and the English players were on their way home.

The covers at Old Trafford, 31 July – A gloomy scene on a gloomy day with a pitch receiving minimal protection.

England 203 (Rhodes 92, Whitty 4-43, Hazlitt 4-77) Australia 14-0
Match Drawn (Full card, Cricinfo Test # 126)

After such a cricketing non-event there was little to be said. Another financial catastrophe and with three games to play all-square between England and Australia with South Africa nowhere. The *Sportsman* reported that the final Test at The Oval 'must be played to a finish'. At least David Denton of Yorkshire had enjoyed his month with 1,000 runs in July, 38-years-old and still 'lucky'.

Leading Averages To 31 July

Batting
Macartney 1696 @ 53.0
Bardsley 1509 @ 48.7
Nourse 1106 @ 36.9
Kelleway 827 @ 33.1
Tancred 751 @ 30.0
Taylor 924 @ 29.8
Gregory 900 @ 29.0
Jennings 879 @ 28.3
Faulkner 730 @ 27.0
Snooke 751 @ 26.8

Bowling
Macartney 29 @ 14.2
Carter 60 @ 15.1
Pegler 116 @ 15.5
Faulkner 91 @ 16.7
Hazlitt 60 @ 18.2
Whitty 67 @ 18.6
McLaren 20 @ 19.0
Matthews 61 @ 19.2
Minnett 31 @ 20.7
Kelleway 44 @ 22.0

Australia: Played 25, won 9, lost 6, drew 10
South Africa: Played 24, won 9, lost 6, drew 9
Monthly rainfall 94.4mm – the worst since 1903

AUGUST

Mo	Tu	We	Th	Fr	Sa	Su
			1	2	3	4
5	6	7	8	9	10	11
12	13	14	15	16	17	18
19	20	21	22	23	24	25
26	27	28	29	30	31	

1912

Jan

Mo	Tu	We	Th	Fr	Sa	Su
1	2	3	4	5	6	7
8	9	10	11	12	13	14
15	16	17	18	19	20	21
22	23	24	25	26	27	28
29	30	31				

Feb

Mo	Tu	We	Th	Fr	Sa	Su
			1	2	3	4
5	6	7	8	9	10	11
12	13	14	15	16	17	18
19	20	21	22	23	24	25
26	27	28	29			

Mar

Mo	Tu	We	Th	Fr	Sa	Su
				1	2	3
4	5	6	7	8	9	10
11	12	13	14	15	16	17
18	19	20	21	22	23	24
25	26	27	28	29	30	31

Apr

Mo	Tu	We	Th	Fr	Sa	Su
1	2	3	4	5	6	7
8	9	10	11	12	13	14
15	16	17	18	19	20	21
22	23	24	25	26	27	28
29	30					

May

Mo	Tu	We	Th	Fr	Sa	Su
		1	2	3	4	5
6	7	8	9	10	11	12
13	14	15	16	17	18	19
20	21	22	23	24	25	26
27	28	29	30	31		

Jun

Mo	Tu	We	Th	Fr	Sa	Su
					1	2
3	4	5	6	7	8	9
10	11	12	13	14	15	16
17	18	19	20	21	22	23
24	25	26	27	28	29	30

Jul

Mo	Tu	We	Th	Fr	Sa	Su
1	2	3	4	5	6	7
8	9	10	11	12	13	14
15	16	17	18	19	20	21
22	23	24	25	26	27	28
29	30	31				

Aug

Mo	Tu	We	Th	Fr	Sa	Su
			1	2	3	4
5	6	7	8	9	10	11
12	13	14	15	16	17	18
19	20	21	22	23	24	25
26	27	28	29	30	31	

Sep

Mo	Tu	We	Th	Fr	Sa	Su
						1
2	3	4	5	6	7	8
9	10	11	12	13	14	15
16	17	18	19	20	21	22
23	24	25	26	27	28	29
30						

Oct

Mo	Tu	We	Th	Fr	Sa	Su
1	2	3	4	5	6	
7	8	9	10	11	12	13
14	15	16	17	18	19	20
21	22	23	24	25	26	27
28	29	30	31			

Nov

Mo	Tu	We	Th	Fr	Sa	Su
			1	2	3	
4	5	6	7	8	9	10
11	12	13	14	15	16	17
18	19	20	21	22	23	24
25	26	27	28	29	30	

Dec

Mo	Tu	We	Th	Fr	Sa	Su
						1
2	3	4	5	6	7	8
9	10	11	12	13	14	15
16	17	18	19	20	21	22
23	24	25	26	27	28	29
30	31					

ARREST OF A LADY JOURNALIST IN LISBON

Miss Oram, the correspondent of the Daily Mail in Lisbon, who was arrested here on Friday, is accused of holding meetings of royalist conspirators at her house and of being implicated in the recent incursion.

BRITISH ATHLETES AND THE OLYMPIC GAMES

THE NEED FOR ORGANIZATION

HIDDEN AND UNDEVELOPED TALENT

HOLIDAY ACCIDENTS
NINE BOY SCOUTS DROWNED OFF SHEPPEY

AUSTRALIAN AIRMAN'S DEATH
ARMY AEROPLANE TESTS DELAYED
'BEAUMONTS' FLIGHTS TO LONDON
THE NATIONAL AVIATION FUND

THE ARREST OF A LADY JOURNALIST

Miss Oram has been set at liberty. She was cross-examined in the presence of the accusing witness, who, after being hard pressed, finally confessed that she was innocent of the charge of being a royalist conspirator, According to even the most advanced Republican journals, both witnesses were very disreputable characters, so that the arrest is incomprehensible.

MOUNT STROMBOLI ACTIVE

The Political Outlook

The unexpectedly great Unionist victory in Manchester must have a far-reaching effect on the political situation and the fortune of the government. What Manchester shows is that the country is fast withdrawing its confidence from the Liberal Party.

DRESS FOR THE SPAS - THE DEVELOPMENT OF THE MODES

"THE TWELFTH"
OPENING OF GROUSE SHOOTING SEASON

NORTH-EASTERLY WIND AND RAIN
NO SIGN OF SEASONABLE WEATHER

THE HARVEST AND THE WEATHER

NAPOLEON'S VILLA FOR SALE

The villa of San Martino, in the Isle of Elba, is to be offered for sale by auction at Porto Ferraio on September 2. It consists of 12 rooms, and contains all the furniture and other things used by Napoleon Bonaparte during his residence in the villa while he was confined to the island. The Napoleonic Museum will be included in the sale, and the reserve price is about £5,500.

MINERS' DISSATISFACTION—THE MINIMUM WAGE AWARDS

Great Britain and Panama
REPRESENTATIONS TO THE PRESIDENT

SEVERE THUNDERSTORMS
SLIGHTLY BETTER PROSPECTS

NEW CINEMATOGRAPH FILMS
LOVE AND ADVENTURE

It is not easy to say which of the two cinematograph films produced at the special matinee at the Palace Theatre yesterday, "With Captain Scott to the South Pole" and "Queen Bess – her Love Story", will prove most popular.

AEROPLANE ACCIDENT IN FRANCE
GERMAN HYDRO–AEROPLANE
COMPETITION
GERMAN NAVY'S FIRST AIRSHIP
SALISBURY TESTS AT A STANDSTILL

THE MID-LOTHIAN CONTEST
CANDIDATES PROSPECTS

CARMARTHEN ELECTION
EVE OF THE POLLING IN A
LEISURELY CONTEST

DEATH OF "GENERAL" BOOTH
THE FOUNDER OF THE SALVATION ARMY

THE KING'S GROUSE BAG TOTAL OF 283 BIRDS ON MALLOWDALE

STORMS AND FLOODS
DAMAGE TO CROP

THE FLOODED COUNTRY
DISLOCATION OF TRAFFIC

At long last, and later than expected, all 500 pages of the mighty and weighty *Imperial Cricket*, edited by Pelham Warner, was revealed for public consumption at a princely six guineas. This was the bibliophile's celebration of the tournament now in progress, containing sumptuous detail of such obscurities of world cricket as the game in the Solomon Islands and Egypt. A truly handsome tome it was, generally well received as a great testimony to a great game even if one newspaper was dubious as to the essence of the entire project. The *Manchester Guardian* complained:

> 'The "Imperial" note is, perhaps, a trifle too prominent. It may be that cricket, like trade, follows the flag: that, as Lord Hawke says in his introduction, "it has had no small part in cementing the ties that bind together every part of the Empire." All the same, we think....cricket is no more than a game when all is said and that it is a mistake to exalt it into an agency for Empire-building'

Nonetheless it was full of fascination, if somewhat elitist in price and size, and remains a remarkable witness to the age which spawned it.

It is doubtful whether such an ambitious publication would find much place in cluttered dressing-rooms, players of all three international teams having enough to occupy their minds.

The first two-thirds of the much-heralded summer of Test cricket had slipped by with more of a whimper than a bang – four one-sided games exposing all the weaknesses of one of the teams and two rain-ruined draws. August offered the chance of, if not a glorious resurrection then at least some healthy competition, a thrilling climax and presumably, at the end of it all, a winner. The general feeling, and it was just a feeling and not a regulation, was that the winners of the ninth and final Test, between England and Australia at The Oval, would be the Triangular Champions. In that case the results of the seventh and eighth games would have no bearing on the final result – this was the perceived wisdom and the English Test Board of Control signally failed to step in and clarify matters. Some sources were claiming that all three August Tests would be played to a finish and others believed some kind of points system was in operation, but apparently nobody knew for sure.

The other Board of Control, that in Sydney, had managed to get itself embroiled in yet another row. The Imperial Cricket Conference meeting in July had established an acceptable provisional Test programme to cover the next five years with the caveat that final ratification would be required from Sydney, Johannesburg and the English counties. Secretary Smith cabled team-manager George Crouch to re-emphasise the Board's opinion that the triangular experiment should not be repeated, particularly as it was completely unfeasible outside England and even in the 'old country' the counties were suffering financially. In other words they were happy with the ICC plan, especially as it made no provision for another three-sided summer.

The *Sporting Life* stirred up trouble by stating that the Board had misunderstood the ICC if they believed that the published schedule signified the death knell of the triangular scheme. The journalist was apparently unaware that Smith was merely echoing an opinion that had been made plain even before the July ICC meeting. It was all much ado about nothing and the *Daily Mail* applauded the Board's stance as 'prudent'. There was one minor detail which Smith and McElhone had allegedly ignored before cabling Crouch in London – they hadn't actually consulted the Board. Mostyn Evan of South Australia was furious at this high-handed behaviour. Not for the first time scant regard had been shown for the Adelaide faction or, indeed, for any kind of democratic process. Clem Hill was quick to record his resentment of such an 'autocratic telegram' and claimed that it was by 'such actions as this that all the recent friction was caused'. Smith's version of events was somewhat different, as reported in the *Age*:

> 'Mr Smith states that Mr Evan kept silence for nearly a fortnight after being specifically asked for his views, and he gave them for the first time in a newspaper… ."His belated complaint seems to me to have been made with a view of assisting his friend the Melbourne Cricket Club in their effort to influence the election of delegates to the Victorian Cricket Association, at the expense of candidates who in the past have been loyal to the board of control. There will be a chorus of denial but that, I believe, is the real reason for it.'"

Apparently the hatchet had not yet been buried. The *Sportsman* did not want to be drawn into the mire of Australian cricketing politics but was adamant that the opinion expressed in Sydney

> 'sounds the keynote to the general views of most people….It is all very well to say that finance should not be considered at all in the matter, but these international affairs require money, and such a lot of it too, for their proper conduct. And where is it all coming from?'

Ironically the *Pall Mall Gazette* was pre-occupied with finance on the same day but took a different tack:

> 'The truth is, the one and only curse of cricket is the "spectator". He was invented with gate-money, Test matches, international sport, and the other enemies of leisure and good fellowship. When cricket is played for profit, and profit alone, it ceases to be a game, and becomes the foolish plaything of the majority….let the mob follow its inclination.'

There was still cricket to be played, hopefully for money, and the two visiting sides had one more county game in August before their third and final meeting, at Trent Bridge, on the fifth of the month. The Australians were in action at Derby on yet another rain-soaked pitch under more relentless grey skies. Less than two hours' play was possible on day one and Charlie Kelleway dropped anchor! The next two were considerably more lively – Jimmy Matthews took 6-23 and Australia went in again with a lead of 49 only to collapse to 89-9. With the pitch easing slightly, defeat was looming until Bardsley and Harry Webster added 48 for the last wicket. Webster was now pressing Carkeek for a Test place as the *News of the World* 'wicket-keeping averages' revealed the senior man to be the second most profligate in the country in the matter of extras as a percentage of runs conceded by his team. There was, however, no time for either side to force a result and the rain returned. The *Times* deemed this game worth just four lines while giving Cheltenham versus Haileybury no less than 50.

The South Africans were at Liverpool and Lancashire was proving to be nearly as wet as Derbyshire. The opposition, however, was much stronger. Play wasn't possible until after lunch on the first day and following the early dismissals of Spooner and Tyldesley the tourists were treated to a wet-wicket masterclass from Jack Sharp, 'quite the best display that has been done against us under similar conditions' recorded Faulkner. With the pitch falling to pieces there was only one possible result – Aubrey Faulkner at least engineered avoidance of the follow-on before taking his second five-wicket haul of the game and completing his hundred for the season. Once again Tancred seemed only to trust two bowlers but when Claude Carter was finally given a chance he picked up two wickets in five overs. Despite the best efforts of Faulkner the target of 270 on a cut-up 'treacherous wicket' was unthinkable and in Harry Dean Lancashire had just the man to deliver the *coup de grace*. Within 75 minutes he had put out South Africa for 44. A local reporter's eulogies on Taylor's fielding and Ward's glovework were scant reward. The toss had been crucial and the enviable unbeaten record against the counties had gone – Lancashire had now won three of four against the two touring teams though curiously they were making no great show in the Championship which was developing into a battle between Yorkshire and Northants with Kent chasing hard. Even in this wet summer, the red rose was feeling the loss of their stalwart veteran pace bowler Walter Brearley.

With just short journeys to make, the two sides arrived in Nottingham in good time to realise that the weather they had been enduring for the last three days looked like staying the same and that their game was attracting precious little enthusiasm either locally or nationally. The *Sportsman's* scene-setting was more than a little downbeat.

> 'I don't know how the good people of Nottingham will take the Seventh Test match, which commences in their midst to-day, but it does seem to me to be asking something for big crowds to patronise a show that has not the slightest local interest, in addition to which the teams engaged are not really up to the desired international standard.'

The *Pall Mall Gazette* was hopeful of a good showing from South Africa. Pegler and Faulkner were 'a long way better' than the opposition attack and, above all, 'they play the game as a club cricketer understands cricket, as a game and a pastime rather than as a business'. This was just one of many publications still confused by the scoring system of the Tournament. 'Even if Australia lose this match both England and Australia are still equal, each having won one rubber'. In Johannesburg, the gallant Welsh Harp was trying to drum up interest by offering three cases of Birch's Black Bottle Whisky to the person coming closest to forecasting the results of the final three Triangular Tests.

So, for better or for worse and for just the third time in its history, following the visits of Australia in 1899 and 1905, Trent Bridge would again host Test cricket.

The Seventh Test
Australia vs. South Africa
Trent Bridge 5 August

Day One

As Louis Tancred and Syd Gregory prepared to toss the coin, the thought uppermost in both men's minds was 'what kind of wet pitch is it this time?' Tancred had rued his decision to insert here against Nottinghamshire earlier in the season and Gregory was a veteran of both previous Tests on the ground and had his own opinions had they been required. Would it be slow and dead getting harder or a spitter and shooter that would then improve? Tancred gambled on the former, suspecting that the wicket was similar to that on which they had played in June.

Gregory and Macartney catch some sun at Trent Bridge, 5 August – A brief moment of warmth amidst the chilly damp that dominated the seventh Test.

Bank Holiday Monday had dawned cloudy and showery. It wasn't until 11 o'clock that the rain stopped completely, allowing the covers to be removed. With no prospect of an early start some of the few enthusiasts who had braved the elements turned on their heels and headed back home. The umpires ordered the rolling, the stiff wind whipped the ground, the captains announced their teams and play was scheduled for noon. Roy Minnett was fit again and returned for Edgar Mayne while South Africa recalled Snooke and Beaumont for Mitchell and Schwarz who had now effectively finished for the season.

On the dot of midday, Tancred and Taylor, buffeted by a nasty breeze and in front of barely 1,000 spectators, walked down the steps of the Trent Bridge pavilion to face the music. Within minutes Tancred, at the non-striker's end, must have felt his heart descend to his buckskin boots as Bill Whitty's wind-assisted yorker crashed into Taylor's stumps. Somehow the captain and his new partner Dave Nourse applied themselves to the matter in hand and doggedly clung on until lunch realising, as each minute passed, that the wicket wasn't so awful after all. The Australians had become rather disheartened and although they maintained a fine length there seemed little zip to their work and most experts agreed that such a diagonal wind should have been ideal for Whitty, Hazlitt and Emery.

The afternoon play was rather colourless and the crowd grew only slowly in the inhospitable conditions but for once a session passed without a break. Nourse moved on to 64 in 165 minutes before being unsettled by repeated interruptions caused by 'chocolate sellers' behind the bowler's arm and then falling to Whitty. This time there was no collapse and as Gregory feverishly juggled his seven bowlers the score grew slowly but surely, only Sid Emery providing a regular supply of hittable deliveries. Snooke and Stricker kept the board ticking over but it was only in the last half hour that the game blazed briefly. Gordon White, showing some of his old form, and Sid Pegler, having been given a 'rousing reception', hit 'like a club cricketer' and, for once, two South Africans were seen taking quick singles. They attacked a tiring team and, with the fielding looking decidedly ragged, took the total to 266-8 at the close.

It was a commendably disciplined effort and, given some luck with the weather, one which might just be a match-winning one. In other respects the day was less satisfactory. A mere 2,365 had paid to enter the ground for a Test match on a public holiday – the fact that the Board at Lord's had set covered seating prices at an exorbitant 7s. 6d. and 5s was certainly a contributory factor (both stands were virtually deserted), the weather was another. A glance at the *Times* the following morning offered a more general explanation.

> 'It would be idle to pretend that the game possesses much interest for the cricketing world, either locally or in general. It would no doubt be pleasant to see the South Africans do something in a Test Match to represent their true cricketing ability, but no victory could, in ordinary circumstances, alter the ultimate position in the tournament.'

As if the entrance figures weren't depressing enough, reports the following morning that county games at The Oval and Old Trafford had attracted 11,000 (even 5,000 were at Leicester) were a clear indication of how the land lay.

Day Two

A couple of morning showers ensured that the pitch was still dead when the unbeaten pair walked out on the second day and they immediately picked up where they had left off. Excepting only Gerry Hazlitt, the Australian attack and fielding was slipshod and, with number 11 Ward joining in, 63 runs were added in 50 minutes before the last wicket was taken. Wicket-keeper Carkeek was reported 'right off it' in conceding

30 byes. Facing a total of 329 in the knowledge that if it stayed dry the pitch would harden and become more unpredictable, Jennings and Kelleway made a steady start until the former decided to test Taylor's arm and, courtesy of some acrobatics by Ward with the gloves, lost. Charlie Macartney emerged to play as if without a care in the world, hoisting Llewellyn fully 100 yards into the stands before falling for 34. Charlie Kelleway, hemmed in by a field set to stifle his fitful stroke-play, stayed for two hours as Bardsley accumulated a skilful but boundaryless half-century at the other end. Then Kelleway fell to Pegler, Bardsley was run out by another piece of brilliant fielding by Taylor and, with the wicket worsening, the score of 171-4 began to look less commanding. The fielding was tight, Pegler and Faulkner began to scent a wilting tail and it seemed that Australia might struggle to restrict their first innings deficit to 125. Then it happened, the rain came at 3.40. The fact that an hour was lost was frustration enough for the South Africans, but worse still was that all the drying of the pitch had now been reversed and it was once again playing slow and easy. Dispiriting as it was, Faulkner and the tiring Pegler plugged away and Australia were removed for 219 in moderate light. It had been a fine bowling performance and prompted Roy Minnett to pronounce Pegler the finest bowler he had faced all summer. A lead of 110 with a day to play and any number of possible ways forward on the last day, with most of them pointing firmly in favour of South Africa. If ever the sun were required this was it; a quick hundred before lunch and then skittle the Aussies on a gluepot in the afternoon!

Day Three

A meeting of Macs, 7 August – Charles Kelleway, Charlie Macartney and Archie MacLaren mull over the unlikely prospect of play.

There was no third day. The rain set in early and the game was abandoned as a draw at two o'clock, the miserable news being compounded by the total gate receipts of less than £250 – when divvied up this would scarcely cover the visitors' hotel bills and train fares.

The Trent Bridge pitch after the seventh Test, 7 August – The line of attack taken by the bowlers is clear, as is the state of the pitch.

South Africa 329 (Nourse 64, White 59*)
Australia 219 (Bardsley 56, Pegler 4-80)
Match Drawn (Full card, Cricinfo Test # 127)

Aubrey Faulkner was naturally despondent at the outcome:

> 'We certainly had the better of the draw but this was scant consolation for the two very severe defeats we suffered in the two previous encounters.'

He found some cause for congratulation in the 'heroic' work of Ward behind the stumps, an improved batting display and, above all, the achievement of bowling out Australia on an easy wicket. Like everyone else he was more then a little concerned about the lack of spectators and reflected ruefully that 'a tournament like this will not be given another trial for a good many years'.

Money was now becoming a serious and public issue for the Australian team. This latest shortfall brought the balance sheet into focus. The *Age* had published the figures for the first two months and they showed a 20 percent decline against the 1909 returns, with worse quite possibly to come. The Australian correspondent of the *Pall Mall Gazette* was clear that the players who had not accepted the flat fee of £400 for the tour were going to be badly out of pocket and at this stage there was the possibility that five months away from home might be rewarded with less than £100. This, of course, led to a further round of misery about the entire contest. The *Westminster Gazette*:

'The poor summer has badly served the first attempt to decide the triangular supremacy and has left it to circumstances in which luck must count almost as much as play.'

Cricket was equally downbeat:

'It [the Tournament] has not gone; and for a good many years to come no one is likely to suggest its revival. Which is a pity in some respects, for the scheme had its merits. But there are other things to be considered. Just as club cricket is the backbone of the whole game, so county cricket is the backbone of the first-class game in this country; and it is quite possible that had the Triangular Tournament been a huge success county cricket would have been given a mortal blow.'

The two bedraggled sides limped away from Trent Bridge with few positive memories and then it was straight on to the next stage of an increasingly punishing schedule. The South Africans were due at Leicester before their sixth and final Test the following Monday and the Australians headed north for a hastily arranged two-day fixture at Sunderland against Durham. The object was quite simply funds and, despite the inevitable poor weather, a crowd of 11,000 was present over the two days for a rare chance to enjoy first-class cricket (although there was some debate about whether this game actually fell into that bracket). A draw was always the likeliest result but Mayne and Bardsley treated local enthusiasts to some excellent batting.

At Leicester, 336 runs for 40 wickets would seem adequate testimony to the nature of the Grace Road square even if Aubrey Faulkner found fault elsewhere:

'The game against Leicester was characterised as being the worst batting on both sides that we have seen so far on this tour....if our display was shocking that of our opponents was certainly worse.'

One could hardly deny their hunger for victory. Spurning the chance to rest his front-line bowlers between the two Tests, captain Mitchell elected to use Pegler and Faulkner for 56 of the 62 overs delivered. Once again Claude Carter, on a wicket to suit, was ignored and the game was completed easily inside two days in favour of the visitors. Then it was back to London for a date with England at Kennington Oval.

For the first time all summer, South Africa had no selection conundrums. They had played well against Australia and anyway it was not as if there were players beating down the doors of the selection committee. The English case was slightly more complex and, as ever, Fry could hardly be accused of leaving matters to the last minute. The team had been announced fully six days before the game was to commence without, of course, any realistic notion of how the pitch might play. The Old Trafford Test had been a washout so it was reasonable to assume that no changes would be made but poor old Schofield Haigh was to be disappointed. Having delivered just six overs at Manchester he was dumped in favour of Surrey's in-form Ernie Hayes, a middle-order batsman. For whatever reason an off-spinner was now deemed surplus to requirements and the batting was bolstered. Surely Fry wasn't adopting a safety-first approach against opponents already twice roundly thrashed? Perhaps he wanted everyone to have a turn or was he trying Hayes out before the ninth and crucial final Test against Australia? The captain was at least in prime county form with the bat and had reclaimed his position at the top of the averages with Bardsley and Macartney at five and six. Haigh and Blythe were the top two bowlers and the feature of domestic form in this wet season was the work of the veterans; Hayward, JT Hearne, Hirst, Denton and Tyldesley were regularly giving the young bucks object lessons in how to exploit or tame rain-affected pitches.

<h1 style="text-align:center">The Eighth Test
England vs. South Africa
The Oval 12 August</h1>

Day One

Seven days earlier Louis Tancred had been looking down at the diminutive Syd Gregory as the captains prepared to toss. This time he was faced by the considerably more impressive figure of Charles Fry on turf that was equally spongy. Tancred had got it right at Trent Bridge but he was much less sure what his decision might be here and he told Fry in no uncertain terms that he hoped to lose the toss. No such luck and, forced to choose, he elected to bat, his reward being bowled for a duck by Barnes who, in Tancred's words, beat him both for pace and break. Taylor and Nourse began a minor recovery, mainly at the expense of Foster, but as the effects of the heavy roller began to wear off it became apparent that the wicket was an absolute stinker and that Syd Barnes was again in top form. The crumbling edifice of South African batting was helpless as Frank Woolley replaced Foster and only the fine technique and footwork of Herby Taylor offered any resistance. Barnes was making the ball turn both ways, kick and occasionally shoot without ever offering the respite of a short-pitched delivery. Eventually it was one of the kickers that accounted for his own wicket-keeper Smith; 'Barney bowled a leg-break fairly wide, Herby Taylor followed it round and the bat and ball hit me in the mouth at the same time'. Smith retired from the field to have loosened teeth examined and his lip stitched and Reggie Spooner took over his unenviable task, wisely not standing-up to Barnes. Taylor fell soon after and the collapse was in full swing. Sibley Snooke asked EHD Sewell "What's to be done?" as he made his way out to bat to which the reply was "Shut your eyes and bang" – joint top score of 23 was the result after some desperate heaves at Woolley. Shortly after lunch, having faced 42 overs in 135 minutes, the South Africans were all out for 95. So much for the 'glorious twelfth', which went into the annals as the coldest on record.

How would England fare on a pitch that was certainly not improving? For the waiting crowd, which had now grown to some 8,000, the prospect of Pegler and Faulkner locking horns with Hobbs, Fry and Spooner promised to be a connoisseur's delight. When Rhodes fell without scoring the tension increased but Hobbs and

Spooner gradually began to right the ship in a partnership that was as illuminating as it was important. The South African bowlers sent down some brilliant and deadly deliveries but the English batsmen were equipped to resist all bar the very best. Footwork above all enabled them to survive, forcing Pegler, Faulkner and Llewellyn, for all their skills, to doubt their length and offer up the hittable ball in a way that Barnes had not. After the pair had added 61, Spooner fell and was quickly followed by Fry and Hayes. Hobbs, supported firstly by Woolley and then by Hearne, moved on to a masterly 68, with eight fours, scored in under two hours. Even without the sun to make it sticky, the pitch was a shocker and *Cricket's* reporter was just one of many to express his admiration: 'Hobbs played one of the very greatest innings of his career'.

The English innings closed at 5.40, 176 all out and a lead of 81. Those 15 or 20 loose balls that had been sent to the boundary were the difference between the two teams. The umpires were all set to re-start 10 minutes later but South Africa were spared a torrid 45 minutes by the persuasive powers of CB Fry who reasoned that he and Tancred were in agreement about the light and that is what mattered. Surely only a temporary reprieve as visions of the gaunt and pale countenance of SF Barnes disturbed South African slumbers that night.

The *Daily Graphic* reports from The Oval, 12 August – Top: Barnes bowls to Stricker. Left: Tiger Smith receives attention after being hit by ball and bat. Right: Smith trudges off to meet the doctor while the remaining players console his replacement – Spooner drew the short straw.

Day Two

The batting side had the temporary relief of seeing the sun was still well hidden but unfortunately a drying wind had been at work on the 'chipped' surface and, worse still, Barnes had a nice little patch to aim for – worn by his own unerring accuracy in the first innings. This time Fry went straight to Woolley whose fourth ball spun several inches before he delivered a 'pair' to the door of skipper Tancred. Thereafter it was Barnes against the rest, although in reality it was only left-hander Dave Nourse who offered any real resistance. Bowling almost exclusively leg-cutters but with the occasional ball jagging back into the right-hander, all accompanied by an undetectable change of pace and the odd lifter for good measure, he worked his way through the opposition. Taylor for six, Faulkner 10, Stricker, Llewellyn, White, Snooke and Beaumont for a combined 14. Nourse stood remarkably firm at the other end.

Aubrey Faulkner described one over to Snooke in detail. Although it lacks the raw pace of Holding to Boycott or Donald to Atherton, it was clearly intimidating.

> 'The first ball pitched on the middle and kicked up wrist high and turned sharply away to the off. The next one came along the right height, but the next one came back from the off and kicked. The fourth one never left the ground but was short enough to enable the batsman to play down on the ball. The fifth was a good length one which hit Snooke on the jaw and stopped play for a few minutes. The last ball was fairly respectable, only hitting him on the hand.'

The South Africans were all over the place and when Dave Nourse finally capitulated, for 42 scored in 100 painstaking minutes, the deed was done. He was given a rousing reception by the crowd, the England players and even WG for he had single-handedly prevented an innings defeat. The real hero though was Barnes. Few doubted he was the best in the world although Hamish Stuart in *Cricket* wanted to see him successful on a plumb wicket before rating him as highly as Lockwood or Richardson. Seemingly he had forgotten Barnes' achievements in Australia seven months earlier.

A mere 13 was required to complete the formalities and it was somehow fitting that the winning runs should come from overthrows as Roly Beaumont shied at the stumps in a vain attempt to remove Jack Hobbs.

South Africa 95 (Barnes 5-28, Woolley 5-41)
England 176 (Hobbs 68, Faulkner 7-84)
South Africa 93 (Barnes 8-29)
England 14-0
England won by 10 wickets (Full card, Cricinfo Test # 128)

The South Africans just had no answers on such a pitch. Taylor and Nourse had battled bravely and Faulkner had bowled well but they had nothing that could match Hobbs and Barnes who described the match as a 'veritable beano'. Furthermore their best bowler, Pegler, and also to a lesser degree Faulkner, had still not quite grasped the basics of bad-wicket bowling. They were inclined to bowl as they would on an unresponsive surface which meant the ball was doing too much. Barnes' method was simple; give away nothing at all and let the pitch do most of the work – Alfred Shaw would have been impressed. The *Daily Graphic* put an imposing action shot of Barnes on its front page accompanied by the simple legend:

8 For 29 - The Greatest Living Bowler

Sydney Barnes, 13 August – The *Daily Graphic* gave over its front page to this shot, and no wonder. A superb study of the effort, aggression and, presumably, pace in a Barnes delivery. Non-striker Aubrey Faulkner seems less than keen to get to the other end – when he did, Barnes bowled him.

Fry immediately announced an unchanged team for the final Test due to start five days later. Once again the logic of such premature selection with the weather so unsettled was, at best, questionable.

Given the amount of rainfall sweeping the country during the second week of August it was probably just as well that the Australian visit to Worcestershire had been arranged for Dudley rather than the county town. Fostershire fielded three of their famous family and two of them, GN and RE, were the best batsmen in a disappointing total of 143. Bill Whitty's 6-57 was a welcome return to form with the final Test now only a week away. The error of batting first was soon revealed as Australia took advantage of an easing pitch; an even greater error was omitting regular wicket-keeper Ernie Bale in order to accommodate amateur Geoff Foster. He missed a simple stumping chance before Warren Bardsley had scored and by the time the innings closed at 407, the Australian had reached an unbeaten 176. A washout on the final day prevented the visitors forcing a win before moving on to a 'wet and cheerless' Cheltenham. The first and third days were again ruined by the weather but in between times Bardsley took another century and became the first man in the country to 2,000 runs. George Dennett gave a masterful example of left-arm orthodox spin on a wet wicket but in the face of competition from Rhodes, Blythe, Woolley and Dean he never stood a chance of international recognition. The Australians also had the opportunity to re-acquaint themselves with one of the founding fathers of South Australian cricket: Jesse Hide was standing in his last season as umpire. A draw was the inevitable result as the weather again defeated the players' best efforts.

The consequence of their crushing defeat at The Oval was that the South African team had an unwanted day off before proceeding to Victoria Station for the short hop down to the fleshpots of Brighton. The decision to put Sussex in on a blustery morning was justified by Dave Nourse's return of 6-16 at lunch and the game took many interesting twists and turns between the showers over the next two days. With the pitch easing, Joe Vine and Albert Relf put on 169 to enable Sussex to set their guests 179 to win. After early reverses, Aubrey Faulkner treated the crowd to a superb exhibition (as he had done in the first innings) and steered his side to a four-wicket win.

The Sunday following this game saw the South Africans (minus Sibley Snooke who had permission to return to South Africa with his wife) negotiating the national rail network on their way to Sheffield where they played out a dull draw on a slow wet wicket in bad light. They then crossed the Pennines and played another draw at an equally sodden Old Trafford where even the decision to change the pitch after each innings could not save the game. In truth, there was now precious little interest in what Pegler, Taylor and Tancred were up to. All eyes were firmly trained on Kennington Oval.

Now was the time to try and figure out by what method the winners of the Tournament would be decided. One thing was decided, this game would be played over six days if required. The authorities were clearly desperate to get a result but they were also prepared to organise a further fixture should these six days prove insufficient. Surely this was at least a clue as to how things would be resolved? On 16 August the *Sportsman* was totally bemused:

> 'A victory for England would, of course, effectively settle the matter. But what is the position should Australia defeat us? They will have won the only game played out by the pair, each having previously won their series with the South Africans, and the wording of the resolution of last August certainly points to the issue being decided by the result of three rubbers of three matches. But there are those who argue that the issue can only be determined by wins in the whole series, and that should Australia win next week it will be a dead heat.
> Seen yesterday at Lord's by a representative of The Sportsman, Mr. F.E. Lacey, the secretary of the MCC, confessed that he was unable to make any definite statement on the controversy though he inclined to the idea that three rubbers were intended.'

The next day the same newspaper was in a bigger lather. It argued that the Tournament was designed to find the winners of three Test series in one summer and that if one team were to win two series then they would be overall champions. But there was nothing in the original plan that required an overall champion; it would be fine to say that England beat South Africa, Australia beat South Africa and Australia drew with England. Why then the talk of arranging a tenth Test? The *Pall Mall Gazette* offered a completely different theory:

> 'The [extra] game would be played at the Oval in the week beginning September 13. The match will, of course, only be played if England and Australia, as a result of the game next week, are equal – that is to say, if England are beaten….England begins her match with Australia at the Oval on Monday next with a lead of one point.'

Cricket was somewhat light-hearted about the absurdity of the debate taking place at all, just two days before the final (or penultimate) game was due to begin.

> '….or whether the fact that England beat South Africa three times and Australia beat South Africa only twice comes into the question – or – but enough!….The Board of Control will meet on Monday in the endeavour to elucidate its own ruling.'

The *Daily Graphic* was simply enjoying the geometry:

> 'It is a Triangular Test match, and people are wondering whether the triangle is our old Euclidian friend the isosceles, with the sides of equal length. It would tax the Major-General in "The Pirates of Penzance" to resolve all the propositions involved in the tangle.'

The Ninth Test
England vs. Australia
The Oval 19 August

At long last the day, or week, of reckoning had arrived. After three months of Test cricket it came down to the old enemies at the Kennington Oval with the fervent hope that this denouement (if that is what this was) would do something to hide the damp disappointment of the previous eight games. The arguments that had preceded the game hardly helped the atmosphere but at least there would be some action on the field rather than in the editorial rooms.

England made two late changes, both of them weather related. Ernie Hayes had picked up a bad cold and it was decided that the pitch had nothing to offer Bill Hitch who was promptly discarded after two Tests in which he hadn't bowled a single ball. The replacements were sensible. Harry Dean was recalled, although some argued for Schofield Haigh in a team already boasting three left-arm bowlers in Foster, Woolley and Rhodes. The other late inclusion (so late that he wasn't actually at the ground when play started) was Johnny Douglas whose dour batting and fast-medium bowling would strengthen any team. Finally the discarded captain of the previous winter had returned.

The Australians elected to field specialist-batsman Dave Smith at seven in place of Sid Emery while wicket-keeper Carkeek retained his place courtesy of an injury to understudy Harry Webster who had looked considerably more assured than his senior colleague over the previous three weeks.

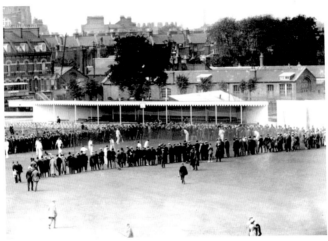

England and Australia practise before the final Test, 19 August – Players from both sides attract large crowds at a net at the Vauxhall end.

Day One

Heavy rain had again fallen on the Sunday before the game, this was then topped up by a storm in the early hours which ensured, once again, a soft surface for the first morning. At least the weather was bright and breezy as spectators began to arrive and a start time of high noon was agreed by the captains and umpires. Surrounded by a throng in front of the pavilion, Fry and Gregory tossed for the third time and for the third time the coin fell in favour of England. The choice was an important one but it wasn't difficult. It was reasonable to assume that the pitch would be slow and docile to begin with before cutting up and then deteriorating to become exceptionally difficult later in the game. The light roller was applied, Jack Hobbs and Wilfred Rhodes buckled on their pads and the crowd of 12,000 settled into their seats in anticipation.

They didn't have long to wait for the opening drama as the English pair chanced a single off the first ball that would have resulted in Rhodes' demise if Bardsley's return had hit. Soon after, Rhodes was again fortunate as Matthews slipped while going for a difficult chance. Gradually, though, this famous pair began to settle down and gauge the pace and bounce even if only eight runs came from the first 10 overs as Whitty, Matthews and Hazlitt kept a steady line and length supported by enthusiastic and athletic fielding. Runs were clearly hard to find but there didn't appear to be any great threat in the bowling either – more than one Australian onlooker sighed for a Spofforth, Turner or Trumble at such a time.

A rain delay after 10 overs was mercifully brief but it brought about a change in approach from Hobbs; he now started to look for runs and Jimmy Matthews obligingly served up two long-hops which were smashed across the slow outfield. At the other end, Rhodes was being kept quiet by an astute leg-side field; hardly a man to be troubled by such things especially with his partner beginning to score freely. There was uneven bounce and turn but it was all so slow that batsmen of this calibre were not going to be troubled by anything except an exceptional delivery. The one Australian who might just have produced such a ball, Sid Emery, was sitting in the pavilion. By lunch, after 80 minutes' play, the score had climbed to 65 without loss of which Jack Hobbs had scored 42.

Another shower during the break ensured that conditions were unchanged when the players re-appeared and the English openers continued in the same vein. Gregory chopped and changed his attack, introducing the left-arm spin of Macartney and the fast-medium pace of Minnett but all to no avail. They could not find a wicket-taking ball and they were now beginning to lose their control as well. Rhodes brought up the 100 with an all-run five off Matthews and Hobbs struck the next two balls for four and three as the run-rate increased. At last a mistake was made and Hobbs fell to a catch behind off Macartney for 66 – a partnership of 107 in 110 minutes had put England firmly in the ascendant.

The crowd had now risen to 16,000 and the most observant of them detected that the wicket had become quicker and more difficult over the previous 15 minutes. Subsequent events bore out this impression. Reggie Spooner was out almost immediately, flicking a ball towards the on-side boundary only to find Gerry Hazlitt diving full length to catch him left-handed close in – his scores against Australia in Tests that summer: one, one and one. Charles Fry now entered the fray to a chorus of booing from the popular enclosures and shuffled around uncomfortably for 45 minutes during which time he missed more than he hit and was lucky that Carkeek fluffed a simple stumping chance. Two rain breaks further fractured the afternoon's proceedings as the Australians began to claw their way back into the game. Fry's ordeal was mercifully ended for five – he had been further barracked for slow play and had cut an untypically ungainly figure. *Cricket* found it 'impossible to praise Fry's innings' although he did find an apologist in EHD Sewell who thought he was 'obliged to play a certain game because he was partner to Rhodes'. The same writer had also bafflingly declared himself unimpressed by the opening partnership because the batsmen were too defensive and failed to punish half-volleys.

Bill Whitty had bowled almost all afternoon and when his reward came with the wicket of Fry it was followed almost straight away by another in the form of Jack Hearne. At the other end, Rhodes' long vigil was terminated by Roy Minnett, one short of a half-century, after three hours at the crease. Tea was taken with England having lost five wickets in scoring 79 runs during the afternoon; 144-5 and evenly balanced.

It was now thoroughly gloomy but the crowd was still growing as some fortunates were able to escape their workplaces early to watch the final session. The rain was holding off and the situation tense. After a good start, England were now facing the prospect of being dismissed for 200 in a game which could, in theory, last for a week. The Australians had stuck to the task well. Whitty's stamina had been sorely tested but he hadn't been found wanting and the fielding, especially that of Macartney, was superb.

The two new English batsmen, faced with the task of righting the lilting ship, were Frank Woolley and Johnny Douglas, who had received a huge ovation from a crowd that clearly felt he had been harshly treated by the selectors and more than deserved his recall. Both men, one naturally the other less so, were cautious and watchful as play began, realising that this partnership might be crucial to the outcome of the entire series. The ground had dried out in the breeze and, as he ascertained the pace of the pitch, Woolley did what was in his nature and found the outfield responsive. The score gradually climbed as Douglas prodded singles and proffered his pads while Woolley punctuated his watchfulness with the occasional flowing drive. The bowlers flogged for a breakthrough but it was almost an hour before Douglas fell to Whitty only for Foster to take his place and prove equally obstinate. The 200 was safely passed and the bowling was becoming ragged before Foster fell and Woolley wisely decided to embark on a late offensive while the going was good. With Tiger Smith blocking manfully at the other end, a succession of loose balls were sent to the boundary and Woolley raced past his 50 before being trapped in front by Minnett for 62. With that the umpires whipped off the bails and called a halt to the day.

It had been enthralling for 12,824 who had paid plus the members and guests. The general feeling was that England had come out marginally ahead by virtue of the opening stand and the late afternoon strokeplay. Australia had given it their best shot – their bowling had been wholehearted, even if the end result showed that they lacked a real match-winner, and the fielding had been in the best traditions of Australian cricket.

Activity in the pavilion had not just been limited to the players and spectators during the afternoon. A meeting of the Test Board of Control had been scheduled with the aim, some might say belatedly, of deciding how the winners of the Triangular Tournament would be decided.

'(a) That in the event of the Test Match in progress being finished it would not be necessary to arrange another.

(b) That in the event of the match now in progress being drawn, with the approval of the Australians, another match should be played, and that subject to Mr S. Cochrane's consent, such match should be played at the Oval, on Thursday, September the 12th and the following days.

The following telegram has been sent to Mr Cochrane:-

"The Board of Control is anxious, if the present Test Match is drawn, but only in that case, to have a fourth match between England and Australia. The only dates are September 12th and the following days, but Australia consider themselves pledged to you. Would you kindly waive your prior claims?"

A reply to the above had been received as follows:- "Will give up date if you play match

SEPTEMBER-
DECEMBER

Sep

Mo	Tu	We	Th	Fr	Sa	Su
						1
2	3	4	5	6	7	8
9	10	11	12	13	14	15
16	17	18	19	20	21	22
23	24	25	26	27	28	29
30						

Oct

Mo	Tu	We	Th	Fr	Sa	Su
	1	2	3	4	5	6
7	8	9	10	11	12	13
14	15	16	17	18	19	20
21	22	23	24	25	26	27
28	29	30	31			

Nov

Mo	Tu	We	Th	Fr	Sa	Su
			1	2	3	
4	5	6	7	8	9	10
11	12	13	14	15	16	17
18	19	20	21	22	23	24
25	26	27	28	29	30	28

Dec

Mo	Tu	We	Th	Fr	Sa	Su
						1
2	3	4	5	6	7	8
9	10	11	12	13	14	15
16	17	18	19	20	21	22
23	24	25	26	27	28	29
30	31					

1912

Jan

Mo	Tu	We	Th	Fr	Sa	Su
1	2	3	4	5	6	7
8	9	10	11	12	13	14
15	16	17	18	19	20	21
22	23	24	25	26	27	28
29	30	31				

Feb

Mo	Tu	We	Th	Fr	Sa	Su
			1	2	3	4
5	6	7	8	9	10	11
12	13	14	15	16	17	18
19	20	21	22	23	24	25
26	27	28	29			

Mar

Mo	Tu	We	Th	Fr	Sa	Su
				1	2	3
4	5	6	7	8	9	10
11	12	13	14	15	16	17
18	19	20	21	22	23	24
25	26	27	28	29	30	31

Apr

Mo	Tu	We	Th	Fr	Sa	Su
1	2	3	4	5	6	7
8	9	10	11	12	13	14
15	16	17	18	19	20	21
22	23	24	25	26	27	28
29	30					

May

Mo	Tu	We	Th	Fr	Sa	Su
		1	2	3	4	5
6	7	8	9	10	11	12
13	14	15	16	17	18	19
20	21	22	23	24	25	26
27	28	29	30	31		

Jun

Mo	Tu	We	Th	Fr	Sa	Su
					1	2
3	4	5	6	7	8	9
10	11	12	13	14	15	16
17	18	19	20	21	22	23
24	25	26	27	28	29	30

Jul

Mo	Tu	We	Th	Fr	Sa	Su
1	2	3	4	5	6	7
8	9	10	11	12	13	14
15	16	17	18	19	20	21
22	23	24	25	26	27	28
29	30	31				

Aug

Mo	Tu	We	Th	Fr	Sa	Su
		1	2	3	4	
5	6	7	8	9	10	11
12	13	14	15	16	17	18
19	20	21	22	23	24	25
26	27	28	29	30	31	

Sep

Mo	Tu	We	Th	Fr	Sa	Su
						1
2	3	4	5	6	7	8
9	10	11	12	13	14	15
16	17	18	19	20	21	22
23	24	25	26	27	28	29
30						

Oct

Mo	Tu	We	Th	Fr	Sa	Su
	1	2	3	4	5	6
7	8	9	10	11	12	13
14	15	16	17	18	19	20
21	22	23	24	25	26	27
28	29	30	31			

Nov

Mo	Tu	We	Th	Fr	Sa	Su
				1	2	3
4	5	6	7	8	9	10
11	12	13	14	15	16	17
18	19	20	21	22	23	24
25	26	27	28	29	30	28

Dec

Mo	Tu	We	Th	Fr	Sa	Su
						1
2	3	4	5	6	7	8
9	10	11	12	13	14	15
16	17	18	19	20	21	22
23	24	25	26	27	28	29
30	31					

THE 40,000TH ISSUE OF "THE TIMES"

THE CRISIS IN THE BALKANS THE THREAT OF WAR DECISION OF THE TURKISH CABINET MOBILIZATION ORDERED	**THE LATE EMPEROR OF JAPAN** FUNERAL CEREMONIES IN TOKYO *An Impressive Spectacle* SUICIDE OF COUNT NOGI AN ACT OF PATRIOTIC DEVOTION

THE NEW CAPITAL OF INDIA

To-day will be memorable in the history of British India as the date of completing the great territorial readjustments involved in the transfer of the capital from Calcutta to Delhi.

RAILWAY DISASTER
EXPRESS TRAIN WRECKED IN LANCASHIRE

FATAL ACCIDENTS TO GERMAN OFFICERS

FATAL PARACHUTE ACCIDENT

FLIGHT TO IRELAND IN A MONOPLANE

ARMY AIRSHIP'S RETURN TO FARNBOROUGH

THE LABOURERS ON THE PANAMA CANAL
WHITE MEN AND NEGROES

MR. LLOYD GEORGE AT THE EISTEDDFOD -------SUFFRAGISTS ROUGHLY HANDLED

THE GERMAN EMPORER **TRIBUTE TO SWISS SOLDIERS**	**CROPS AND LIVE STOCK** **A DISHEARTENING HARVEST**

PLANS FOR THE TREATMENT OF TUBERCULOSIS

THE SKULL OF DESCARTES

It has recently been suggested that the skull said to be that of Descartes, which is kept in the Museum of Natural History, has been lost.

A POST-IMPRESSIONIST EXHIBITION - MATISSE AND PICASSO

This exhibition, held like the first at the Grafton Galleries, contains a few beautiful works by Cézanne; but otherwise it is entirely given up to living artists, French, English and Russian. It contains a large number of pictures by H. Matisse and a good number by M. Picasso, and as these are the most notorious and abused artists in the movement it is worthwhile paying particular attention to their works. M. Matisse has been freely called a charlatan, which means that he is incompetent or a mediocrity affecting a wilful eccentricity in the hopes that he may be mistaken for a genius.

ATTEMPT ON THE LIFE OF MR ROOSEVELT

OUTBREAK OF WAR
FIGHTING ON THE FRONTIER
DECLARATION TO TURKEY BY MONTENEGRO

DUEL IN PARIS

A duel took place in the Parc des Princes this morning between M. Leon Blum and M. Pierre Veber, as the result of a quarrel at the Theatre des Arts over M. Veber's new play, *Une Loge pour Faust*

A BULLET WOUND IN THE CHEST

THE OLYMPIA MOTOR SHOW - LOW-PRICED CARS

MR ASQUITH ON THE BALKAN WAR
THE MAP OF EASTERN EUROPE TO BE RECAST

British Policy & British Power

Firmly as we trust that peace will be maintained, a moment has come in European affairs when every nation with interests and friendships to preserve must look to its resources and strive to appraise their worth. Is British power still adequate to hold its great position and guard its heritage? We believe that it is.

THE ADVANCE ON ADRIANPOLE
BULGARIAN COAST BOMBARDED

DANGER OF ELECTRIC BATHS

The End of the Year

The year 1912.... is passing away in an atmosphere of anxiety, though, as we all know, a cloudy sunset does not always mean an impending storm.

The Defence of the Empire

We live in breathless times and every morning presents us with so varied a diet of news that those who mark it all must have robust and eager minds.

AN ATTEMPT TO KILL THE VICEROY - BOMB THROWN IN DELHI

THE ARCHDUKE FRANCIS FERDINAND IN BERLIN
"A HAPPY INTIMACY" WITH ENGLAND
GERMAN POLICY IN THE BALKANS

ROUT FOR TURKS
ANXIETY FOR CONSTANTINOPLE
KILLED AND WOUNDED: - 25,000

PRISHTINA CAPTURED BY SERVIANS
DESPERATE FIGHTING IN KOSSOVO

After the sodden summer of 1912 it was hardly surprising that the subject of covering wickets had intermittently risen to the surface. Not only were games frequently delayed or curtailed by wet wickets but they were often decided by the arrival of rain and its effect on what had previously been something benign. Hardly a series had passed in the previous 40 years without at least one Test being decided largely by who had the misfortune to get caught on a spinner's paradise, a gluepot or sticky dog and even 1912, with its damp uniformity, was no exception. The ninth and final Test might have been won by the best team but they had also had the best of the luck.

In 1910 MCC had, at Surrey's instigation, framed explicit rules for covering pitches but only as a resolution, hoping 'that the counties will make it a practice':

> 'After the actual commencement of play the ground may be protected when necessary, and shall be protected every night during the continuation of a match, but the covering shall be removed each morning, if fine, at seven o'clock.'

This was fine as far as it went, but:

> 'The covering must not protect a larger area than 18ft. by 12ft. at each end, and must not protect a space of more than 3ft. 6in. in front of the popping crease.'

Put simply, the area where the ball would pitch would not be protected. Did this mean that luck played too great a part? Was it unfair to spectators? Would a change have altered the nature of how the game had always been played and was intended to be played? The majority accepted that the question of covering pitches was a fundamental one that the summer of 1912 had brought into sharp relief. The *Times* addressed the question in early September:

> '....it must be said that if the effect were to be that wickets were practically always plumb the suggestion would hardly be welcomed by the player....a long succession of wet wickets are perhaps more monotonous than a long succession of dry, but variety of wicket makes the most interesting season.'

The potential ramifications of adopting full covering were enormous, not the least of which was the fear of endless drawn Test matches and the need to adopt the Australian example of no time-limits. Pelham Warner was one of the few who believed this to be the right way forward. It soon became clear that one spoilt summer was not going to cause a radical about-face from the rule-makers.

These rules were rigidly adhered to in competitive fixtures but, with the serious business now over for the touring teams, the majority of the remaining games fell into the category of festival cricket and the rules were bent on more than one occasion.

The main points of discussion in Australia were less about covering pitches and more about the covering of backs. The epic war of words in pamphlet form had lulled since McAlister and Laver had crossed swords in May but the silence was only temporary and, in late August, Melbourne CC finally replied to the statement the Victorian Cricket Association had issued in March.

Then, at the beginning of September, 'A Few Facts for Fair-Minded Sportsmen' appeared in print under the signatures of Board stalwarts Ernie Bean and Harry Rush. It was a fine example of the massaging of statistics and a series of selective averages, cherry-picked newspaper quotes and wishful thoughts that led to the conclusion that 'the present team….has more than answered expectations' contrary to anything that the *Age* and others might say. The East Melbourne CC AGM was another particularly nasty evening with Frank Laver refusing to 'shake hands and put the past to rest' with his old enemy Peter McAlister. Laver was furious that the club secretary had been working against him in the elections to the committee and the secretary's skill was advertised when the result was announced; Laver voted off after 25-years service. Throw in a banquet in Sydney in honour of Billy McElhone, complete with the rhetoric one would expect, and then rumours of some kind of coup involving the presence of Armstrong, Trumble, Ransford, Hill, Noble and Cotter in Sydney and it was clear that there was precious little sign of a healing process between players and officials, clubs and Board or Melbourne and Sydney taking place. In fact it was sounding more like Dodge City with a Randolph Scott figure urgently needed to settle the warring factions.

Of more immediate concern to the men still in England, and carrying the Australian colours, was money. On this the *Pall Mall Gazette* had unearthed some interesting titbits. At the beginning of the tour the players had been offered a simple choice: a £400 plus expenses flat fee or a share of the profits which, based on previous experience, might be double that amount. Four had opted for the former and 11 chose the latter. An 'insider' was now reporting that some of the larger group had initially been 'apprehensive' of the drawing-power of a team shorn of Trumper, Hill and the others but 'on the advice of one of the members of the Board' they had accepted a share of the profits. Now they were facing the prospect of a return less than half the guaranteed sum and 'some of those interested state that they have more than a moral claim' to have the shortfall made good by the Board. The newspaper rightly doubted that the Board would see it this way. It's hard to imagine an air of harmony accompanying the team on their last lap.

Both teams had four more matches to play, though given the weather compounded by the general exhaustion after four months non-stop playing and travelling they would have happily skipped the last lap. But commitments were commitments and the first of the month found the depleted South African party assembled at Bournemouth. On a difficult wicket, only one batsman from each side was able to prosper in the first innings. Louis Stricker hit 99 in his only commanding innings of the summer and Phil Mead, inevitably, held the Hampshire innings together. The pitch improved dramatically after the first day, allowing Dave Nourse to belt a double-century in 220 minutes before the home side were set an unlikely and ungenerous target. For a short time it looked as if they might be skittled but Mead, again, stood firm to force a draw, remaining twice unbeaten, as he had done against Australia six weeks earlier.

The South Africans at Bournemouth with the mayor, 2 September – From left: Ward, Campbell, Pegler, Carter, White, Faulkner, Tancred, Taylor, Cox, Stricker, Nourse.

A quick trip to Attleborough saw the South Africans next pitted against a mixed bag of a side collected by Lionel Robinson (and presumably his secretary, one Archie MacLaren) at his beautiful and luxurious country estate. Dean and Sharp from Lancashire, Tarrant from Australia via Middlesex, Roy Minnett's brother Rupert, father of the googly Bosanquet and a young Patsy Hendren were amongst the gathered XI on a pitch that had been so well protected that it was hard and fast enough to shock almost everyone into submission. Hendren, batting at nine, gave an inkling of a career to come by hitting 80 in 75 minutes before the rain beat the covers, leaving the wicket ruined and South Africa were skittled by Tarrant and Simms in the fourth innings.

The Australians were showing understandably little enthusiasm for the last leg of their English marathon, excepting only the tireless Warren Bardsley who had yet to miss a game. A strong Surrey and Middlesex XI gave them a good hiding, Frank Tarrant showing no mercy to his countrymen, and only Bardsley saved them from complete humiliation on a perfectly presentable Oval pitch that had, again, been well protected. 'The absence of resolution in much of Australia's batting was very noticeable' wrote the *Times* which was then equally damning about the bowling: '[It] neither deserved nor received anything more than momentary respect'. William Caffyn, 85-years-old and a veteran of the first two trips to Australia half a century earlier, can hardly have been impressed with what he saw from his place of honour in the pavilion. If their morale was low after this ten-wicket defeat, a long journey to a 'windy and chilly' Scarborough was hardly the tonic they were seeking. Lord Londesborough had not done his guests any favours by inviting Ranji to captain a team that included Spooner, Rhodes, Mead, Douglas, Haigh and Hirst but in the event the Australian mettle was scarcely tested as what should have been an interesting contest fizzled out between downpours into a meaningless draw.

One week to go and the South Africans now replaced Australia at Scarborough where the cruel Lord Londesborough had seen fit to invite their nemesis Syd Barnes to join his side. The weather was no longer just chilly, it had turned bitter and in the little time available for play Barnes picked up 6-32 before the rain saved the long-suffering tourists from further punishment. Meanwhile the Australians, with the exception of Emery and Webster who were injured and had taken a jaunt to Paris, were on the South Coast at Syd Gregory's favourite place – Hastings. Once again a covered wicket produced a sound surface and the batsmen made hay over the first two days once the shock of Jack Hobbs hitting his own wicket off the first ball had worn off. Joe Vine led the South of England to 420 before the Australians tucked into the slipstream of Charlie Macartney in full flow as he flayed all and sundry for 176 and moved past 2,000 for the season. The third day was merely an exchange of pleasantries before stumps were drawn early. The Australian party had the little matter of a train to London, another to Holyhead and then a boat to Dublin for the game the following day against CB Fry's XI. Relf and Hobbs were making the same journey while Barnes and Rhodes were travelling from Scarborough to Dublin on the same evening.

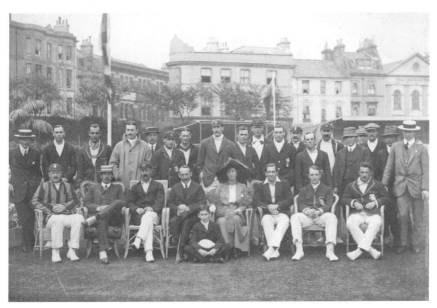

The Australians at Hastings, 9 September – The South of England and Australians gather together as an arduous tour nears its end.

On that same afternoon the Board of Control in London, with Lord Hawke in the chair, had met and passed the accounts for the summer, taking the opportunity to thank Charles Fry for his captaincy and work as a selector. Lord Harris, in abstentia, wrote that the lack of adverse criticism showed how well the selectors had performed, certainly there was none of the 'madness' that had accompanied the decisions of

1909. However, Fry's insistence on announcing teams a week before the game only to change them at the last minute when the weather dictated a different approach was somewhat questionable plus his sense of loyalty to men such as Haigh and Hitch was non-existent. One other piece of business at the meeting was to consider two letters from the seven professionals and two umpires who had participated in the final Test of the summer. They argued, as Barnes alone had done *during* the match, 'for increased payment owing to the fact that the Test Match at The Oval had lasted beyond three days'. The application was, in a display of miserly ingratitude, denied. Hobbs, Barnes and Rhodes may have been new professionals in many ways but they needed to know their places. Why should they receive an extra day's pay? After all, they had only led England to victory in the Triangular Tournament and with it retained the Ashes.

These were, however, relatively minor niggles compared to the issues still being hotly debated in Australia. On the same day, the *Age* branded the tour an 'absolute failure' and was clear where the fault lay and how it should be fixed.

> 'Surely it is for those who love the game for its own sake, and who are nauseated with cricket politics, to be up and doing. They must vote against those who represent the present board of control in this state'

The sniping didn't stop there. When the *Age* wrote, rather uncontroversially, that 'the batting averages make poor reading and the bowlers have proved very uneven', the *Bulletin* accused it of 'hawking stale fish and trying to push trade by misrepresentation'. That same sober journal then bafflingly set out to prove that Bardsley was no match for Macartney. The former was 'a good bat of the stolid sort but on neither of his English tours has he been the best man in big things whatever newspaper averages may allege.' What the averages showed, rather than alleged, was that Bardsley had scored twice as many runs as Macartney at double the average in precisely those 'big things'.

Back in England, Hastings week continued over the next three days with the Gentlemen of England providing the opposition for the South African's 37th and final game, and an extraordinary match it was too. After two days the Gentlemen led by 239 runs with six wickets in hand before a final flourish from Pegler and Faulkner followed by carefree and aggressive batting from Taylor, White and Faulkner again saw the tourists finish their arduous schedule on a winning note.

The Australian finale was considerably less impressive. After their long journey to Ireland, incorporating various excesses that would later come to light, they were put in to bat by Fry and subsided to 72 on a perfect wicket. SF Barnes made light of his trek from the Yorkshire coast by taking 6-27. A young onlooker, 'Father' Marriott later of Kent, wrote: 'I learned more about the art of bowling in those twenty overs than I did in all the rest of my life'. After that first morning it was always a lost cause in spite of better batting second time around and on the final morning, the Jacks – Hobbs and Hearne – cleared matters up with a partnership of 78 in an hour. The Australian's 38th and final match had ended in an eight-wicket defeat and Jack Hobbs had the pleasure of having played for no less than four different teams that had beaten Australia during the course of the summer.

Leading Averages At Tour End

Batting

	Bowling
Bardsley 2441 @ 51.9	Pegler 189 @ 15.3
Macartney 2207 @ 45.0	Faulkner 163 @ 15.4
Nourse 1762 @ 35.2	Macartney 43 @ 16.3
Kelleway 1300 @ 30.9	Carter 67 @ 16.6
Taylor 1340 @ 25.8	Whitty 109 @ 18.1
Hartigan 372 @ 24.8	Hazlitt 101 @ 19.0
Faulkner 1075 @ 23.9	Matthews 85 @ 19.4
Gregory 1055 @ 23.4	McLaren 27 @ 23.0
Jennings 1060 @ 22.5	Minnett 41 @ 23.6
Snooke 800 @ 22.2	Emery 67 @ 23.9

Leading English Averages

Fry 1592 @ 56.8	Barnes 69 @ 11.3
Johnston 1044 @ 54.9	Carr 61 @ 12.0
Mead 1933 @ 50.9	Blythe 178 @ 12.3
Sharp 1375 @ 44.3	Haigh 125 @ 12.3

Tourists' End-Of-Term Report

Australia

Gregory: Made a fine start with 300 runs in his first four innings but he added a mere 760 more in the next 47. His cheerful disposition and longevity made him popular wherever he played but it soon became clear that both his batting and his fielding were not what they had been. As a captain he stood little comparison with his predecessors, Monty Noble and Joe Darling.

Jennings: After beginning the tour in the middle-order, he was promoted to opener and enjoyed a good spell during June when he attracted praise more for his style than substance. Despite being unable to sustain his form as the wickets became wetter, he played in all six Tests with little success and eventually reached his 1,000 runs in the penultimate game without once passing three figures. Did not help himself by being run out no less than eight times in 47 completed innings.

Macartney: The record of the Governor-General was a marvellous one and showed how far he had progressed since the 1909 tour. He was capable of the brilliance of a Hobbs or Spooner at their best and his early form was so good that it seemed he might match WG's 1,000 runs in May. With the odd exception he became rather stale in the middle of the summer as his bowling was increasingly demanded on wet wickets but he bounced back with some marvellous innings in the last month. He was at his best at Lord's when taking 99 from the English attack in the manner of Trumper himself.

Bardsley: It was later said 'he simply couldn't get enough cricket' which was just as well because he played in all 37 games and was the most reliable and consistent run-getter in the team. His final aggregate was second only to Victor Trumper in 1902 and his average was the best ever achieved by an Australian. Eight centuries were spread across the season and, but for a run of eight matches without a 50 in June, he would have certainly reached the magical 3,000-run mark. A fine fielder and a masterful on-side player, he was a worthy successor to the other great Australian 'mollydookers', Hill and Darling.

Smith: Didn't appear in the first five matches and thereafter rarely did more than fill in for injured or resting first-teamers. His only innings of note was marred when he ran out his partner with victory in sight and that century accounted for nearly one third of his total runs. Would have been better suited by hard wickets but generally appeared out of his depth.

Minnett: Another who would have benefited from firmer wickets although he did show some flashes of brilliance which gave an indication of why he had attracted such praise at home before the tour. Alas, an overall batting average of less than 20 and little to show from four Test appearances did nothing to enhance his reputation even if his bowling was an unexpected bonus late in the tour.

Mayne: In and out, a rather peripheral figure for most of the summer, his best scores seemed to come in minor matches or when the game was already dead. Made little impression and played only one Test.

Kelleway: Arrived in England largely unrecognised but soon received plenty of attention for his combination of defensiveness and perceived lack of style. During the course of the next four months most observers were won over by his resolution and determination which proved of enormous value to his team, especially in international games. He averaged only 30 in all matches but double that in Tests, despite suffering from terrible nerves, and was a useful change bowler.

Matthews: His place in cricket history was secured by the double hat-trick at Old Trafford in May but the magic deserted him after that. He managed only nine more wickets in the remaining five Tests and the fact that his place was never under threat says much about the strength of the squad. He remained one of the three main bowlers without ever appearing to be of genuine Test standard although his hard hitting was occasionally useful as was his enthusiasm and bravery in the field.

Whitty: Hard-working and reliable, he led the attack as best he could although in reality he would have been better suited as a foil for a genuine strike-bowler. He sent down 860 overs and was Gregory's first choice in the most difficult or important situations and, after being given a break in mid-June, he was still bowling with plenty of verve in September. After two operations for appendicitis in 1911 he was close to re-capturing the form that saw him destroy South Africa at home two years earlier.

Hazlitt: One of the mainstays of the Australian attack, he displayed admirable consistency and stamina despite a long-standing medical condition and problems with his eyes and teeth. It was a shame that frequent questioning of the legality of his 'slower ball' overshadowed the early part of his tour and it would appear he made a successful effort to eradicate this defect. Also unfortunate was that his finest bowling spell, in the final Test, got his side back at the wicket sooner than was good for them.

Emery: Started superbly, with no less than 31 wickets in his first three games hopes were high that Australia had unearthed a secret weapon. His sporadic brilliance was mixed with expensive dross and after three Test failures it was felt that his bowling was too much of a risk on wet wickets where runs were in short supply and gifted boundaries were unacceptable. By the end of the tour, with injury having interfered, he had collected only another 36 wickets to add to his haul from the early games.

McLaren: Never came close to achieving even the most modest hopes that had been held out for him. There was little or no evidence of genuine pace even on the rare occasions when the wicket was fast and his excellent out-fielding was scant compensation as he became one of the forgotten players.

Carkeek: Reliable at best and prone to off-days, his record was a mixed one. Giving away 61 byes in the first two matches was less than auspicious and, although conditions were often difficult, he frequently lost out in comparison to his counterparts and also made little contribution with the bat.

Webster: Struggled with fitness throughout the summer and never really came to terms with the conditions. Like Carkeek, he started poorly, with 59 byes in his first two games, and thereafter watched more cricket than he played. A record of 1,018 extras conceded by the two glovemen was testimony to their shortcomings.

South Africa

Mitchell: The role envisaged for him was that of the experienced middle-order batsman whose knowledge of English conditions would make him a rock of stability for wet-wicket novices. For the first fortnight this plan seemed to be working well, culminating in a superb innings against Yorkshire. Thereafter there was next to nothing – he slipped down the batting order and then in and out of the team. All this, together with slow fielding, made him, by the end, almost a non-playing captain who played. This was compounded by some highly questionable on-field decisions.

Tancred: A slow start was followed by illness and injury, but he found form in June and frequently assumed the captaincy, including for three of the Tests. However, he failed to reach 1,000 runs, his best scores tended to be against easy opposition and he generally fell well below expectation.

Taylor: Moved up to opener through the failure of others and his partnership with Hartigan prospered briefly. Most experts recognised his potential but he was prone to disappointing due to impetuous hitting early in his innings. A brilliant 93 against Australia at Lord's confirmed his reputation as the coming man but considering his ability, and even allowing for inexperience, he should have managed at least one century in 57 attempts. Fielding was consistently excellent.

Hartigan: Started brightly and it seemed that he and Taylor might form a useful youthful opening partnership. He was taken ill in mid-June and then broke his arm in his comeback game thus robbing South Africa of one of her best fielders and a potentially exciting batting all-rounder.

Snooke: Much was expected of this experienced batsman but he delivered precious little. He started with plenty of good cameos but no big scores and in five Tests contributed almost nothing. Left for South Africa after the last Test with his bride of four months.

Stricker: Began the tour as an opener but after repeated failures was dropped down the order. His poor form throughout the summer was punctuated by the odd glimpse of his real capabilities and his knock at Bournemouth was described as 'masterly'. He played all but six matches, still failing to reach 1,000 runs and averaging less than 20.

Beaumont: Began the tour as an aggressive lower-order batsman who, it was hoped, might swing a game in 30 minutes. He never did and was rarely given a chance to prove himself higher up. Like so many of his fellow batsmen he was unsuited by the wet wickets and, unable to adapt, he managed just 500 runs and did little in three Tests.

Nourse: One of the few players in the party who could have been considered a success though even this was only relative, despite his appetite for work. The heaviest run scorer, with a respectable average, as well as a useful bowler who could offer some relief to the big two. In Tests, however, he managed just one half-century in 11 innings yet still topped the team averages.

White: Had been out of cricket for two years and his original notion of taking a holiday and playing when specially needed would have been more suitable. A late arrival, he was then injured in the first Test and, like many others, spent most of the tour under a cloud both literally and metaphorically. His bowling seemed to have melted away to nothing and there was little evidence of his renowned free-swinging stroke play. He did enjoy a few brighter moments in the last matches but overall it was a pretty disastrous summer.

Faulkner: After the brilliance of the previous five years it was hoped that he would be able to shepherd the side. His century in the first Test seemed to confirm both form and fitness. This was, however, an illusion. Ludicrously over-bowled, his batting suffered and he managed barely 1,000 runs. Seven wickets in the eighth Test showed what he could still do but the weight of responsibility, the workload and the constant disappointments ground him down until he was mostly a shadow of his former self.

Llewellyn: With Lancashire League commitments he only played once outside the Tests and it was soon clear that his bowling skill had largely deserted him. Two half-centuries, both at Lord's, showed that his abilities as a forceful batsman were still intact but he never had the luxury of a tiring attack to dismantle.

Schwarz: After an elbow operation, encouraging comments and early wickets, it was hoped that he might repeat his performances of 1907 and 1910-11. However most experts (and opposing batsmen) realised that there was something vital missing. He laboured on until mid-July before dropping out with a mere 18 wickets. It later transpired that he had been reluctant to play at all.

Pegler: The one unqualified success in the South African team although even here there were questions to be answered. He was criticised for trying to do too much on bad wickets which was harsh because his haul showed he was doing much more right than wrong. Like Faulkner he was completely over-bowled and by August was clearly tiring. He should have been rested in minor matches but instead completed nearly 1,300 overs during the 130 days of the tour.

Carter: If Pegler was over-bowled then here was the complete opposite. On pitches that generally suited his methods, his average was good yet he delivered only one third of Pegler's total and in his two Tests was entrusted with a mere 13 overs. His overall record was quite respectable, with more bowling he would surely have improved and taken some strain off his senior colleagues.

Cox: May as well have stayed at home for all the opportunities he was given. Ignored for the first four games, bowled well against Oxford University and then delivered just eight overs in the next seven matches; and so his summer continued. In a team where the two main bowlers were so overworked, his total of 170 overs was absurd.

Campbell: After starting the tour as first choice, his position gradually deteriorated due to rheumatism in his fingers and the form shown by Ward. Played only 13 times and after losing his Test place never looked like regaining it.

Ward: Had a shaky start and then that infamous 'king-pair' at Old Trafford. After that his form improved slowly but surely until by the end of the tour many judges believed him to be the best of the three national wicket-keepers. Adapted well to new conditions, occasionally managing some useful runs.

With the cricket finished, a veritable flood of statistics, verdicts, views and summaries filled the newspaper pages of the three participating nations – the watchword was 'failure'.

PUNCH, OR THE LONDON CHARIVARI.—August 21, 1912.

THE TRIANGULAR FARCE.

Scene—A blasted pitch.

Chorus. "WHEN SHALL WE THREE MEET AGAIN
IN THUNDER, LIGHTNING OR IN RAIN?"

Punch sees the Triangular Tournament as a Shakespearian tragedy.

George Allsop: 'I have never seen such bowling in my life as that of Barnes. He delivered the ball in such an extraordinary fashion that it made it absolutely impossible for our side to score. He bowled the leg breaks much faster and more accurately than anyone I have ever seen. He is undoubtedly a marvellous bowler with a distinct style of his own – a style no other bowler possesses.'

The *Times*: 'They showed us no great bowler, not more than four batsmen above the ordinary standard, and no great captain. In fielding they were good, but, with exceptions, not strikingly so: and, although Mr Carkeek has improved immensely, as a wicket-keeper still he cannot be said to be up to the highest standard….It was in batting that the weakness of the South Africans was most apparent, but their bowling has been but a shadow of the terrors it presented to the England batsmen in 1907….As some compensation there was Mr Pegler, a young bowler of real class.'

Frank Mitchell (in the ***Star***): 'As captain he had been let down by the failure of the batting of GA Faulkner, GC White and SJ Snooke. Despite the results he considered the South African eleven equal to the present Australian team and is of the opinion that it would have done better in a drier season.

Mitchell praised the batting of AD Nourse though sometimes, he said, the Natalian had failed when a big effort from him was needed….SJ Pegler was one of the best bowlers now before the public, GA Faulkner towards the finish of the tour bowled as well as ever. He predicted a brilliant future for T Ward as wicketkeeper. Regarding the fielding the captain said that the difficulty was that so few members of the side could throw well….the side had been a very happy family and he emphatically denied that the comparative failure in the field was due to demands on players socially…. he was in no way despondent as to the future….there being plenty of young talent there. There was, however, a great need for turf wickets and first-rate coaching.'

Cricket: 'This season has been all against the bowler who needs a pitch with some life in it, and that partially accounts, no doubt, for the very small show given John McLaren and Joseph Cox….These two must be thoroughly disappointed men….. Cox has had only four real trials….while McLaren has certainly not been a complete failure when given a show.'

The *Sydney Morning Herald*: 'Judging by the tests, the Australians have nothing to regret, and their prestige has not been lowered. In the lesser games their record was not so good. The batting was somewhat disappointing, the fielding not being as brilliant as expected. The bowling was not very convincing and the wicket keeping was of a low standard.'

Cricket: 'Who is the man to whom the Tournament has brought the greatest access of fame? I should say, without a moment's hesitation, Charles Kelleway. Bardsley did splendidly; so did Hobbs, Barnes, Woolley. But of these great things were expected. Others did well, but scarcely well enough to increase their reputations. Kelleway stands to-day far higher than he did when he landed in England.

The ***Daily Telegraph***: 'The colts did not fulfil expectations; still, in the tests, they [Australia] did remarkably well. Probably if proved players had gone, England would still have won triangular supremacy because no great bowler was left behind.'

The ***Pall Mall Gazette***: 'In any case, the season has been one on which we can look back with a great deal of satisfaction. And – best of all – as it has produced a number of young players of the most brilliant promise, the immediate future of the game seems as rosy as its immediate past.'

Cricket: 'The outstanding successes of the two teams are to my mind Bardsley, Macartney, Kelleway, Hazlitt, Nourse, Taylor and Pegler. Others have done pretty well, but on the whole – even in Faulkner's case and Whitty's – certainly not better than, if as well as, one had expected.

Ernie Vogler: 'But I quite admit that England were the best side. Hobbs and Rhodes as an opening pair of batsmen, understanding one another so thoroughly, making many short runs that would be mere folly for others to attempt, formed a big asset. Then there were Barnes and Foster as bowlers and with these I should place Dean, and Woolley must not be overlooked.'

The ***Sportsman***: 'But the wet, cheerless days of the last three months completed the effect which labour unrest in the spring had exercised on the attendances at some of the earlier matches and added to the unsatisfactory situation of a side that can scarcely be said to have left their own shores under happy auspices....Like their fellow colonials, the South Africans have come, have played but failed to conquer. At least in one quarter it was thought that they stood a good chance of figuring at the head of the results of the Triangular Tournament, the idea of which had emanated from that quarter of the globe, though it was difficult to see how, bearing in mind the results when they visited Australia and the fact that no fresh stars of magnitude had arisen, this impression was likely to be realised. As a matter of fact the actual course of events proved that they fell lamentably short of the Test standard.'

The ***Natal Witness***: 'I know of men in Natal who openly stated before the tour commenced that favouritism had been shown....and that some incompetents were included. I am not wholly with them. For one thing they scoffed at Pegler.... rather for the source of failure one can point to the old hands: Faulkner has been good in spasms, Llewellyn has been completely under a cloud and Schwarz can apparently "google" no more....even granting....say, the English team of to-day, the African eleven of 1907, and the Australians of 1909, it seems that there would be very many difficulties to overcome before success could be claimed; before, indeed, there would be any certainty as to the interest being maintained throughout the whole course of nine Test matches in one season....It was a sportsman's idea, but optimistic sportsmen have always had a way of painting bright views. South Africa must agree with her sister countries – the Triangular Test scheme has been a rank failure.'

Syd Gregory (in the ***Manchester Guardian***): 'he thought his team would have done better in a dry summer, Jennings, Minnett and Smith being essentially hard wicket batsmen. The bowlers also were better suited to hard than to soft wickets. Mr Gregory expressed his conviction that England had an incomparably better team this season than either Australia or South Africa.

He thinks that if he had won the toss at the Oval last month his side might possibly have beaten England, but victory in that match would not have affected his opinion as to the relative merits of the sides. He even goes so far as to say that he thinks England would have beaten the best team Australia could have sent over.'

The *Star*: 'Though the Triangular series of matches cannot be said to have realised the expectations of those who promoted the scheme, the competition might nevertheless have been a great success, alike from the playing and financial point of view, but for the inability of Australia to send over a representative team, the signal failure of the South Africans to do their powers even approximate justice in any of the Tests and the cold, cheerless and wet character of the summer.'

Ernie Vogler: 'I put the South African failure down as largely due to the absence of Percy Sherwell. One man cannot make a side, it is true; but the material was there, and it is astonishing what an influence a captain of the real "lifting" type can exert…. apart from the absence of Sherwell, I consider that the chief cause of the failure was the presence in the team of too many young and inexperienced players.'

The *Times*: '….there can be no doubt that England were very much the strongest of the three – sounder and more dependable in the body of the team in batting, stronger in bowling with bowlers more suited to the wickets that prevailed, for on sticky wickets the bad ball that is a "gift" four means as much, and both the Australian and South African bowlers were apt to give far more of these than the English.'

George Allsop: 'Everything possible has been done to make our visit enjoyable and we shall carry back to South Africa very many pleasant memories of the tour.'

George Crouch: 'Hazlitt bowled quite up to his reputation in England. He was thought a lot of there; in fact, Jessop told me Hazlitt and Emery were the bowlers most feared by the English batsmen. Emery bowled remarkably well right up to the time of our entry into Scotland, when, running in the outfield one day, he had the misfortune to twist his leg, and was not able to play for two or three weeks. [Macartney] was marvellous. He has a wonderful eye.'

FE Lacey (MCC secretary): 'If we had had anything like a normal season the tournament would have been a big success, not only financially, but in other respects despite what has been written to the contrary in many of the newspapers.'

FE Lacey: 'We may feel gratified that the arrangements for the Triangular Tournament, which had been left to us, have been carried out satisfactorily and without any friction whatever. Our guests may have had a poor opinion of the English climate, but they have been convinced that we have some very great cricketers.'

Syd Gregory (In the *Sun*): 'He had never in his life seen anything like some of the innings played by Macartney....He could not find words good enough to praise Bardsley....Whitty was their main bowler but Hazlitt and Emery (till his break-down) were also splendid.'

Now was the time to say goodbye, and possibly even heave a sigh, for the players who had arrived 21 weeks earlier. The Australians had arrived back in London from their Irish trip and attended two functions before their departure. Monday was at their headquarters at the Howard Hotel and Tuesday at the Nag's Head Hotel in Covent Garden as guests of Mr E Penfold whose son was to accompany the 10 players who had opted for the American trip. The morning of Wednesday 18 September found 11 of the original party at Waterloo waiting for the Southampton train. Roy Minnett had travelled to see his colleagues off (Hazlitt, Bardsley, Macartney, Jennings and manager Crouch hadn't) and there was a small and rather undistinguished group on the platform. No Warner, no Fry, no Ranji, no Harris; a poor show that almost ended in disaster when Jack McLaren narrowly avoided injury after hurling himself into the moving train at the last minute. Jennings and Minnett elected to prolong their stay in England but the other four sailed for home shortly afterwards.

The South Africans were in slightly less of a hurry, also travelling in two main groups. A much larger and more distinguished gathering was to be found at Waterloo on 21 September to wish the first batch *bon voyage*. Tancred, Taylor, Nourse, Pegler, Ward, White and Cox were seen off by, amongst others, Lord Hawke, Henry Leveson Gower, Albert Relf, Walter Lees, Roy Minnett (again) and also the rest of the South African party. George Cox of Sussex was present in a different capacity, off to Durban for a winter of coaching. Seven days later it was the turn of Stricker, Campbell, Hartigan, Carter and manager Allsop to wave *adieu* on their way to join the *Walmer Castle* at Southampton docks. Frank Mitchell elected to stay longer as his father was gravely ill, so too did Roly Beaumont who wished to see more of the country. Faulkner, Schwarz and Llewellyn were now British residents.

On 24 September the summer's accounts were made public and pretty depressing reading they were too. The total receipts from the nine Tests and the two trial games amounted to a mere £12,463. 4s. 2d. The Australians would have to be content with £2,986 and the South African share was just £1,878. 10s; neither would there be any great sum to be added from their labours in all corners of Britain. With three Tests (England's two at Lord's and the final one) producing nearly two-thirds of the total it was clear that the other games had been little more than a financial catastrophe. It was not only the accountants in Sydney, Johannesburg and London that would face the unenviable task of balancing the books, the English counties would not be receiving any windfalls either. They could expect just £157. 12s. 4d. apiece – for the previous Australian tour in 1909 the figure had been in excess of £300, a telling difference.

The Australian Board had already been apprised of the situation and volunteered to forego its share thus raising the earnings of the 11 who had opted for the profit-share to £190. 14s. 6d. This figure was poor compensation when measured against the £800 of the golden era or even the £400 of the 1909 tour; Macartney, Whitty, Hazlitt and Mayne were the four wise men that had chosen the £400 fixed fee.

As an English autumn drifted towards winter and the new cricket seasons were commencing in Australia and South Africa, the financial calamities in England were becoming clear with the publication of county reports. Northamptonshire, despite their best ever season on the field, were in severe difficulties. Somerset launched a 'shilling fund' in a bid for survival. Lancashire showed a small profit but described the season as disastrous and Middlesex were £500 in the red. Leicester and Hampshire were struggling: Kent alone seemed to have ridden the storm although they had now to reckon with the retirement of the architect of their success, Captain William McCanlis. The AGMs weren't exclusively financial however. The Lancashire committee severely criticised the Yorkshire side for gamesmanship (or cheating) in their fixture at Old Trafford. In the closing stages, the Yorkshire batsmen were alleged to have repeatedly broken the two-minute rule for the new man to arrive at the crease in order to slow down the game and secure a draw.

In November the summer's activities were brought back to public attention by the publication of EHD Sewell's book *Triangular Cricket*, complete with in-depth descriptions of the nine Tests and photographs taken by the author of his friends and acquaintances, the players. His 'best eleven of the Triangular Tournament' was interesting and somewhat different from either a team selected largely by using the Triangular averages or a 'World XI' for 1912.

Sewell's Team	Average's Team	World XI
Hobbs	Hobbs	Hobbs
Rhodes	Rhodes	Trumper
Macartney	Macartney	Macartney
Spooner	Spooner	Bardsley/Hill
Bardsley	Bardsley	Armstrong
Fry	Kelleway	Woolley
Woolley	Woolley	Faulkner/Hordern
Faulkner	Pegler	Sherwell
Pegler/Foster	Whitty	Foster/Pegler
Barnes	Ward	King
Ward	Barnes	Barnes

The Australians in North America were now well into their tour and had been busy from Winnipeg to New York, having suffered at the hands of the renowned Philadelphian swing bowler John Barton King (17-152 in two games), now aged 39, to the degree that both Edgar Mayne and Syd Gregory claimed they would rather face Barnes. They arrived home in late November; Dave Smith, having injured his knee in Bermuda, was delayed in landing as the authorities regarded him as a cripple. He was set for a long spell away from cricket which just about rounded off his horrible eight months on the field. The others, who had travelled directly home, had mixed luck. Warren Bardsley elected to spend a week in Ceylon and Charlie Macartney probably wished he had. Somewhere between Colombo and Fremantle a thief got into the ship's baggage room and cut into his suitcase stealing £100 worth of goods including 'a gold locket set with diamonds', a gift from Ranji expressing his regard for the Governor-General's batting.

The South Africans were, with differing degrees of commitment, back with their club sides (except for Gordon White who had announced his retirement), mostly tanned from the sea trip rather than the cricket. The critics were discussing the ramifications of the poor show in England and how matters could be improved. One cause for optimism was the plethora of professional coaches now employed at centres other than Johannesburg. Cities such as Cape Town, Durban, Port Elizabeth and Bloemfontein had all attracted British professionals and three more were hoping to follow suit. If only the question of matting wickets could be so speedily addressed. Some believed that turf wickets in the Cape or Border were not inconceivable but further inland, with drought an annual issue, there was no immediate possibility of progress being made.

Just when it seemed that the events of the two simultaneous tours were now becoming part of cricket history the events of the previous summer were suddenly back on the front pages and not for any positive reason.

On 25 November the *Sun* in Sydney ran a front-page story which was to open up another miserable chapter in Australian cricket even before the previous one had been closed.

'Australian XI
Charges Against Cricketers'

The Australian players lately active in America had returned from their long journey, beginning at Vancouver and continuing via Auckland, the previous day. Several passengers had tales to tell of what had gone on aboard the RMS *Marama*. In short, two members of the Australian party had disgraced themselves with drunken and loud behaviour. The various witnesses agreed that this was not in itself so terrible but the fact that they were national representatives made the episodes worthy of criticism. These same witnesses defended, to a man, the team captain while admitting his demeanour was clearly that of someone who had lost control.

> 'My sympathies in the matter are chiefly with Syd Gregory....Though he said nothing about it, I think he must have felt the action of the players keenly, for on several occasions when they were betraying their lack of good manners at the dinner table he rose and left the saloon before finishing his meal.'

The intrepid *Sun* reporter was quick to buttonhole Gregory but he

> 'declined....to admit that any members of the eleven had been guilty of such misconduct. When specific instances were related to him he refused to discuss them. "You may be sure" he said evasively, "that nothing of the kind occurred during the English tour. If it had the offenders would have been sent back home.'"

Time was to show that Gregory was lying. His motives may have been fine but when he was caught in a position that left him nowhere to turn, he chose to attempt concealment. The *Sun* tried to elicit a fuller response from his team-mates. They were 'likewise loath to talk on the subject' until eventually a 'damaging statement' was forthcoming from one (unnamed) player:

> 'There has been a little trouble in the team but only since we started on the American tour, and then only in respect to two of the players. These fellows certainly deserve to be censured. Syd Gregory, who is one of the finest fellows that ever played the game, has done his best, both by example and by personal suasion, to keep the men in check, but they got beyond all control, and have of late completely defied his authority. Syd is too good a fellow, however, to "squeal". He says nothing but he feels a lot and I believe he is deeply hurt by the matter. Naturally the rest of the team all resent such conduct, and feel very sensitive about it, for if only one man plays up the honor of the whole team is involved.'

The story took on a much more legitimate and serious form 10 days later as soon as it became known that team-manager George Crouch would submit a report to the Board of Control at its annual meeting of 6 December which seemed to bear testimony to the rumours that had been flying around. The main business of the evening was expected to be the financial accounts of the series in England and these revealed a serious, if expected, deficit. Expenses of £4,567 did not tally well with an income of £7,367. With payments to players and manager of some £4,400 the Board was facing a £1,600 shortfall.

Further discussion followed on the inadvisability of a further Triangular experiment and the desire to adopt the programme of tours for the next five years that had been proposed in London in July. The election of a chairman for the next 12 months was a straightforward victory for Ernie Bean but it was Crouch's report which dwarfed all that had preceded it. In England, the *Daily Mail* had already been tipped the wink by cable, its report appearing on the same day as the meeting, having been telegraphed from Sydney on 4 December, i.e. two days earlier:

'The Australian Cricketers Manager's Remarkable Accusations

> Mr Crouch....reports to the Board of Control that the conduct of certain unnamed members of the team was so disgustingly bad in England that the side as a whole was socially ostracised and even the non-offenders recognised the justice of this treatment.

He recommends in the interests of Australia's good name that the selectors of future teams be instructed to consider other matters besides merely playing ability. The board will receive this report at the meeting in Melbourne on Saturday, when the chairman, Mr McElhone, in order that the whole team shall not be under a cloud, intends to demand the names of offenders, and to propose an inquiry into the matter.'

If this were not enough of a scandal, readers might have been interested to know who on earth had leaked such sensitive information, and even how the Board would respond, fully two days before the meeting actually took place. The fact that the Board's response was so confidently predicted is perhaps an indication of the source. The *Daily Mail's* own comment on the actual day of the AGM in Sydney expressed genuine surprise at the accusations:

> 'This report of Mr Crouch will come as bombshell to the public in England. It is true that the majority of the Australian team on the tour over here last season were not great "diners-out" nor, indeed, in the past have they been "society lions" but they attended the banquets given by the MCC and Surrey County CC and certain members of the team were freely entertained.
> There were no complaints heard as to the behaviour of the team and no hint of ostracism, though doubtless the knowledge that most of the members of the team preferred dining in their own quarters led to fewer invitations than usual being offered.'

Once the Board meeting had actually taken place, the Australian press took up the story. The *Age* described Crouch's report as being of 'a very voluminous nature' before analysing its main points. Finances were, as ever, a major issue. He defended the increased hotel costs and the decision to insist on a 'shilling gate' in some county fixtures, pressing for a hard-and-fast rule to be adopted in future. The difficulty encountered with this charge in the first game against Lancashire was largely because the games against Derbyshire and Yorkshire had been played before a 'sixpenny gate'. Crouch was also concerned about the fitness of some of the men under his charge and suggested that all players should be medically examined before departure, a procedure that MCC had already adopted. But the crux of the report was the issue of behaviour and the *Age* quoted Crouch directly.

> "The conduct of the team on the whole was good, but from experience gained during the tour I feel it is absolutely necessary in the interests of Australian cricket to say that it is my firm opinion that in the selection of future teams to visit England or South Africa qualifications of a candidate other than individual cricket ability should be weighed. There were members of the team with whom it was difficult to work, and an element of this nature is detrimental to the whole side. Further I would remind you that the members of the Australian Eleven come prominently before the public eye while they are in England, and from a national point of view it is desirable that you shall send men who realise the responsibilities of their position and be a credit to their country."

In reply, the Board agreed to adopt the suggestion of a medical examination and then appointed a five man sub-committee to enquire into the conduct of the players. Crouch was asked to submit a more detailed supplementary report and by the time this news reached the general public the word was that his 'complaints against certain members are said to be definite and....will be substantiated by statutory declarations'.

Syd Gregory was now in great demand as the man most likely to know where the bodies were buried but he wisely declined to comment on the report. He did, however, have plenty of advice to the men looking into that very document. He advocated that any enquiry should be held in public and hoped that 'the fullest light would be thrown upon the whole situation'. He then went a step further:

> 'If the board does not see its way clear to hold the meeting as I have indicated, I will then be prepared to make a full statement on my own account, as captain of the team.'

These were the words of a man who had had a bellyful and wanted everybody to know what he knew thereby ensuring that the culprits would be suitably punished. Not only that, he was warning the Board that he would not partake in any cover-up. His earlier cautious statements were now well and truly forgotten. The *Bulletin* had, of course, its own animal-orientated style in dealing with the growing scandal:

> 'Most of them were gentlemen; but as a very small proportion were hooligans at heart, the whole team has to suffer in reputation for the doings of the scallywags. A sub-committee has been appointed by the Board to inquire into the matter and deal it out to the hogs who put both feet in the trough and squealed while eating.'

The *Daily Mail* had been given to believe that the report chiefly concerned just two players while the *Pall Mall Gazette* stated that English cricketers were surprised at a display of ill-temper on the field by one player which actually upset his captain more than anyone else. This was presumably a reference to Bill Whitty losing his temper with the wet ball and slippery run-ups at Bradford and was always likely to be something of a red herring. Quite simply, the newspapers were casting around for answers and were largely forced to admit that they had little idea what the hullabaloo was all about. The same paper went on to freely admit 'we certainly never heard of the ostracism of any of the players'.

But the flood gates were now open and the details pouring through made pretty ugly reading. The *Daily Chronicle* fanned the flames by publishing an authoritative letter on 7 December from 'an ex-state captain' who had clearly been given information by one of the players present:

> 'Englishmen who came in contact with the team during its recent tour will not have experienced that much difficulty in discovering that all was not well with it. The fact was that practically from the time it reached this country it was divided into two almost openly hostile camps. And the trouble naturally increased as time went on....it is a fact that the acceptance of certain limited invitations given in all courtesy and kindness by English gentlemen was one of the leading means of fomenting the internal ill-feeling. The result was that much of the "social ostracism" was

self-inflicted, for towards the end of the tour it became almost a habit of various members of the side to decline all invitations in which the whole team as a body was not included.

But one can only regret that is has been thought necessary to give publicity to what should at the worst have been a confidential report to the board and it will be interesting to ascertain in what manner it came to be given to the Press. While in England the team had periodical meetings to discuss the business of the tour, and at one of the last of these, one of the members, whose conscience was not quite clear on the subject, referred to it and suggested that an undertaking should be given that the trouble should be hushed up as far as Australia was concerned.'

It was curious that the *Daily Mail* and *Daily Chronicle* in England should have been so fortunate with their sources of information. 'Hushing up' in Australia did not, apparently, include talking to someone who would cable stories back to London. But then someone broke ranks in an already faltering line. It was as if the question on everyone's lips was: 'What did they actually do that was so terrible?' On 9 December the *Sun* answered that question in detail so precise that it can, again, only have come directly from one of the players on the tour though this time there was neither reticence nor evasion. The newspaper was cautious not to commit itself to claiming the six incidents it cited were in Crouch's report, but one thing it was sure of was that these events had actually taken place. Evidently they had it first-hand.

'....in a public dining-room, a player was asked by a waitress what his next dish would be. His answer, given so loudly that it could be heard in the contiguous street, was of so disgusting a character that he was promptly ejected. He was wearing the colors of the team, and it soon became known by other diners that he was an Australian cricketer.'

'On another occasion it is alleged that one of the players insulted one of the housemaids in one of the hotels in which the team was staying, and that on a complaint being made the manager stated that he would not allow any future Australian team to put up there.'

'The doings of some of the players on the steamer trip from Ireland will also be investigated. On that occasion the master of the ship suspended the sale of liquor.'

'Certain proceedings at Cardiff, Wales, where there was no play on the opening day because of rain, will also form the subject of inquiry.'

So far so bad, but it got considerably more serious as far as polite society and the game of cricket were concerned.

'One of the most serious relates to a Victorian member of the team. A dinner was given by Ranjitsinhji, and the Australians were present. The host, during the inevitable speechmaking, made reference to CB Fry, and followed conventional lines when he expressed the view that he of all batsmen was more likely to make runs than any other player. The Victorian, in loud voice, then gave his opinion of Fry. It is unfit for publication.'

'Early in the tour they split up into distinct groups and it is stated that some of the bowlers had no hope of securing a wicket by means of a catch when the ball went to certain players who were not friendly disposed towards them. "Lolly" catches, after much juggling, were invariably dropped.'

The charge of deliberately dropping catches when representing one's country is a fairly stiff one and, even given Edwardian morality and codes of conduct, it is surprising that this was not the most damning indictment. It's hard not to cast back over the tour and think of occasions when an inordinate number of easy chances were dropped in an unimportant game or how often Bill Whitty was involved as both culprit and sufferer.

Then, on the next day in the *Adelaide Advertiser*, Edgar Mayne stepped in with some blindingly stupidly-timed words of his own, attacking the quality of umpiring in England. He described the standard as 'awful' and, while never going so far as to make an accusation of cheating, he gave a number of examples where the English players had been favourably treated. The Bardsley run-out in the final Test was the first object of his ire as he claimed that the batsman was in the process of turning and looking for possible overthrows when the ball hit the stumps, causing tears of vexation. In the same Test, Fry was accused of calling out to the umpire that he had trodden on his wicket in the act of running and was therefore given not out. On another occasion, in Ireland, an umpire, who had earlier given Hobbs not out when plumb, joined in the applause for his 2,000[th] run saying "Good old Jack". Mayne's final broadside was perhaps the most damning:

'I don't suggest that they were purposely unfair, but they were all keen on being selected for future teams.'

He did considerably more than 'suggest' in this one utterance. Perhaps the timing wasn't remotely foolish after all. Was this a conscious attempt from an intelligent man to deflect interest away from the tawdry tales of life on tour and engage some good old-fashioned anti-English feeling?

With the Australian Board sub-committee now engaged in 'collecting information' pertaining to its investigation and with Christmas approaching, it was announced that the enquiry would not be held in public but that the findings would be published should it be deemed necessary. It was also pointed out that the Board itself had no power to punish any miscreants except by 'instructions to selectors' although it could make recommendations to the association responsible for any player concerned. Meanwhile the *Bulletin* treated its readers to a colourful summary of the current rumours:

'There are lurid stories floating around regarding the goings-on of a section of the Australian XI. The team was divided into two lots, and between them was a great gulf, that was never bridged even when they were travelling together. According to report, one section consisted of the men who knew how to conduct themselves; the other of hogs, who put both feet in the trough – hoodlums who were thrown out of hotels and cafes for using bullocky language to waitresses; who requested total strangers to pass the crimson bread; and who spoke of the other portion of the team as the vermilion ***** elite. Whether this dissension had any bad effect on the playing is hard to say, but it is a moral certainty that it did it no good.'

Felix, in the *Australasian*, dealt with the same issues in more sober tones:

'When you hear one member of a team referring to another as belonging to the "toff" brigade it does not need any profound reasoning powers to infer that the team are not likely to be a band of brothers. As a fact they were distinctly other than so....From what I can gather, the use of foul and filthy expressions form a major part of the indictment. As to a member being called a "cheat" by another member, and reported for it, I have heard that word used, with copious adjectival embellishments, concerning the decisions given by English umpires....That is not so, unfortunately, in the case of filthy language on the present tour. It seems to have been used in banquet halls and on board ship in the presence of women.'

As if this weren't enough, there was still 'rancour' and 'smouldering fires' that needed attention in Victorian cricket circles as Warwick Armstrong was deposed from the state captaincy in favour of Bill Carkeek who was, of course, high on the list of suspected miscreants from the English trip. When Armstrong made it clear he would not play under him, JA Seitz of East Melbourne was elected in a vote of distinctly political and diplomatic nature.

The year of 1912 in Australian cricketing circles was ending as it had begun. Nothing had really been solved in the old dispute and now there were new scandals to reckon with.

In South Africa there was plenty to consider if their national side was ever to become the equals of its big brothers but at least it was domestic cricket, not in-fighting and blood-letting, that was making the headlines.

In England the cricketing world was largely at peace with itself but outside that cosy world the mood was considerably less serene and the challenges that were to be faced were considerably more serious.

changing balance of power in South African domestic cricket had been re-confirmed. Herby Taylor hit an unbeaten 250 (a new Currie Cup record) in a crushing defeat of Transvaal.

At the end of the season, in March 1913, the South African Cricket Association met to consider the events of the previous year, the way forward and also to literally count the cost of failure. The secretary commented on 'the complete inability of the South African team to perform up to expectations' before moving on to individual players. Pegler, Taylor and Ward were 'the only members of the team to enhance their reputations' although a modicum of praise was offered to Nourse and Hartigan. Faulkner's performance was 'disappointing for a player of such outstanding ability' while Stricker, Beaumont and Carter met 'with some success'. As for the veterans:

> 'Mitchell, Tancred, White, Snooke and Schwarz could [not] find their old form, and the failure of such men was the primary cause of the disastrous record of the team in the Triangular contest.'

Manager George Allsop's report was presented to the Association in which he quoted the words of a 'well-known England cricketer', quite possibly Pelham Warner:

> 'If they proved themselves by far the weakest team in the Triangular Tournament, the South Africans have earned great fame for their sportsmanlike conduct. From first to last, from Captain and Vice-Captain to the last-joined recruit, they have played the game in a delightful spirit, and this will be remembered long after their defeats have been forgotten. It has been a pleasure to meet them and to play against them, for they were a charming lot of men.'

Allsop's main criticism concerned the amount of matches and the need for gaps in the programme to allow the players to conserve their strength over the duration of the tour. He recommended removing at least four of the fixtures on the next tour and taking greater care over the arrangements 'in order to eliminate as far as possible unnecessarily long railway journeys'. Attention was then given to the tour accounts and they made miserable reading. The receipts of £4,004 for the 37 games were particularly depressing when compared to the £6,376 earned in 31 games by the 1907 touring team. Fortunately, there was an impressive list of guarantors of the tour who were now about to foot the bill. At the top was Sir Abe Bailey who would hardly have to dig deep for his portion, amounting to £750, and in truth the amounts were minor for the men who had signed on the dotted line 12 months earlier. Of greater concern was the image of a national side being bankrolled by Randlords and the consequent feeling that South African cricket had just stepped backwards.

The following South African summer saw the arrival of an MCC team under the leadership of the ever keen and willing Johnny Douglas. While not the absolute strongest possible team it was nevertheless still a pretty formidable combination: the batting was led by Hobbs, Rhodes and Mead followed by all-rounders Douglas, Hearne and Woolley. The bowling would be shared by Relf, Booth, the all-rounders and SF Barnes. As it turned out, the latter was quite able to do the job alone. Young

THE SOUTH AFRICAN CRICKET ASSOCIATION.

THE SOUTH AFRICAN CRICKET TEAM IN ENGLAND, 1912.
REVENUE AND EXPENDITURE STATEMENT OF THE TOUR.

EXPENDITURE.		REVENUE.	
To Steamship Fares	£837 19 2	By Gate Receipts	...£4,004 4 3
,, Railway Fares	496 8 11	,, Balance being loss	.. 2,467 8 11
,, Hotel Expenses	1,272 16 1		
,, Allowance to Players and Salary of Mananger	2,811 10 0		
,, Baggage—handling of	94 1 0		
,, Baggage Man's Wages	54 0 0		
,, Washing	107 11 10		
,, Tips	263 0 0		
,, Medical Expenses	115 15 11		
,, Petty Expenses	122 15 5		
,, Colours, etc.	87 4 0		
,, Stationery and Printing	38 19 3		
,, Entertainment	56 9 1		
,, S. J. Snooke...	9 10 0		
,, A. D. Nourse	3 12 6		
,, Cost of Arranging Fixtures	100 0 0		
	£6,471 13 2		£6,471 13 2

G. ALLSOP, Manager.

Certified correct,
C. L. ANDERSSON & CO.,} Incorporated Accountants. } Auditors.
ERNST DANCKWERTS,}

Johannesburg, 21st April, 1913.

SACA accounts for the tour of England 1912 – roughly one-third of the tour expenditure was met by the guarantors, led by Sir Abe Bailey.

Herby Taylor had now taken on the leadership of the national team at the age of just 24 and the responsibility brought new depth to his batting just as it had the previous year at Durban. For home supporters the only real hope was that the English players would fail to adapt to the matting wickets but this was clutching at straws to say the least. Hobbs, Mead, Woolley and Barnes, amongst others, had all played before in Africa. Furthermore, the South African team now had none of the googly bowlers that had caused the tourists endless trouble in 1905-06 and 1909-10.

There were no great surprises. Taylor, Nourse, Hartigan, Ward and Cox from the 1912 team appeared in the first Test which was lost by an innings. They were joined by Beaumont and Tancred for the second which was lost by the same margin. By this time Syd Barnes already had 27 wickets! The third game went the same way and in the fourth Carter returned to the team as Hartigan and Beaumont dropped out. Thanks largely to Taylor's batting a draw was salvaged and Barnes now had 49 wickets in four games. The fifth was won again by England and the relative merits of the two sides had been savagely exposed. The achievement of Herby Taylor in scoring 508 runs in such a prolonged rout and against possibly the finest bowler in history on a surface made-to-measure, was one that quite rightly placed him into the list of great batsmen to represent South Africa, following Faulkner and being, in turn, followed by men such as Dudley Nourse and Barry Richards. But Taylor was only one man and the national side as a whole had slipped back to the level at which it had been 10 years previously. Those who had lifted them to near parity with Australia and England, Vogler, Schwarz, Faulkner, Kotze, Sinclair and Sherwell were now finished, their replacements were not of the same calibre. For two South African debutants in the final game, Reginald Hands and Bill Lundie, and MCC's Major Booth there would be no more Test cricket as they were to lose their lives in France.

The MCC tourists in South Africa 1913-14 – Back: AE Relf, H Strudwick, ID Difford (manager), MW Booth, CP Mead, SF Barnes, FE Woolley; middle: JB Hobbs, MC Bird, JWHT Douglas (captain), Hon. LH Tennyson, W Rhodes; front: EJ Smith, JW Hearne.

Critics cast around for causes and there were plenty to be found. The size of the cricketing population was number one followed by the matting wickets, lack of professionals and over-reliance on googly bowling. Herby Taylor was inclined to blame batting shortcomings on the inability to play on the back-foot, something that didn't come naturally on a matting surface but, as Taylor himself proved, could successfully be employed on any surface. As to googly bowling, the problem was not the style but the standard. Hordern had shown that a good wrist-spinner could still excel in Tests and after the War Mailey, Grimmett and Freeman would continue the tradition. Artificial wickets were another matter. Only the very greatest of early South African batsman had been able to translate their home form into runs on tour. This problem would continue well into the 1930s by which time turf wickets had finally arrived. As if these factors were not enough, there was the problem of retaining the players that had proved themselves. Faulkner had settled in England, Vogler and Sherwell were prematurely lost to the game and there was no sign that Sid Pegler, the great discovery of 1912, would play international cricket again.

When the MCC side left for home in March 1914 the situation in the Cape was bleak and the visit of Australia eight months later was hardly being anticipated with relish. But within six months the world was at war. Writing in *The History of South African Cricket* in 1915, Free Lance was certain of the way forward:

> 'South Africa has struck a bad patch. But South Africa will come again if those who govern her cricket steadfastly keep in front of them the International ideal. It led to her success in the past, and it will lead her to victory in the future. Its pursuit must be followed for all time if South Africa is to be a world-factor in cricket. It is the only way.'

In 1915 nobody could have conceived of the self-imposed barriers to this 'pursuit' that would isolate the greatest of all South African teams at their very peak some 60 years later.

Australia

The new year began quietly with attention, for once, focussing on events on the field though even there everything seemed slightly tainted by the controversies of the previous 18 months. Trumper was in wonderful form and Clem Hill belied his veteran status with a series of fine innings for both club and state as he led South Australia to the Sheffield Shield title. Of the Big Six, only Tibby Cotter seemed to be past his best; the other five were busy showing the Australian public just what the 1912 tourists had been missing.

Two major events were now looming, one an occasion for celebration and the other the complete opposite. On the positive side, a benefit match for Victor Trumper, between New South Wales and the Rest, was fixed for early February at the SCG. Considerably less salubrious was the imminent meeting of the Board's sub-committee which was due to hold its enquiry as soon as it could collect statements from all the relevant sources. The row that Edgar Mayne had provoked on the subject of English umpiring was also showing no sign of abating. Interviewed in the *Australasian* in mid-January, he wasn't inclined to retract his earlier accusations:

> 'Umpiring in England in test and county matches has been inefficient for several seasons. One has only to hear statements of such men as Joe Darling, Victor Trumper and Frank Iredale to know what goes on. I saw enough during the last tour to convince me that a radical change is absolutely necessary. I think the decisions given are due to incompetency, but good judges in England say that they are due to the method by which the umpires are selected….We admit that we were beaten by a stronger team on paper, but we merely point out how we were handicapped by wretched decisions by umpires.'

Mayne was not alone in wanting the Australian system (of the captains agreeing from a list) to be adopted in other countries but his methods were singularly undiplomatic. It had, meanwhile, become apparent that George Crouch's report to the Board did not contain any criticism of the umpiring in England and a week later Syd Gregory felt it necessary to say his piece.

> 'Mistakes were made no doubt but they were no worse than cases which occur in first-class cricket in Australia. Bardsley's run out in the last test was very glaring…. but the mistakes were probably genuine ones. Umpires are not infallible, but my experience is that they do not openly make flagrant breaches of the rules….I think English umpires are quite as fair as those in Australia.'

No obvious signs of love lost between Gregory and Mayne. The English press had

'The team sent over by South Africa was not nearly as good as the 1907 side....
players who, in 1907, had made reputations failed badly. After Faulkner's wonderful
success in Australia in 1911, it was a big blow to the side when he could not get into
his stride with the bat....Nourse headed the batting averages in all matches but was
not the success in the Tests we expected. White, Tancred, Snooke and Llewellyn,
who were expected to make some of the runs, never seemed to strike form. Mr
Frank Mitchell was a good captain but no run-getter. Of the new comers to English
cricket Pegler, Ward (and perhaps I may be permitted to include myself) did well.'

Pelham Warner had little new light to throw on proceedings although he did
question Fry's judgement on two counts. Why did he not use Woolley on a wet Lord's
wicket against Australia and why did Johnny Douglas not feature in the England
team until the final Test?

And then there was *Life Worth Living*, the thoughts and memories of CB Fry,
published in 1939. How to tackle his account of 1912? Fry was not one to be
restricted by modesty and neither was he overly concerned with allowing facts to
cramp a good story but, as captain and chief selector of England, he was at the
heart of things and for this reason his account is most revealing. His version of the
selection process must count as highly dubious: the three-man committee met once
in May, 'chose a definite team with definite substitutes if required for the whole series
of six matches, and we never met again'. This may have been how Fry liked to imagine
business being done but not only was it impractical it was also incompetent. Was
there no consideration of county form and how did he account for the treatment of
Bill Hitch, who was selected twice and delivered not one ball? Like all other writers
Fry commented on the ghastly weather but his opinion on the various merits of his
opponents was less predictable.

'We beat South Africa in all three Test Matches but because of their difficult bowling
I myself feared their eleven more than I feared the Australians. The South Africans
did not realise how strong a batting side they were, and they did not do themselves
justice either against England or against Australia.'

Fry did indeed struggle against Pegler but his estimation of the relative strengths
of the two teams is unusual and the South Africans were, quite categorically, not
a strong batting side. In a similar vein he recollected that the Australians had three
dangerous batsmen on a wet wicket: Macartney, Gregory and Smith. The latter was,
of all the Australian batsmen, most at sea on wet wickets and Gregory was little
better. Fry neglected to mention Bardsley who was quite a different matter. Most
contemporaries that had seen him on two continents agreed that he was at his most
impressive on soft English wickets.

One of Fry's oddest tactics had been the extended use of Jack Hobbs as a bowler
in the second innings of the Lord's Test against South Africa. His reasoning was that
he thought he could make a Test bowler of Hobbs which seems fairly unlikely in one
morning although no more unlikely than the angle taken by Tiger Smith that Hobbs
was put on to bowl 'seam up' to extend the game. Either way it was a dangerous ploy
because the end of the game was closely followed by a colossal storm which flooded

Claude Jennings 1884-1950

Another who was finished with first-class cricket after 1912, aged just 28. This was a severe loss to Queensland. A successful career in the civil service followed and in 1938 he was appointed a delegate to the Board of Control. Johnnie Moyes' summary was both brief and pertinent: 'A neat batsman, lacking real power, sound but not Test class'.

60, 2453 @ 25.55

Claude Carter 1881-1952

On returning from the 1912 tour he showed fine domestic form and played in two of the Tests against England in 1913-14, taking nine wickets. After the War he continued to lead the Natal attack, took 15 wickets against the visiting Australians in 1921 and was selected to return to England under Herby Taylor in 1924 in what was to be his last season. Soon afterwards he was offered a professional position in Cornwall where he stayed until the late 1930s, playing for the county and Penzance CC.

107, 1333 @ 11.68, 366 @ 18.56

Ernie Hayes 1876-1953

After serving in the Sportsman's Battalion of the Royal Fusiliers, including on the Somme, he received an MBE before returning to Surrey as an amateur only to find that long-standing hand injuries prevented him from finding his best form. He succeeded Schofield Haigh at Winchester College before taking a coaching post at Leicester where he stayed for five years during which time he returned to the first-class game, aged 50, for seven matches in 1926 including being run out for 99 against Larwood's Nottinghamshire. He was then invited back to The Oval where he worked for five years before taking over a pub in West Norwood. He may still be credited as the first batsman to 'switch-hit', pulling the ball past a bemused point fielder after scoring a century in a county match.

560, 27318 @ 32.21, 515 @ 26.70

Warren Bardsley 1882-1954

Continued as a lynchpin of the Australian side until well into his forties thus, with Macartney, neatly bridging the years between Trumper and Bradman. He was not quite the batsman that he had been after the War but remained a prize victim for English bowlers and, after a run of 17 Tests without a century he carried his bat at Lord's in 1926 for a remarkable six-hour 193 to ensure Australia would avoid defeat. This at the age of 44 and against Tate, Root, Kilner and Larwood. On this same tour he twice captained his country in the absence of Collins and also received a fearsome blow on the head from Ted McDonald which left him partially deaf. His enthusiasm and pessimism remained equally undimmed, but 'Warren made pessimism pay'. It was somehow fitting that he should take up playing the bassoon of all instruments. His response to seeing the covers brought on at the SCG after his retirement was to turn to Charlie Macartney and say "Charlie, we were born a generation too soon". According to Johnnie Moyes he was a fine but not great batsman because he never assumed complete mastery – 'he commanded the respect but never the fear of the bowlers'. Was awarded a shared NSWCA testimonial with Jack Gregory in 1937, married seven years later and remained a keen gardener and surfer well into his retirement.

250, 17025 @ 49.92

Gerald Hartigan 1884-1955

He finally recovered from the injury sustained in Ireland and regained his place in the national side for the visit of Douglas' team in 1913, managing little in three Tests. He continued to play for Border until 1927 but was never capped again and sadly failed to live up to the promise of his youth.

37, 1535 @ 29.51, 92 @ 21.08

Gilbert Jessop 1874-1955

All the talk of his imminent retirement in 1912 proved wide of the mark and he continued until the outbreak of war when he immediately joined up, as a captain in the Manchester Regiment, using his popularity to encourage others to do the same. The prognosis was not good when he was invalided out with a damaged heart in 1916 after over-exposure to steam treatment for lumbago, but he again routed the opposition by surviving into his 80th year. The Croucher's legend remains, mainly for his outrageous hitting but also for his remarkable fielding. Tiger Smith recalled the strength of his returns lifting him off his feet and spinning him around – Smith only came into the game when Jessop was in his mid-thirties.

493, 26698 @ 32.63, 873 @ 22.79

Roy Minnett 1888-1955

Such had been his reputation leading up to the Triangular Tournament, it was hoped that his play would flourish back on hard Australian wickets. It wasn't to be as he gradually wound his career down in order to devote more time to his duties as a doctor. He did, however, sign off with 8-50 against Victoria in December 1914. He turned down the pre-war South African tour and then used his medical skills in the forces – a genuine case of 'what might have been?' There was no doubt that he was 'a delightful comrade and opponent'.

54, 2142 @ 28.94, 86 @ 25.02

Charles Fry 1872-1956

Lack of money and his devotion to the training ship *Mercury* had always made cricket something of a luxury and his career petered out after the partial triumph of 1912, although his reputation as one of the cricket's greatest theoreticians and practitioners remains. Following the War he remained a keen observer of, and writer on, the game and famously penned a speech for his old friend Ranji to deliver at the League of Nations before declining the throne of Albania, dependent as it was on a £10,000 annual income to bolster the country's exchequer.

394, 30886 @ 50.22, 166 @ 29.34

Harry Dean 1884-1957

His Test career did not continue after 1912, however the following year he had the satisfaction of taking 17-91 in a roses match at Aigburth that had been specially arranged to coincide with the visit of King George V to Liverpool. After leaving Lancashire he continued to play for Cheshire as his red hair turned grey, before taking up a coaching position at Rossall School.

267, 2559 @ 10.31, 1301 @ 18.14

Rolland Beaumont 1884-1958

Was only seen intermittently on the field after 1912, including his one first-class century in 1913, but did make two Test appearances against England in 1913-14 albeit without any success. His career finished when war broke out. He is commemorated by the Beaumont Pavilion at Hilton College in Kwazulu Natal.

32, 1086 @ 25.25

Frank Foster 1889-1958

Continued in fine form for Warwickshire until the outbreak of war, culminating in a remarkable triple-century at Dudley in just 260 minutes. Unfortunately he was unable to accept an invitation to tour South Africa under Douglas and in 1915 a motor-cycle accident effectively ended both his military and cricket careers. It's doubtful that any other five-year involvement in the game had such impact both at home and abroad. However, this was not enough to convince Warwickshire to pay him £1,000 per annum as 'Team Manager'. Douglas Jardine sought his advice on field-placing for a leg-theory attack prior to the 1932 trip to Australia but his later life was peppered with personal difficulties involving court appearances and mental instability. Few finer compliments have been paid than that of Herby Taylor: 'Barnes did not worry me as much as Foster….he was downright unpleasant to bat against'. His quick arm sounds reminiscent of Wasim Akram, and Tiger Smith put his pace above fellow left-armers Garry Sobers and Alan Davidson.

159, 6548 @ 26.61, 717 @ 20.75

Charlie Macartney 1886-1958

Brilliant as he was in 1912, this was just a foretaste of what was to come after he came through the War unscathed. In 17 Tests he hit six centuries including three in a row in his last series against England and he averaged well over 50 on tours in 1921 and 1926. It wasn't just the weight of runs but also the manner of scoring which made him one of the finest batsmen in Australian history. His triple-century against Notts. in 1921, scored in just four hours, remains one of the most remarkable feats of sustained hitting in the history of the game. The Triangular Tournament was really the turning point in his career when he moved from orthodoxy to genius. Johnnie Moyes spoke of his cheekiness and impertinence: 'His stroke-play often left me gasping and his audacity sent shivers down my spine'. What a T20 player he would have been!

249, 15019 @ 45.78, 419 @ 20.95

Louis Stricker 1884-1960
Dropped out of first-class cricket after the 1912 series, aged only 28. His younger brother played three times for Transvaal but died fighting in East Africa in 1917.
60, 2107 @ 22.90

Reggie Spooner 1880-1961
Business continued to prevent him giving his full attention to the game as he missed tours both just before and after the War (in which he was wounded in 1914). His career started to wind down in the early 1920s leaving him with just one Test century, against the South Africans at Lord's. He finally retired in 1923 but kept an active interest in the game and was president of Lancashire CCC for two years just after the Second World War. Like many other genuine amateurs of his generation there is no knowing what he might have achieved but the certainty remains of what Neville Cardus termed 'the sheerest poetry of cricket'.
237, 13681 @ 36.28

Edgar Mayne 1882-1961
On returning to Australia he became involved in controversy with an attack on English umpires and then again when leading an unsanctioned tour of America. After the War he switched to Victoria, touring England and South Africa under Warwick Armstrong but was, again, a peripheral figure and played Tests only at the end of a long trip in Cape Town and Johannesburg. In 1923 he and Bill Ponsford set a state opening-partnership record of 456. He then made history as one of the first radio commentators, covering the two Tests played at Melbourne by Gilligan's England side, for 3AR radio. 'He lived for cricket, and made a big success of it.'
141, 7624 @ 32.72

Dave Smith 1884-1963
His only cricketing exploit after 1912 was failing to appear to give evidence at the Board disciplinary enquiry, pleading ill health and simultaneously incriminating himself in most eyes. Hardly surprising that he never played first-class cricket again. Moyes' verdict was that 'he could bat capably enough without being top class'.
46, 1764 @ 23.83

Jack Hobbs 1882-1963
When he finally retired in 1934 he had amassed more runs than any man will ever score in first-class cricket, at an average of over 50. This despite suffering from migraines and often giving away his wicket when he thought he had done enough in scoring a century, something he achieved 197 times. His batting after the War was slightly less thrilling than it had been before though even in his mid-forties his skill was undiminished (11,000 runs in four seasons) and the last of his Test centuries came at Melbourne in 1929. It was typical that his last first-class century should come in a testimonial match (for George Duckworth) on a bitterly cold day. His knighthood, awarded in 1953, reflected not only his achievements but the manner of their attainment. CB Fry summarised his art perfectly: 'He sailed through sunshine and storm on a perfectly even keel with an

alert pair of aristocratic hands on the helm of the game'.
834, 61760 @ 50.70, 108 @ 25.03

Pelham Warner 1873-1963

Although his Test career finished with the Triangular Tournament, his career in cricket most certainly did not. After two bouts of serious illness during the War, he returned to the game to lead Middlesex to an unlikely and dramatic Championship victory in 1920. He then retired and founded the *Cricketer* magazine as well as writing numerous books and articles and becoming an early pioneer of live radio commentary. His work as an administrator reached its peak as manager of the infamous bodyline touring side and he was president of MCC in 1950 and then the first ever life vice-president in 1961. He was the fourth man knighted for his services to cricket but the first who had played the game at the highest level.
521, 29028 @ 36.28

Charlie Llewellyn 1876-1964

Although the 1912 series showed that he was not the all-rounder of old, his career still had plenty of life left in it. He returned to Accrington in 1913 and hit a Lancashire League record 188 against Bacup that stood until the year before the Second World War when Learie Constantine surpassed it. He continued to play professionally in the Bolton and Bradford leagues until well into his fifties. Controversy has continued to dog his wonderful career but it is now generally agreed that, in spite of his daughter's denials, he was the first coloured cricketer to represent South Africa.
267, 11425 @ 26.75, 1013 @ 23.41

Bill Hitch 1886-1965

Prospered after his personal debacle in the 1912 series and the following season was his most successful for Surrey. His big hitting became well renowned and even after the War, in which he served with Hayes, Sandham and Hendren in the Sportsman's Battalion, he was considered good enough (or maybe there were no alternatives) to tour Australia, though with predictably little success. After leaving Surrey in 1925 he played as professional for Todmorden before settling and coaching in Glamorgan.
350, 7643 @ 17.81, 1387 @ 21.56

Jack Hearne 1891-1965

Having played for England 10 times before he was 22 it is surprising that his international career was not a great one. He toured Australia twice but never re-captured his form of 1911-12, his Test career often being interrupted by a proneness to hand injuries. His Middlesex record was quite different and he continued at Lord's until 1936 whereupon he was offered a coaching position and thereafter a life-membership of MCC.
647, 37252 @ 40.98, 1839 @ 24.42

Sibley Snooke 1881-1966

Despite the disappointments of the 1912 tour, his career was far from over even though he missed the MCC series in 1913-14. After the War he was a Currie Cup regular for Transvaal for many years but the biggest surprise came when he was recalled to the national side in 1923 at Durban where he took five English wickets for 58 in 35 overs. Later still he managed the successful 1935 tour of England.

124, 4821 @ 25.91, 120 @ 25.14

Syd Barnes 1873-1967

The best bowler ever? When Richie Benaud selected his 'greatest XI' it included just two players he had not seen play: Hobbs and Barnes. After mauling South Africa just before the outbreak of war he quietly returned to minor county and club cricket, continuing to mow batsmen down until well into his sixties. He made few excursions into the first-class game; in 1929 (aged 56) he played twice at this level and collected 19-150! In the absence of film footage there will always be questions as to his speed and method. Taylor thought his spin bowling about the same speed as Bill O'Reilly but he bowled cutters as fast as Eddie Barlow. Fry put his average pace above that of Maurice Tate but with huge variations, a verdict which is open to any amount of interpretation. Moyes concentrates on his away-swinger/cutter although the ball moving back in to the right-hander was also difficult. Ian Peebles emphasised that this 'cut' was illusory because it was in fact medium-pace spin using a classic first-and third-finger grip and not relying on the condition of the ball or a green wicket. With this variety, uniqueness and almost metronomic control it's hard to envisage anything better.

133, 1573 @ 12.78, 719 @ 17.09

Sid Emery 1885-1967

The hope that the eccentric 'Mad Mick' would eventually find a consistent length to match his speed and prodigious spin was never realised and he dropped out of cricket even before war broke out. Monty Noble once told him he would be a great bowler if he could control his googly to which he replied "I'd be a great man if I could control myself". Placing a lighted match on the stumps after an unsuccessful appeal against the light was a measure of his flamboyant humour. He was afflicted by blindness in his final years.

58, 1192 @ 18.33, 183 @ 23.79

Joe Cox 1886-1971

After missing out on all six Triangular Tests he showed good form back on matting wickets and got his international chance in 1913 against England. He was unable to make any great impact in three matches and his career finished shortly after the War. His nephew, Lindsay Tuckett, played nine Tests for South Africa shortly after the Second World War.

42, 357 @ 8.30, 120 @ 22.53

Sid Pegler 1888-1972

After wonderful performances in England it seemed that he was destined to lead the South African attack for many years to come but he soon dropped out of the game and played no part in 1913-14 series. After winning the MC and being badly the square. In the Lord's Test against Australia Fry again adopted an unusual course and was roundly condemned for not using Frank Woolley on a wicket apparently ideally suited to his left-arm spin. Australia faced 119 overs and easily saved a game they couldn't win. Furthermore England's most effective bowler was another left-armer, Wilfred Rhodes, who was generally considered, at this time, less effective than Woolley. Fry's reasoning was that England could not possibly bowl Australia out twice in a day to win the match so why show them a bowler who might just be a trump card on a wet wicket at some point later in the season? Sound thinking in a sense and seemingly vindicated when Woolley took 10-49 in the ninth and deciding Test. On the face of it a masterstroke and it's hard to think of any other explanation for ignoring Woolley at Lord's. Two nagging doubts do, however, occur. Could Charles Fry really have waited 27 years to answer his critics and why did he then give Woolley six overs in the completely dead Test at Old Trafford?

His recollections of the ninth and final Test are the most 'hazy'. According to the England captain, the huge first-day crowd was sitting in the sun at the appointed starting hour, having no idea that the pitch was a 'quagmire' and wondering why there was no sign of play about to begin. Then, 'early in the afternoon', Gregory approached Fry with a mind to toss and make a start. The English captain realised that he had the much stronger team and that only the vagaries of pitch and weather could beat them so he wasn't about to risk Australia batting on an easy mud patch before catching England on 'a drying sticky wicket'. He refused Gregory's invitation 'until the turf was genuinely fit [and] we did not start until late in the afternoon'. Word got around the packed enclosures that Fry had delayed the start and 'I was unanimously booed by our 30,000 supporters'. That was of CB Fry's account.

The reality was quite different save in respect of the reception received by Fry. The pitch was indeed wet at eleven o'clock but a start time of midday was agreed by the captains and officials, the toss being made in front of the pavilion. Fry may have justifiably engineered this delay but the duration was one hour at the most. The game did not start 'late in the afternoon' and the crowd was certainly nowhere near 30,000; most estimates placed it at half that number. Artistic license? Maybe. The passage of time? Doubtful. Self-aggrandisement? Probably. So why the booing? Johnny Douglas was cheered when *he* went to the wicket in a spontaneous display of affection for the man who had won the Ashes the previous winter and had been harshly replaced – by Fry. It was Fry, of course, who had the last laugh. He won the toss, played a masterful innings and led England to Triangular victory, but after the game he would, as has already been noted, acknowledge none of the crowd's plaudits. Now he could reveal his reasons:

> 'But when the crowd gathered around the pavilion and shouted for me I would not go on to the balcony, because I felt that the time for them to cheer was when I was walking out to bat as captain of my side to try to win the match on a foul wicket. Ranji was in the dressing-room and he said to me, "Now Charles, be your noble self." But I said "This is not one of my noble days."

wounded in the War, he became a district commissioner in Nyasaland (now Malawi) and spent his leave in England where he played occasional games before being co-opted onto the 1924 tour and taking 100 wickets. He made one more tour, as manager in 1951, thus completing the unenviable record of participating in the three most disappointing tours of England in South African cricket history.
103, 1677 @ 12.70, 425 @ 19.58

Wilfred Rhodes 1877-1973

The most prolific bowler the game will ever see and yet he was an opening batsman in 1912. After the War the Yorkshire attack was thin following the loss of both Drake and Booth in France and he returned to bowling as if he'd never been away, topping the Championship averages in four out of five seasons. In 1926 his fellow-selectors convinced him to return to the England side in the decisive fifth Test: he scored invaluable runs, took six wickets and England regained the Ashes. Leonard Crawley of Essex likened a comparison of Rhodes and Verity, both of whom he faced, to 'a glass of fizz' against 'a cup of cat's piss'. Rhodes was in his dotage and Verity approaching his prime when Crawley played. In 1930 he went on the first Test tour of the West Indies and at Georgetown, in searing heat, he sent down 91 overs in taking 4-189. His batting wasn't quite so prolific now that he was 53; he only managed 51 runs in the four Tests – for an average of 51!
1110, 39969 @ 30.81, 4204 @ 16.72

Herby Taylor 1889-1973

If 1912 saw the last of most of the South African team, this was certainly not the case with the batsman of whom great things had always been expected. He assumed the captaincy of Natal on his return; such was his success he was the obvious choice to lead his country against England in 1913 and he embarked on an epic series-long tussle with Syd Barnes and enjoyed the presence of his elder brother under his command in two of the Tests. He claimed the secret of his success was a mixture of forward and back-play (rare amongst matting-trained batsmen) and watching the spin from Barnes' fingers. He also adopted the unusual stance of having his bat in the air *a la* Graham Gooch. After being awarded the MC in the War, he picked up where he had left off, captaining, and often carrying, the team before gratefully handing the leadership to Nummy Deane after the 1924 tour of England. Under his captaincy the South Africans won only one of 18 matches but he managed to average almost 50. He continued playing Test cricket until 1932, finishing his domestic career with a century at the age of 45 and retiring as the first great South African batsman. In the words of Johnnie Moyes 'he was orthodox in the best line of orthodoxy'. He later coached schoolboys with great success and lived long enough to add Graeme Pollock to the list of great batsmen he had seen, following Hammond, Bradman, Woolley and Hobbs.
206, 13105 @ 41.86, 22 @ 25.45

Bill Whitty 1886-1974

He never quite regained the speed, swerve and control with which he had tormented the South Africans in 1910-11 although he continued to play first-class cricket until the mid-1920s. After serving in the Light Horse during the War, the emergence of Gregory, McDonald and Mailey meant that he was never seriously considered for Test honours again once the proposed 1914-15 tour of South Africa had been cancelled. He continued in State cricket until the mid-twenties and club cricket until the mid-thirties. A feisty and active octogenarian, he can be remembered for his altercations with an umpire who turned down an appeal for caught behind – his next ball was well wide but he appealed anyway, exclaiming "just thought you might make two mistakes in one day".

119, 1465 @ 11.53, 491 @ 23.40

Frank Woolley 1887-1978
Having played the last 22 Tests before 1914, he then proceeded to play the first 32 after 1918 (August 1909 to August 1926) and was even recalled for one last time in 1934, when in his 47th year, to face Grimmett and O'Reilly. Four years later he retired from the game with an unbeatable record. For a man remembered primarily for his languid strokeplay it was a remarkable feat to take 1,018 catches (his nearest pursuer was WG Grace with a mere 874) and a whole stack of cheap wickets. Equally convincing are the testimonies of those lucky enough to have seen him play; Johnnie Moyes described him as he emerged from the pavilion, 'his bat hung like a toothpick in the hands of a giant'. He later coached at King's School Canterbury for a time and the finest description of his skills came from the pen of JM Barrie, 'Woolley whispered his wishes to the ball and it understood'.

978, 58959 @ 40.77, 2066 @ 19.87

Tiger Smith 1886-1978
On the 1913-14 South African tour he lost his international place to Herbert Strudwick but, although he never regained it, he didn't lose his enthusiasm for the game. He continued with Warwickshire until 1930 and then stood in eight Tests as an umpire during the thirties before returning to Edgbaston as coach, overseeing a Championship victory in 1951 and the early careers of men such as Tom Cartwright and Dennis Amiss.

496, 16997 @ 22.39, 722/156

And so the 1912 Triangular Tournament passed into history and has been largely forgotten. Its palpable failure as either a spectacle or a financially-viable festival sounded its death-knell but its importance in the history of cricket, and beyond, remain. It had been intended as a symbol of the brotherhood of Empire but it sank almost without trace amid a welter of arguments and shadow-boxing which occasionally blossomed into full-scale sabre-rattling. The unremitting bad weather was very unfortunate; the inability of both visiting nations to bring their best teams was disastrous. What Vogler, Trumper, Sherwell and Hordern might have brought to the wet fields and turnstiles is anybody's guess – they would certainly have brightened any summer, even that of 1912. Over-taxing tour schedules and poor leadership also hampered two of the sides as did the inability to decide on a tournament scoring system which further alienated the public.

There were, however, memorable events. Faulkner's century and Matthews' hat-tricks at Old Trafford; the vastly contrasting batting of Bardsley, Kelleway and Macartney and the brilliance of Sid Pegler. England could boast the skill of Hobbs, miniature masterpieces from Spooner, Rhodes, Fry and Woolley and, above all, the menace of the imperious Syd Barnes – at the age of 39 he had reached his peak.

Only two years later the world tumbled into a general conflagration that had been long predicted, even if the scale was grotesque beyond imagination. The fact that the Empire soldiers played a significant part in the war against Germany was in itself a justification of Triangular cricket for the organisers if not the players. The Empire had pulled together in its greatest hour of need.

Afterword - 16 September 1916

The war had already taken a monstrous toll and the names Gallipoli, Tannenburg, the Somme and Verdun had entered a modern lexicon of horror and disaster. The two greatest names in cricket, WG Grace and Victor Trumper, had died the previous year and active players Percy Jeeves, Kenneth Hutchings and Major Booth were just tiny additions to the casualty lists that were now filling pages rather than columns of national newspapers in France, Germany and Britain.

EHD Sewell, author of *Triangular Cricket* back in the days when such things had been of importance, was still busily writing for various publications including the *Graphic*. In September 1916 he turned his attention to 'Bowling & Bombing: Cricket as a Training for Campaigning'.

> 'I have been asked whether cricket is any good as a training for bomb-throwing. Being, unavoidably and unfortunately, no bomb-thrower I cannot write from experience, but I hazard cheerfully the guess that an able cricketer would make a very much better bomb-thrower than a man who is so unfortunate as not to be a cricketer. And, of all cricketers, the regular bowler ought to make as good a bomber as any, except the habitual outfield or coverpoint….it may not matter, except to the bomber, whether a bomb is bowled or thrown up to a distance of thirty yards. If he is wise he will bowl it, as he will feel fewer protests from his arm if he does.
>
> As to the matter of accuracy of aim, to bowling must be awarded the prize in the long run. For a dozen shots it may be that a man throwing would beat himself bowling, and if the target was fifty yards or more away he would surely do better if he threw. But the number of shots come in here, and a bowling action up to fifty yards would last longer than a throwing action….I cannot think of a more likely bomb thrower than W. Brearley, who, whenever he had to send the ball in from the long-field, always *bowled* it in. A bomb propelled by C. J. Kortright in his best days would have damaged a platoon of thick-skinned Huns. From his hand a bomb would become *ipso facto* a super-bomb. The majority of Australians could take on the rest of the Army at bomb-throwing with every probability of success. They are the finest throwers I have seen on the cricket field.
>
> The game of cricket, and its quite priceless teachings, have stood sterner tests in this ghastly and trying war than whether one or other of its disciples can fling a bomb accurately, or whether he can catch such a hurtling missile and return it to the sender. It is the other things taught by cricket which have been done daily wherever Britons are fighting that will endure.'

Bibliography

Contemporary Press

Primary Sources:
Australia: *Sydney Sun, Age, Australasian, Bulletin*
South Africa: *South African News, Rand Daily Mail, Star, Sunday Times*
Great Britain: *Times, Manchester Guardian, Daily Chronicle, Daily Mail, Pall Mall Gazette, Sportsman, Daily Graphic*
New Zealand: paperspast.natlib.govt.nz

General History

Blom P – *The Vertigo Years*
Briggs A – *Victorian Cities*
Dangerfield G – *The Strange Death of Liberal England*
Davenport R & Saunders C – *South Africa: A Modern History*
Ferguson N – *Empire*
Feuchtwanger E – *Democracy and Empire: Britain 1865-1914*
Hattersley R – *The Edwardians*

Judd D – *Empire*
Macintyre S – *Australia*
Rickard J – *Australia, A Cultural History*
Searle G – *A New England?*
Seeley J – *The Expansion of England*
Thompson L – *A History of South Africa*
Trevelyan G – *A History of England*
Welsh F – *Great Southern Land*
Wheatcroft G – *Randlords*

Sport And Society

Archer R & Bouillon A – *The South African Game*
Birley D – *Land of Sport and Glory*
Casman R & McKernan M (ed) – *Sport in History*
Holt R – *Sport and the British*
Inglis F – *The Name of the Game*
Inglis G – *Sport and Pastime in Australia*
Mangan J – *The Cultural Bond*

Mangan J – *The Games Ethic and Imperialism*
Nauright J – *Sport, Cultures and Identities in South Africa*
Polley M (ed) – *The History of Sport in Britain 1880-1914*
Stoddart B & Sandiford K (ed) – *The Imperial Game*
Various – *Sports and Sportsmen: South Africa*

Cricket History

Altham H & Swanton E – *History of Cricket*
Arnold P & Wynne-Thomas P – *An Ashes Anthology*
Bassano B – *South Africa in International Cricket*
Bassano B – *Aubrey Faulkner, His Record*

Batchelor D – *CB Fry*
Batchelder A – *Hugh Trumble*
Beldham G & Fry C – *Great Batsmen and Fielders*
Beldham G & Fry C – *Great Bowlers*
Birley D – *A Social History of English Cricket*